A BEGINNER'S GUIDE TO COMPUTERS & MICROPROCESSORS
—with projects

A BEGINNER'S GUIDE TO COMPUTERS & MICROPROCESSORS
— with projects

BY CHARLES K. ADAMS

TAB **TAB BOOKS Inc.**

BLUE RIDGE SUMMIT, PA. 17214

FIRST EDITION

FIRST PRINTING—AUGUST 1978
SECOND PRINTING—AUGUST 1979
THIRD PRINTING—JULY 1980

Copyright © 1978 by TAB BOOKS Inc.

Printed in the United States of America

Library of Congress Cataloging in Publication Data

Adams, C. K.
    A beginner's guide to computers & microprocessors.

Includes index.
    1. Microprocessors. 2 Microcomputers. I. Title.
QA76.5.A3332   001.6'4   78-15617
ISBN 0-8306-9890-6
ISBN 0-8306-1015-5 pbk.

Preface

++

Up to now, computers have been beyond the means of the average person, but recent advances in semiconductor manufacturing technology have lead to large scale integration at a price the average consumer can afford. The time is coming when the microcomputer will be common, and every family will be able to have one, complete with video screen, printer, and keyboard. On this machine the children will be able to do their homework, the mother will be able to plan meals, the father will be able to keep track of family expenses and finances, and everyone will be able to play games.

Even today, the parts to put together a small computer are available at a very reasonable cost. The advanced microprocessor families are, in reality, a computer on a chip, requiring only a few discrete components to assemble a working computer. The illustration on the following page shows such a microprocessor, but these are the advanced units, expensive and hard to get. However, by using available parts, a simple computer can be constructed with seven integrated circuit chips at a reasonable cost. This is a simple computer by today's standards, but when compared to the systems available twenty years ago,   it is very advanced and more than capable.

This book has been designed to introduce the reader to the fascinating world of the microprocessor. The basic parts of the

Single chip microcomputer. Courtesy of Intel Corp.

computer are coverd, and considerable attention is given to programming and how to use the instructions to do what you want them to do. Finally, the assembly and programming of a simple computer are described.

Charles K. Adams

Contents

Chapter 1
Introduction to
Computers & Microprocessors

++

A computer is a machine capable of making decisions based on inputs and program conditions. Early computers were mechanical, using gears, cams, and clutches to make their calculations. Later systems were electrical, using large numbers of relays to do their computing. Then came the early electronic computers, made from vacuum tubes. All these early computers were large, bulky devices, hard to keep running and very expensive. They were built and used largely by universities and research organizations because no one else could afford them.

The ENIAC, developed at the University of Pennsylvania's Moore School of Engineering and put into operation in 1945, is generally accepted as the first programmable electronic computer. It was housed in cabinets 10 feet high, 3 feet deep, and 100 feet long, contained 18,000 vacuum tubes, and required tons of air conditioning equipment to keep from overheating.

The advent of the transistor led to physically smaller computers (Fig. 1-1) with increased capabilities at reduced cost. The space program gave further impetus for ever smaller minicomputers at still lower costs, until a computer could be small and inexpensive enough to be dedicated to a single purpose (Fig. 1-2). The demand for minicomputers spread, and new uses were found for them. These applications include:

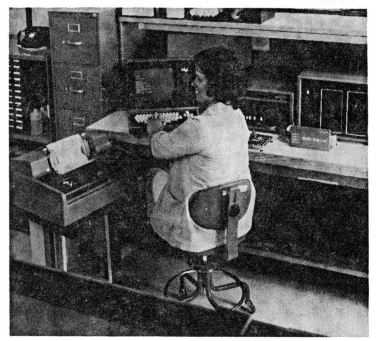

Fig. 1-1. An operational microcomputer development system complete with video terminal, printer, and disk system. Courtesy of Intel Corp.

1. Accounting and inventory control, where the computer has taken over the routine everyday tasks.
2. Scientific, research, and engineering, where the computer solves long complex problems and monitors tests and processes.
3. Medicine, where the computer can monitor a patient's vital signs and alert the staff if the patient is weakening.
4. Simulation, where the computer program is designed to simulate anything from stresses on a bridge to population growth.
5. Navigation, where the computer supplies navigation information to the pilot of an aircraft, boat or spaceship.

The development of the microprocessor has increased the uses and potential uses tenfold. Already the microprocessor has found widespread application in such things as traffic lights, gasoline pumps test equipment, programmable control panels, typesetting, medical monitoring, security alarms, scales, instruments, and process controls. This is just the start: new applications are being conceived daily. The applications are limited mainly by the ingenuity of the users. Not that the microprocessor is without some drawbacks. Being designed for simple applications, both the number of memory words available and the number and type of instructions are limited, compared to the larger computers.

HARDWARE AND SOFTWARE

Modern computers are separated into *hardware* and *software*. *Hardware* refers to the components which are permanently assembled into the system. *Software* refers to the information which is changeable. Information is of two kinds: instructions and data. Instructions tell the hardware what to do, and control the system to handle the data in the desired manner. Data is the raw material of numbers and facts which represents information for the program.

Software

The program makes the computer a versatile tool, giving it the ability to perform a series of logical operations. The program is a

Fig. 1-2. A system containing the single board microcomputer. Courtesy of Intel Corp.

series of step by step instructions to the hardware, telling it what to do to accomplish the desired function. An instruction is one operation (such as add, move, or input) which is an entity in itself.

The same computer can run many different programs, and perform many different operations. The programs may be stored in the computer's memory, as with modern computers, or may exist on a set of punched cards or cogs on a wheel, as with earlier machines.

Programming is the art of writing programs for a given computer and entering them into that computer. Since most types of computers are different, the methods of programming are slightly different, but programs written for one machine can be modified to run on others. Programs may be entered into the computer by a keyboard, paper tape, magnetic tape, magnetic disk, punched cards, or any of several data transfer methods.

Hardware

The program contains the steps required for the computer to accomplish the assigned task; the hardware decodes and executes the instructions from the program. Figure 1-3 shows a basic block diagram for the hardware of a typical modern computer. It has the five following major areas:

1. Central control unit: This controls the operation of the system, decodes the instructions, and does some of the basic operations.
2. Memory: The memory stores data, programs, and program variables.
3 & 4. Input/Output: This section of the hardware controls the data flow to and from the system.
5. Timing: This section provides the timing signals required to keep the system operating in the proper sequence.

Central Control Unit. The central control unit (CCU), sometimes called the central processor unit (CPU), is the central part of any computer. It contains the arithmetic logic unit (ALU), the instruction decoder, the program counter, several registers, and the control circuits. The CCU is the heart of the system, controlling everything that goes on, as directed by the program.

14

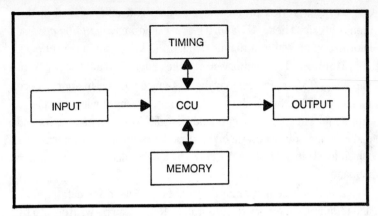

Fig. 1-3. Simple computer.

The ALU performs all the arithmetic operations, such as ADD, SUBTRACT, logical AND, and logical OR. The instruction decoder provides the signals required to execute the instructions.

The program counter keeps track of the memory location of the instruction being executed. This counter keeps the program execution in the sequential order unless a program transfer instruction is executed, which would initiate a program transfer by changing the contents of the program counter.

Registers are temporary storage locations used by the program and the hardware to hold information. The accumulator is the register used by most of the instructions requiring a register. The results of most of the ALU operations end up in the accumulator, and it contains one of the numbers required for the operation. For example, an ADD instruction adds the contents of the accumulator to the contents of another register, and places the results in the accumulator. Most of the data which is transferred to and from the system and memory starts or ends up in a register. Other registers are used for memory addressing for the transfer of data.

The control circuits provide the control signals required to run the system. These include signals to the other parts of the system as well as to the internal circuits of the CCU.

The program is the brains of the computer, telling the CCU what instructions to execute, and in what order. All the system is under its control. The program, as all information stored in memory, consists of a series of 1's and 0's (on's and off's) stored in the memory cell. These 1's and 0's are called *machine language*, or information stored in a manner which the CCU can interpret.

Memory. The memory stores the program, data, and program variables. This memory may be a semiconductor memory, core memory, disk storage device, tape unit, or any device capable of storing information and being addressed. Normally, tape units and disk storage devices are used to store large volumes of information which are transferred to the core or semiconductor memory upon demand.

Random access memories (RAMs) are used for data storage and temporary memory for programs. RAMs can be written into by the system under program control. A program, stored on tape, is transferred to the RAM under program control. When the program has been executed, another program can be written into the same RAM locations from the tape unit and executed. In this manner, several programs can be run on a system with a relatively small memory. Also, large volumes of data, stored on tape, can be written into RAM memory as required.

Read only memories (ROMs) cannot be altered by the program. These take a special programmer to load information into the memory locations. Therefore they are reserved for permanent storage, such as for the programs for addition and subtraction.

Input/Output. For a computer to be useful, it must communicate with the outside world. The input/output (I/O) provides a link between the machine and the external equipment. The external equipment may be a computer terminal, traffic light, gas pump, cash register, controlled tool, display device, on any of the hundreds of devices used with a computer.

The input may be tape units, keyboards, data inputs, readers, or even other computers. The output may be printers, cathode ray tube (CRT) displays, machines, lights, punches, or any device which can be controlled. The I/O circuitry is under program control, and the information to and from the I/O circuitry is sampled by the program.

Timing. Timing keeps the system operating in the correct manner. A sync pulse is issued when the instruction read starts.

Using this pulse as a starting gate, timing pulses are generated by a countdown circuit operating from a basic clock generator.

Compatibility

The hardware and program must work together to accomplish the desired results. There are several different configurations of hardware, with the exact system being determined by the application, but the program must always be compatible with the hardware, if it is to exercise the input/output in the proper manner to convey meaningful information to and from the system.

Large, general purpose machines have a general, or universal configuration, with the input from some mass storage device, and the output to tape units or printers. These machines can run several programs at the same time, and are used for problem solving, simulation, accounting, payroll, and other such applications.

Most microprocessor systems are nearly identical as to the hardware for the instruction decoding and execution. Computer games, machine controlled tools, and monitor systems all use the same hardware for their particular applications. The difference is in the input/output and in the program, both of which are tailored to the specific application. A general purpose system, with a keyboard input and a printer output, is often used to develop the programs for specialized systems. In these applications, the inputs and outputs are simulated by the program, allowing the operator to test the program under all possible conditions.

Figure 1-4 shows a simple system for controlling traffic lights dependent on the traffic flow and direction. The system's job is to control the sequencing of the lights for optimum traffic flow, and to sequence the yellow lights from 11 pm to 5 am.

The inputs are the car sensors mounted in each traffic lane. The outputs are the traffic lights. The program reads the time of day from an internal clock, and determines the optimum sequencing of the lights.

No matter what the computer is assigned to accomplish, the hardware and the program must be compatible. In this example, the traffic sensors would be useless to the system if the computer could not read the data from them. One method of reading the data is to use counters to count the number of cars. When these counters are

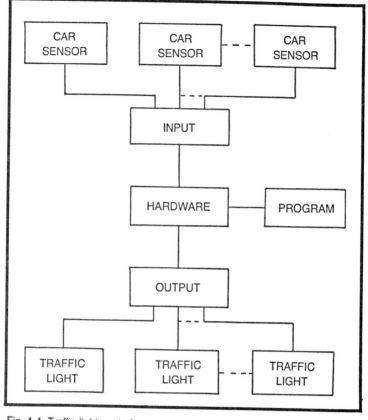

Fig. 1-4. Traffic light control.

read by the computer, they are set to zero, so the program will know how many cars have passed over the sensor.

If the input is raw data, the data is placed in a register then read by the computer. While the computer is reading the data, new data is inhibited from entering the register. Once the data has been read, the register is freed to accept new data. If the input data is from a keyboard, the program must be able to decode the keyboard into the language used by the system. This is done by using look-up tables and conversion routines.

The same rule of compatability applies to the output: the information sent by the program must be usable to the device. In the above example, drivers are used to turn on and off the different colors of lights for each traffic signal. These drivers are similar to relays, where a small control voltage turns on the relay, turning on the light. Figure 1-5 shows this circuit, with a relay driver. If the drivers are controlled by a single bit in the output word so that there is a different bit for each color and a different word for each light, then setting one bit on in one word will turn on one light.

The program must set the selected bit on for the desired length of time, for each output word. The bits will not be the same unless the same color light is to be turned on for all lights. The computer output circuitry must recognize the command to turn on a specified light and color. This is done by assigning each light a different output address so that by addressing one output and sending it the proper bit combination, the desired colors on a specified light will be turned on.

INTRODUCING THE MICROPROCESSOR

The typical microprocessor is not itself a microcomputer, but the brains of a microcomputer, its CCU. It processes all the information and controls the remaining components which make up the system. It reads the program, decodes the instructions, and conditions the system to execute these instructions.

The Development of the Microprocessor

The microprocessor evolved from the transistor, which was the first major semiconductor device. Several transistors were then

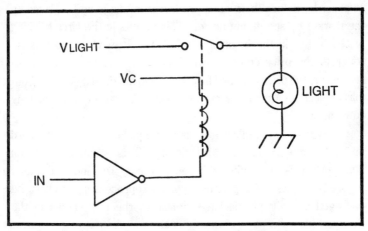

Fig. 1-5. Controlling a high intensity light with a microprocessor output.

put on one semiconductor substrate, and the integrated circuit (IC) evolved. This was a major advance in the electronics world, but it only paved the way for greater things: the evolution of the many analog circuits and the more complex digital circuits which contained several transistors and other components.

The number of components which can be stacked on one chip determines the complexity of the circuit. A chip is a small piece of substrate, usually silicon, upon which the total circuit is made. These chips are so small that it takes a strong magnifying glass to see the components.

Techniques were developed to put more and more complex circuits on the same chip, evolving into medium scale integration (MSI). Because these MSI circuits are more reliable, cost less, and use less power than the transistor equivalents, they are easier and cheaper to use. These circuits have found widespread use in the electronics world.

It was the evolution of the large scale integration (LSI) circuits that opened the door for microprocessors. To develop the LSI capability required new concepts in circuits, manufacturing methods, and testing. New techniques were developed to improve the yield of the manufacturing and testing processes. All this required hundreds of thousands of dollars worth of engineering and development time.

Because the technology is changing so rapidly, the companies try to write off their research and development expenses as quickly as possible, before their latest product is outdated and replaced on the market by something newer. This results in the circuits being priced higher in the beginning. When the R & D expense is recovered, the price comes down drastically. For one type microprocessor, the price dropped from over two hundred dollars to about thirty dollars. Other units are cheaper yet, and most are coming down in price.

A typical 40 pin microprocessor is equivalent to 450 standard integrated circuits or 110 MSI circuits. This equates to several hundred transistors. Quite a difference in cost, size, and ease of use. Figure 1-6 shows the chip for one type microprocessor, which will be packaged in a 40 pin package similar to the one shown in the Preface.

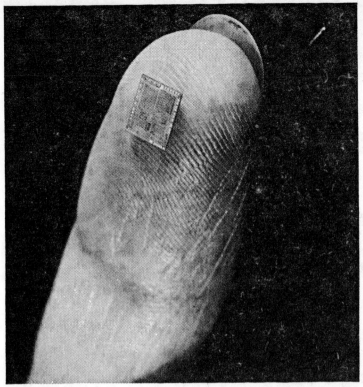

Fig. 1-6. The actual chip from the microcomputer shown in the Preface. Courtesy of Intel Corp.

In addition, several supporting circuits have been developed, such as the semiconductor memory and input/output chips. Development is continuing on support chips, memories, and interface circuits. Presently a microprocessor system can be assembled using mostly LSI and MSI circuits, with only a few discrete components.

The Microprocessor System

A microprocessor system is a small computer, called a microcomputer, with limited capabilities compared to the larger computers. The CCU of the system is the microprocessor, one integrated circuit, measuring about one-half inch by two inches, which replaces many circuit packs in a standard computer.

Most microprocessor systems are 8 bit systems. This means that one computer word (byte) is 8 bits long, and all memory words are 8 bits long. Normally they have the capability of addressing 64,000 words by the use of 16 address bits. Normally the 8 bit systems have about 75 different instructions. Some of these instructions require 2 or 3 program words to give the detailed instructions to the CCU. For example, a program transfer instruction normally requires 3 words. The first 8 bit word is the instruction, while the second and third words give the 16 bit transfer-to address. In the larger computers, these are normally one byte instructions.

Several systems are 4 bit systems, making up simple systems with a minimum system, but their capability is severly limited. There are also 12 and 16 bit families, which offer greater capability than 8 bit systems.

The number of instructions is limited for microprocessors, and some types of instructions are not available in the microprocessor because of hardware limitations. This includes multiplication and division, but most of the instructions not available can be simulated by the program.

In spite of the limitations, the microprocessor makes a good small computer. Most applications do not require more than the 64,000 memory words available, or more than the 75 instructions provided. Also, the microprocessor system requires less power than the larger systems, even less than a 150 watt bulb. Better yet, you can build one yourself.

Chapter 2
The Functional Diagram

++

A microprocessor is a complex device, comprising hundreds of logic gates to accomplish its many complex operations. The detailed schematic of a microprocessor covers many pages and is difficult to understand. Add to this the complexity of the other circuits which make up a system, and the detailed schematic of a small system can be very long indeed. If detailed schematics are used, their complexity and sheer mass will require an electronics expert to put the system together and to understand how it operates.

FUNCTIONAL BLOCKS

The functional diagram was conceived as a shorthand method of representing a complex system by a series of functional blocks. This is a type of block diagram, but it is based on functions and not on hardware divisions. Each functional block represents one function required for the system operation whether this function requires one chip, several chips, or a complex circuit. The interconnection of the blocks is shown and the control requirements are noted; however, none of the internal workings of the block are given, which greatly simplifies the presentation of a system.

Different microprocessor families break down the functional blocks in different manners, but the general rule is to let each complex integrated circuit, such as the microprocessor, represent a block. Circuits required between the blocks may be shown as small blocks or as discrete parts, and are treated separately from the blocks. Complex circuits having a function of their own, such as input/output circuits, are represented by functional blocks. When two or more functions are combined into a single chip, this is represented as one block. The interface and control signals define the level of the combination.

Figure 2-1 shows the functional diagram of an 8080 type microprocessor. Compare this with Fig. 4-1, which is the block diagram of the same microprocessor. There is quite a difference in the complexity of the diagrams. Project this difference to a schematic of the individual components, and the simplicity of the function block diagram becomes even more desirable.

Notice on Fig. 2-1 that only the interface signals are shown, and that these signals are identified. This diagram does not show how the signals interact, nor what conditions are required to produce the various signals. To obtain this information, the description and specification sheets of the individual chips must be consulted. Always study them for the chips used.

The standard functional blocks which make up a system are:

- Microprocessor
- Clock generator
- System controller
- Memory
- Bus drivers
- Input/output
- Address decoders

These are the basic blocks which make up a family. The microprocessor is the CCU of the system. It provides addressing, instruction decoding, controls, and instruction decoding. This is the active part of the system, with the rest of the hardware supporting it. The clock generator provides the clock signals required, the system controller takes the output from the CCU and generates system control signals, the bus drivers provide drive and isolation for the buses, and the memories provide information to the CCU while under the control of the CCU. The program tells the microprocessor what to do, and the CCU determines how to do it.

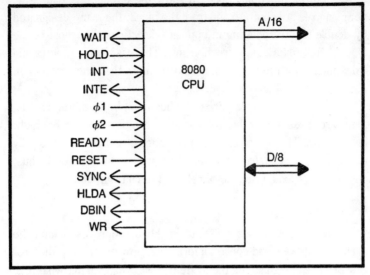

Fig. 2-1. Functional diagram for the 8080 microprocessor.

A large complex system may use all the blocks and more than one of some of them, but not all of the blocks are required for all systems. A simple system may use only five of the blocks. For the 8080 family, a minimum system consists of the clock generator, microprocessor, system controller, memory, and I/O. Figure 4-2 gives the functional diagram for a simple system. Only those signals required for operation are shown; those signals that are not required are not shown.

Some families have special blocks, such as timers. Other families combine several functions into one chip. For example, the 8085 combines the clock generator, microprocessor, and clock generator into a single chip, and its input/output circuits are combined with memory (RAM, ROM, or EPROM) and a timer.

BUSES

The functions and designations of the interconnecting signals are slightly different for the various families of microprocessors, but most of the functions are standard. A *bus* is a representation of a group of individual lines in the functional diagram that have a common function, such as address, and it transfers information around the system. The bus may contain many individual lines or few. The arrows on the functional diagram show the direction of data flow. Some signals flow both to and from the block; these are designated by double arrows pointing in opposite directions, but most of the blocks handle data in one direction only. There is always a source and a destination for the data. There may be more than one destination, but never more than one source.

All devices which can drive the bus must be tri-state. That is, there are three states that the output of the device can take: high, low, and off. The off state is the high impedance state, and basically disconnects the chip from the bus. This prevents loading of the bus, and prevents loading of the unselected circuit outputs.

Control Bus

The control signals originate in the microprocessor and the system controller and control information flow external to the processor. These signals tell the system what is happening, what is to happen, and when. They control the operation of the system; for example, the I/O read signal gates information from the addressed port to the data bus.

A control signal has two states, high and low, which can convey commands. Either state can be designated as the *active state*, the state which causes the function to happen for inputs, and indicates that function is commanded to happen for outputs. Active low signals are represented by a bar over the signal name, such as $\overline{WR}$. This indicates that a low represents the function happening. Signal names with no bar over them usually represent active high signals, such as RESET. A high level into this input causes RESET to happen. Sometimes an active low is indicated by a small circle between the signal line and the functional block.

A control bus is used to designate the control signals as a group. The individual control signals can be broken out from the bus as single lines as required, and these control functions retain their individual designations; the total bus does not go to any of the using blocks.

Data Bus

All data is transmitted to and received from the system over the data bus. Information which is read from memory is transmitted over this bus to the microprocessor. The data bus is bidirectional; that is, data can go both directions on the bus: from the processor to the memory, or from the memory to the processor.

In Figs. 2-1 and 2-2, the lower bus, designated D/8, is the 8-bit bus. Notice that the arrows point both directions, indicating that it is a bidirectional bus. An 8-bit microprocessor system, such as the 8080, has 8 data lines, so the data bus is 8 bits wide (D_0 thru D_7). Over this bus travel the instructions, read from the program in memory, the data to the outside world via the output device, and the data from the outside world via the input block. Notice that this bus connects all blocks which are involved with data.

Address Bus

The memories and the input/output blocks are selected by the processor control signals and by the address bus. Normally there is an address associated with the chip, and a select signal to select the chip. The chip may have more than one address, but only one select. The select signal determines the addresses of the memory by enabling the chip for the proper block of memory addresses.

The address information is generated by the microprocessor, and transmitted to the rest of the system over the address bus. The address bus carries the address information to memory and the I/O circuits. This bus selects which address location is read or written into, and which input/output circuit (port) is enabled. Most microprocessor families have sixteen address lines. These sixteen lines will address up to 64K words of memory. Most systems do not require all sixteen lines. Twelve address lines will address 4K words, while fourteen lines will address 16K words. A small system usually does not require more than 4K words, while a general purpose expandable system requires the capability of addressing all 64K words.

The double line and large arrow, designated A/16 in Figs. 2-1 and 2-2 represent the address bus, all the address lines represented by a single bus. The A indicates that it is the address bus, and the 16 means that it is comprised of 16 lines, containing signals A_0 through A_{15}. The arrow indicates direction of data flow.

An address expansion bus is sometimes used. This bus is generated by an address decoder, and is used in the addressing of

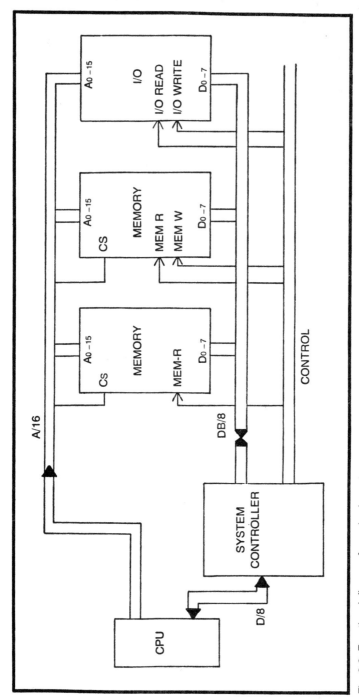

Fig. 2-2. Functional diagram for a simple system.

28

memory and I/O. The address expansion bus is usually designated as AE and may contain up to 8 lines, O_0 thru O_7. Large systems may have more than one expansion bus, and the buses are separated by subscripts such as AE_1.

Let us trace a few instructions through the system shown in Fig. 2-2. This will illustrate how the system and the buses work together. At the start of the instruction cycle, the program instruction is read by placing the address of the instruction on the address bus and generating a memory read (MEM R) pulse. This reads the selected memory address, and places the contents of the memory location on the data bus. This information is read from the data bus by the microprocessor and decoded. If the instruction is an output instruction, the port number is placed on the address bus, and an I/O write pulse is generated. This places the information on the data bus on the selected output port.

From this, it can be seen that all instruction cycles require the address bus, control bus, and data bus to transfer the instruction from memory to the microprocessor. During the execution of the

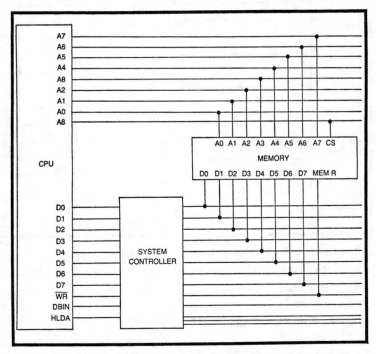

Fig. 2-3. Detailed functional diagram for a simple system.

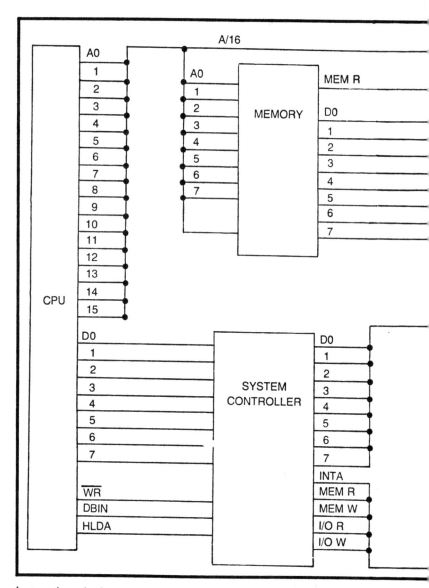

instruction, the buses may or may not be required. Some instructions, such as an ADD instruction, are executed completely within the microprocessor, so no buses are required for the execution of the instruction.

MODIFIED FUNCTIONAL DIAGRAMS

There are many ways of presenting the functional diagram. Figure 2-2 is a simplified functional diagram, showing how the sys-

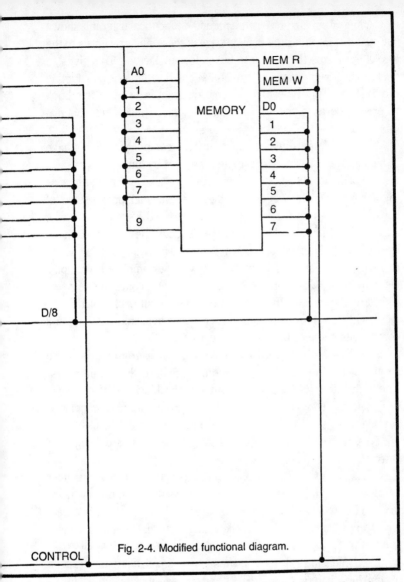

Fig. 2-4. Modified functional diagram.

tem works and its required signals, but not giving any of the interconnecting details, such as pin numbers for the individual circuits. So to get the system running or to troubleshoot the system, the individual diagrams for the chips used must be consulted. One way around this is to use the detailed functional diagram, shown in Fig. 2-3. This gives all the interconnecting lines, but does not use the bus concept. The result is quite cluttered, and can be confusing.

A logical compromise is the modified functional diagram, shown in Fig. 2-4. This gives the pin numbers of the individual signals to the blocks but forms the lines into buses for simplicity. This gives an uncluttered diagram which is useful in building and troubleshooting the system. This type of functional diagram is used in this book whenever detail is required. Otherwise, the simple functional diagram is used to show concepts and systems.

For the simple functional diagram, the components do not have to be specified by part number and type, just by function. A system can be constructed from this diagram using available parts, as long as the control signals are compatible. The normal progression of hardware design is to specify the capabilities of the system and draw the simplified functional diagram, then specify the parts and make up the modified functional diagram. This will provide the information to make the system. Figure 2-5 shows the simplified functional diagram for the CPU portion of a microprocessor controlled test set. This circuit pack is connected to an output circuit pack which interfaces with the item to be tested. The data bus, address bus, and control bus connect the two circuit packs.

Figure 2-6 shows the modified functional diagram for the same circuit pack. The numbers inside the blocks are the pin numbers. The alphanumeric designations outside the blocks are the signal designations. The A and B numbers in the circles are pin numbers for the board edge connectors. The large numbers inside the blocks are the type numbers of the individual chips. The buses are designated as to function and number of lines.

This circuit pack is a small general purpose computer without input or output facilities. It contains 256 words of temporary memory and 512 words of permanent memory. The total memory capacity is expandable to 64K words using external memory boards connected to the buses. The circuit pack on which this circuit is mounted measures 4 by 7 inches; so a small computer can be assembled using two circuit packs and power supplies, and mounted in a 6 by 8 by 8 inch cabinet.

When the system is turned on, a reset pulse is generated by the clock generator. This forces the address bus to zero, so when a memory read pulse is issued, memory address 00 is read. The contents of this location are placed on the data bus, and transferred to the processor which then decodes and executes the instruction.

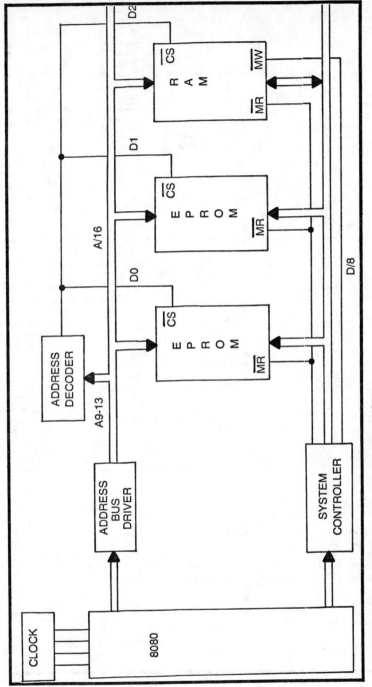

Fig. 2-5. Simplified functional diagram of an operational CPU.

33

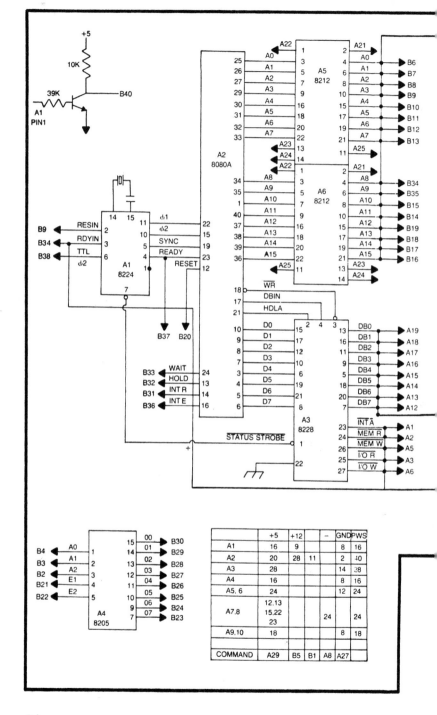

34

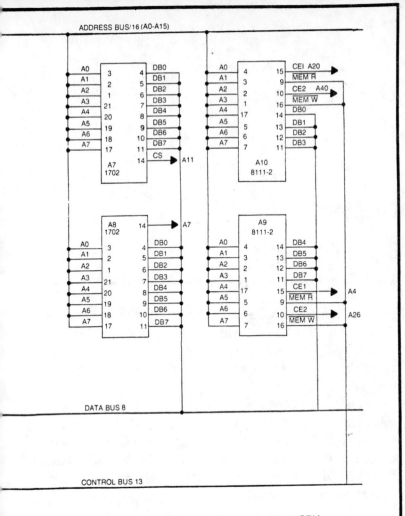

Fig. 2-6. Modified functional diagram of an operational CPU.

Once this instruction is completed, the address is incremented and the next memory location is read. Address 01 corresponds to address line A_0 being high, and all other address lines being low. This instruction is read and decoded by the microprocessor.

Chapter 3
Computer Logic

++

All digital computers, including microprocessors, operate on the digital concept. That is, the electrical signal which transmits information around the computer is either on or off, with no in-between state. These signals represent binary numbers to the circuitry and program.

Analog computers operate on varying input voltage, so the voltage level of the input is important. Figure 3-1 shows a typical analog computer circuit. The output voltage level and waveshape is a function of the input and the response of the feedback circuit. Integrators, differentiators, amplifiers, and other circuits are made by changing the feedback circuit.

DIGITAL COMPUTERS

The on state is typically 4 to 5 volts and the off state is 0 to 1 volts, although some families of circuits do use other voltage levels. The circuits are designed so that the circuit is unstable between the on and off state, forcing the output of the circuit to be either on (sometimes called a high) or off (sometimes called a low). Steady state inputs between the on and off voltage levels are not defined, so if they exist they must be conditioned to one of the defined input states. This is done with amplifiers, Schmitt triggers, or comparators. Figure 3-2 shows a simple NAND gate made from discrete

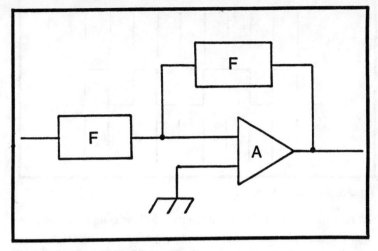

Fig. 3-1. Typical analog computer circuit.

components. This circuit provides a low output as long as all the inputs are high. If any input goes low, the transistor turns off and the output goes high.

Serial Computers

Serial pulse trains were used in the older electronic digital computers. These computers were called serial computers, and

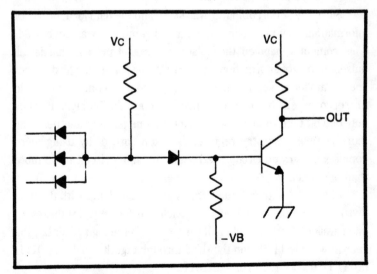

Fig. 3-2. Simple digital NAND gate.

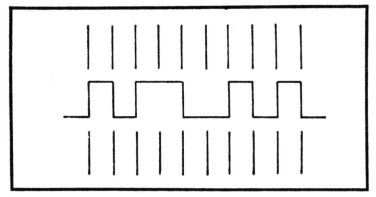

Fig. 3-3. Serial pulse train.

were relatively slow, but the circuitry was less complex because in many cases only one circuit was required for data handling.

Figure 3-3 shows a serial pulse train divided into equal time slots. Each of the time slots is defined as one pulse time, or one bit. Since pulses are read in the same manner as numbers, the right hand pulse is the first pulse, and the lowest order pulse. Using this guideline, the pulse train in Fig. 3-3 represents the binary number 101100101. This is a serial pulse, and it takes 9 bit times to transmit or move this number around the system.

Parallel Computers

Since the serial computer was slow, and the data load, or bits of information, was increasing, the parallel computer was developed. This computer handled the pulses as parallel pulses; that is, all pulses, or bits of information, appeared at the same time on different lines. Parallel pulses are used in most modern computers and in microprocessors because the speed of operation is high. It takes only one bit time to move one word from one place to another. The more complex circuitry required is taken care of by using more complex integrated circuits and using the same circuit to do more than one function.

Figure 3-4 shows 4 pulse trains each 8 bits long, with the time divisions. The first (left) pulse on each line (pulse train) makes up one parallel 4-bit word, 1111. If the top line is the high order bit, the second word is 1110, and the third through eighth words are 0111, 0011, 1101, 0001, 0110, and 1011.

In parallel machines, time must be allowed between pulses to allow for the operation to take place. This is done by conditioning the circuits to perform the next operation, so the bits are gated into and out of the circuits. This gating consists of another pulse, whose width is less than the bit width, and which occurs once during each bit time. Figure 3-5 shows data on a 4-bit data bus, along with the gating pulse. The pulses are read when the gating pulse is high, and the pulses are operated upon between the bits. For the data bus, the timing pulse is the read or write pulse. This results in data being transferred when the gating pulse is high, and the levels between the pulses are not important. It is during this time that the pulses change levels.

For the address bus, the gating pulse is also the read or write pulse. This pulse commands a memory or input output circuit read or write. For a memory read pulse, the address is put on the address

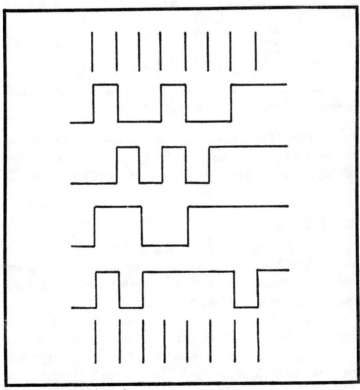

Fig. 3-4. Parallel pulse train.

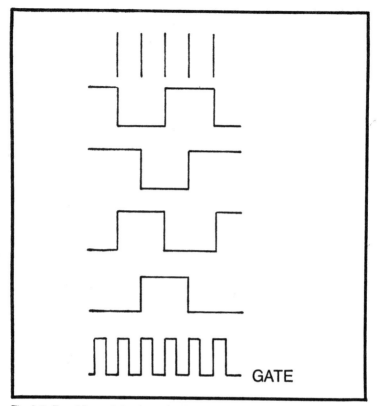

Fig. 3-5. Four bit parallel pulse train with gating pulse.

bus, then the memory read pulse is issued. This gates the address into the memory addressing circuit. So the information stored in the memory location addresses is placed on the data bus, where it is gated by the memory read pulse.

LOGIC CIRCUITS

Before proceeding, a review of basic digital logic circuits is in order. Digital logic circuits respond to the digital inputs, giving outputs depending on their function. Figure 3-6 shows the standard representation of some of the basic circuits.

The buffer, or *driver*, is used to increase the current drive of an input. For this circuit, the output is the same as the input. The inverter inverts the input. So the output is low for a high input, and the output is high for a low input. The circle on the output of the

40

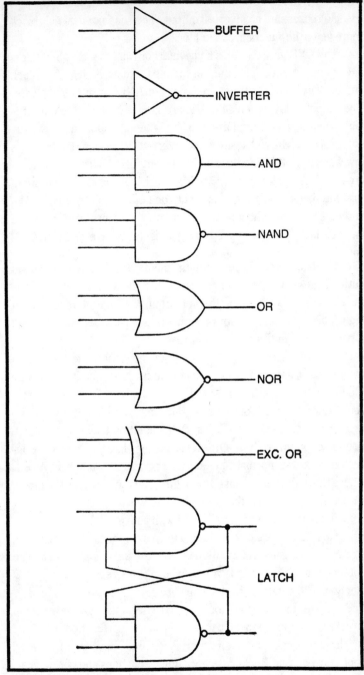

Fig. 3-6. Logic diagrams for some digital circuits.

triangle represents an inverted output. The shape of the basic block represents the function of the block.

The AND gate output is high when both inputs are high. If this is a 3 or more input AND gate, all the inputs must be high for a high output. The NAND gate is the 'inverted AND' or 'not AND' gate. The output is low when all inputs are high. The OR gate output is high when any of the inputs is high. When all inputs are low, the output is low. The NOR gate is the inverted OR gate, so the output is low when any of the inputs is high. The output is high when all inputs are low. The exclusive OR gate is a special OR gate. The output of this gate is high when one, and only one of the inputs is high. The output is low when the inputs are low, or when more than one of the inputs is high. The exclusive NOR gate is the inverted exclusive OR gate.

The latch circuit is set when the input goes low, making the set output high and the reset output low. When the reset pulse goes low, the circuit is reset, making the set output low and the reset output high. This circuit is used for remembering pulses, because once set it remains set until the circuit is reset.

Sometimes a small circle is drawn on the input to the gates. This means that it takes a low to perform the function, and it can change the function of the circuits. For example, if a NAND gate is used for active low inputs, the output is high when either input is low, so the function becomes OR NOT. The NOT notation following the function description, such as OR NOT, means that the inputs are inverted from the normal function. A shorthand notation is $\overline{A} + \overline{B}$ where the + designates an OR function, and the line over the inputs ($\overline{A}$ and $\overline{B}$) designates that the low is active.

Similarly, if a NOR gate is used with active low inputs—that is, if the small circles are on the input of the gate—the function becomes an AND NOT gate. All inputs must be low for a high output. The notation for this function is $\overline{A} \cdot \overline{B}$ where the · represents an AND function. The notations for the standard gates are shown in Fig. 3-6. The line over the total function $\overline{(A + B)}$ designates that the output is inverted, as opposed to the bar over the individual functions ($\overline{A} + \overline{B}$) which represents that the inputs are inverted. There are many good books on logic and Boolean algebra (logic equations and operations). Consult one of these books if you desire more information in this field.

receivers depends on the function of the circuit, and what it is driving.

Each instruction is a unique bit combination which must be decoded as such by the hardware. The pulse from the decoder is an enable pulse for the decoded instruction. This enable pulse gates the circuits required to execute the instruction. Since most instructions require several circuits for the execution, this enable pulse feeds several circuits. Most of the circuits are used for several instructions, so more than one enable pulse feeds these circuits.

The circuits shown here have been simplified versions of computer circuits. Normally 8 bits are decoded for instruction decoding, and additional gating and timing is used to control the enable pulse width for different applications.

Figure 3-7 shows a simple gating system for a 4-bit parallel data bus. One input to each NAND gate is one line of the bus, and the other input line is connected to the gate pulse. When the data line is high, the output of the NAND gate goes low when the gating pulse goes high. This sets the latch, so the output is high. It remains that way until the reset pulse goes low, resetting the latch. If the data line input is low, the output of the NAND gate remains high when the gating pulse goes high. So the latch remains in the reset condition, with a low output.

This circuit is but one of many possibilities for data receiving circuits. Another version is to replace the latches with drivers. Yet another is to use only the NAND gates. The circuitry of the data

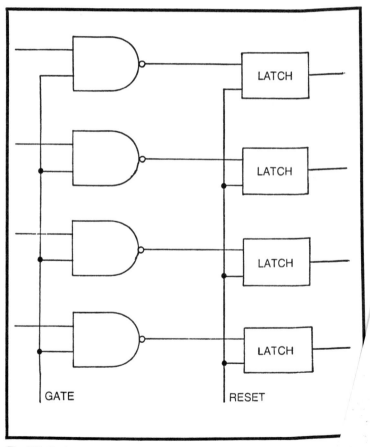

Fig. 3-7. Gating system for a 4 bit parallel data bus.

Chapter 4
Microprocessor Architecture

++

The term "architecture" is often applied to the organization of the microprocessor, to refer to how the internal blocks of the unit are tied together, and how they work together.

The microprocessor is the CCU of the system, providing addressing, instruction decoding, and controls. It is the active part of the system, with the rest of the hardware supporting it. The clock generator provides the clock signals required, the system controller takes the output from the CCU and generates system control signals, and the bus drivers provide drive and isolation for the buses.

THE MICROPROCESSOR

For the first part of the discussion, the 8080 microprocessor shown in Fig. 4-1 will be used. Then some of the differences with the other systems will be presented.

This CCU consists of the following major functional units:

- Register array and address logic
- Arithmetic and logic unit
- Instruction decoder and control section
- Bidirectional 3-state data bus buffer

The arithmetic unit contains the ALU, the accumulator, the status flag flip flops, and the associated circuits. This section of the

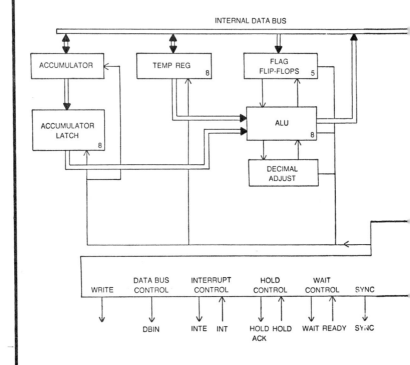

INTERNAL DATA BUS

ACCUMULATOR

ACCUMULATOR LATCH 8

TEMP REG 8

FLAG FLIP-FLOPS 5

ALU 8

DECIMAL ADJUST

WRITE	DATA BUS CONTROL	INTERRUPT CONTROL	HOLD CONTROL	WAIT CONTROL	SYNC
	DBIN	INTE INT	HOLD HOLD ACK	WAIT READY	SYNC

Pin	Signal	Function
1	A10	Address bus bit 10
2	GND	Ground
3-10		Data Bus: D4, D5, D6, D7, D3, D2, D1, D0 respectively;bidirectional.
11		-5V
12	Reset	High resets system and sets program counter to zero.
13	HOLD	Suspends machine operation at the end of the current instruction cycle;input
14	INT	Interrupt request;input to processor to request processor recognize interrupt at end of current instruction;input
15	φ2	Phase 2;Timing input
16	INTE	Interrupt enable;indicates the state of the interrupt enable flip/flop;output

46

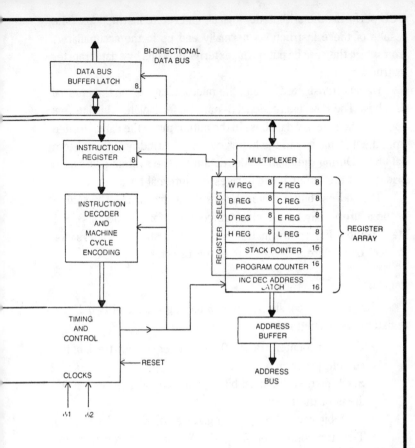

17	DBIN	Data bus in:indicates to the external circuits that the data bus is in the input mode:output
18	$\overline{WR}$	Write:data from processor on data bus is stable when this signal is low:output.
19	SYNC	Synchronizing signal:provides a signal to indicate the beginning of each machine cycle:output
20		+5V
21	HLDA	Hold acknowledge:indicates that the processor is responding to the hold input:output
22	φ2	Phase 2:timing signal:input
23	Ready	Indicates that valid memory or input data is available on the data bus:input
24	Wait	Indicates that the processor is in the wait state
25-27		Address bus bits 0, 1, and 2,respectively
28		+12V
29-40		Address bus bits 3-9, 15, 12, 13, 14, and 11,respectively

Fig. 4-1. 8080 functional block diagram.

CCU performs the arithmetic, logical, and rotate instructions. The results of these instructions normally end up in the accumulator, from which they can be put on the external data bus by a data transfer instruction.

Data is transferred around the microprocessor on the internal data bus. The 8 bit bidirectional 3-state buffer isolates this internal bus from the external data bus. In the output mode the data is loaded from the internal bus to the buffer, which in turn drives the system data bus. During the input mode, data from the system data bus is loaded into the buffer, which drives the internal bus.

The address buffer drives the system address bus. The source of the address may be the program counter (for instructions), the stack pointer (for return instructions), the H and L registers (for indirect data addressing), or any of the registers.

Registers

The registers consist of eight 8-bit registers and two 16-bit registers, as defined below:

- Program counter (PC): 16-bit register to keep track of the current program address
- Stack pointer (SP): 16-bit register containing the top address of the stack
- Six 8-bit general purpose registers (B, C, D, E, H, & L)
- Two temporary registers (W & Z): 8-bit registers for internal use.

Program Counter. The program counter maintains the program memory address of the current program step. It is incremented by the hardware during every instruction fetch, and during the execution of multibyte instructions. Program transfer instructions, when executed, load the transfer to address (contained in bytes 2 and 3) into the PC. So the next instruction is read from this address. This register is not used for data transfer instructions, but is addressable by the program.

Multibyte instructions require more than one memory location; these instructions require an address which takes types 2 and 3, or data. The added memory locations are read during the execution of the instruction. Some multibyte instructions give the capability of

48

entering a constant unto the program by the multibyte immediate instructions.

Stack Pointer. The stack pointer maintains the address of the top available memory location in the stack. The stack is a series of temporary memory locations reserved for temporary address storage. The call instruction, which is a 3-byte program transfer instruction, places the next program address in the stack. Then the return instruction, a single-type instruction, reads the top address of the stack and executes a program transfer to that location. This provides an automatic program return to the next address after the call instruction, considerably reducing the programming required.

The low order 8 bits of the address is moved into the address contained in the stack pointer, minus 2. The high order 8 bits are moved into the next higher address. The stack pointer is decremented by 2, setting it to the low order 8 bits. So a RETURN instruction loads the contents of these two addresses, with the stack pointer providing the low order address, into the program counter. This affects the return to the instruction after the CALL instruction.

The stack pointer must be initialized by the program, and is usually the last address in temporary memory. Care must be taken not to let the stack and the data storage overlap, which could result in destroying the stack address, and the program wandering when RETURN is executed. Realize that the stack can contain several addresses, and grows downward from the initialized address.

General Purpose Registers. The six 8-bit registers are general purpose registers for use by the program, and are under program control. These registers can be used as 8-bit registers, denoted B, C, D, E, H, and L, or be combined to form 16-bit register pairs (rp), B, D, and H. The B register pair uses the B register for the high order 8 bits and the C register for the low order 8 bits. The D register uses the D register for the high order 8 bits and the E register for the low order 8 bits. The H register pair uses the H register for the high order 8 bits and the L register for the low order 8 bits.

When using the registers, care must be taken to keep the registers identified so as not to use one for two purposes at the same time. Any of these registers can be used as an 8-bit or a 16-bit register, but *not* at the same time.

One of the major program uses of the H register pair is for indirect addressing of memory. The memory address is preloaded into the H and L registers. When certain data transfer instructions are executed, these registers will then supply the address.

Temporary Registers. The temporary registers W and Z are used in the execution of some of the instructions. These registers are under hardware control, and cannot be addressed by the program.

Some systems have a test input. The program can sample this input to determine if it is high or low. This can be used by the program as a direct single-bit input to command the program.

Some systems have the status lags, either all or some, or other programmable flags brought out to pins. These are for use by the external hardware to indicate status, or to give a direct programmable, single-bit output.

Size

The size of the microprocessor is the number of data bits available in the data bus. There are 4-bit systems, 8-bit systems, 16-bit systems, and bit-slice systems.

The 4-bit systems are small systems with limited capabilities. The microprocessor is usually in a small package, such as a 24 pin DIP. Some of these units use the data bus to address the memory and to transfer the data by multiplexing the data. This is accomplished by using timing to keep the data and addresses separated. Data appears on the bus only during a data transfer instruction, and only during the data transfer portion of the instruction execution. Memory control signals expand the memory addressing capabilities beyond the 4 bits of the data bus. Using this, several memory chips can be addressed. Some 4-bit systems use 8-bit data words by transferring the data in two bytes, the upper 4 bits and the lower 4 bits. Other systems use 8-bit memories and address the upper or lower 4 bits by using an address control signal.

By far the most common microprocessor size is 8 bits. This offers a good data bus size, and 16 address bits. The address and the data buses may be multiplexed to reduce the number of pins required on the microprocessor. These systems have a wide selection of instructions, and the data handling capability is good. Most of

8080—	8224 Clock generator
	8228 System controller and data bus driver
	1702A/8702A EPROM
	2708/8708 EPROM
	8111-2 RAM
	8102-2 RAM
	8212 8 bit I/O or 8 bit bus driver
	8255 24 bit programmable I/O
	8251 USART
	8205 One of 8 decoder
	8213 Priority interrupt control unit
	8214/8226 Four bit bi-directional bus driver
M6800—	XC6875 Clock generator
	MC6820 Peripheral interface adaptor
	MC6850 UART
	XC6852 USRT
	MCM6810 RAM
	MC6880 Data bus driver
	MC6889 Data bus driver
	XC 6886 Address bus driver
2650—	2102 RAM
	2602 RAM
	82S115/123/129 PROMs
	8T95/6/7/8 Hex buffers
	8T31 8 bit bi-directional port
	8T26 Quad transceiver
	8250 Decoder
SC/MP—	MM2101 RAM
	81LS97 Buffer
	DM8551 Latches
	DM 8839 Data transceiver
	DM 7442 Memory select
	DM8095 Buffer
	DM8833 Bi-directional buffer

Fig. 4-2. Microprocessor families.

the development work under way is to improve the characteristics of 8-bit systems, making some of them a universal system. Although 8-bit microprocessor systems offer good capability for data handling and control, their mathematical capability is limited, so anything beyond add, subtract, and logical operations requires subroutines or special routines.

To increase the data handling capability and simplify the instructions, larger machines are available. Some 16-bit systems are available which have an expanded instruction set and can perform additional mathematical operations. The 16 bits allow more information to be included in the instruction, requiring fewer multibyte instructions. These systems are new on the market, and their acceptance is slow for control and most data uses although they are being used where the expanded capability is required.

Families

There are several different microprocessor chip families, and several manufacturers of each. Normally, chips from the same family are compatible even if made by different manufacturers, but some of the chips from the different families are not compatible. This does not apply to memories, and normally not to the input/output chips, but the control functions must either be compatible or be made compatible by external circuitry.

Figure 4-2 lists several families, the support chips available, the size, and other characteristics of the family. The selection of the family to use is usually biased by availability, knowledge about the family, past experience, and the application. In this chapter the individual functional requirements are examined for the common families, and the control requirements are detailed. Circuits can be built up using discrete parts, such as transistors and IC's, but this is more expensive, time consuming, harder to implement, and leads to serious problems getting the system running.

Figure 4-3 lists the characteristics of several microprocessor types. Figure 4-4 shows the block diagram for a 4-bit 4040 type. The active level for the signals is given by the dash over the designation for active low. All other signals are active high; that is, when the signal is high, the function is true. For example, when the signal reset is high, the system is in the reset condition. If the signal had

Type	Word size data/inst	Max memory size	Max clock freq(MHz)	Inst time shortest/ longest	Number of internal general registers	Number of stack registers	On-chip clock	DMA	Voltages required	Number of basic instructions
4040	4/8	8K	.74	10.8/21.6	24	7X12	no	no	15	60
8008	8/8	16K	.8	12.5/37.5	6	7X14	no	no	5,-9	48
8080	8/8	64K	2.6	1.5/3.75	8	RAM	no	yes	5,12,-5	78
8085	8/8	64K	3	1.3/5.85	8	RAM	yes	yes	5	80
M6800	8/8	64K	2	1/3.5	0	RAM	no	yes	5	89
SC/MP	8/8	64K	4	5/10	0	RAM	yes	yes	5,-7	46
2650	8/8	32K	1.2	4.8/9.6	7	8X15	no	yes	5	75
PACE	16/16	64K	2	2.5/5	4	10X16	no	yes	5,8,-12	45
1802	8/8	64K	6.4	2.5/3.75	16	RAM	yes	yes	3 to 12	91
Z80	8/8	64K	4	1/5.75	14	RAM	no	yes	5	150

Fig. 4-3. Characteristics of several microprocessors.

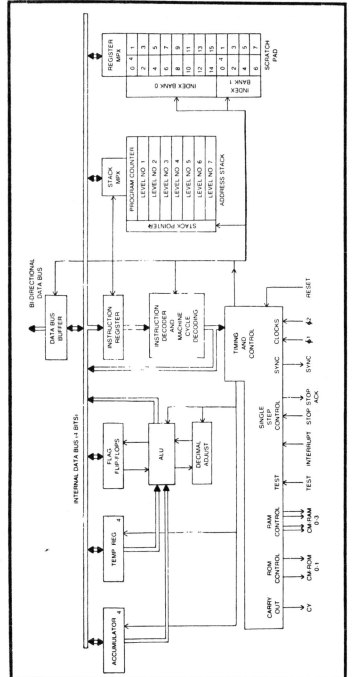

Fig. 4-4. 4040 functional block diagram (see parts list on page 55).

Pin	Signal	Function
1-4	D0-D3	Bidirectional data bus
5	STPA	Stop acknowledge; indicates the processor has entered the stop mode; output
6	STP	Stop; a high causes the processor to enter the stop mode; input
7	INT	Interrupt; a high causes the processor to enter the interrupt mode; input
8	INTA	Interrupt acknowledge; indicates that the processor has recognized the interrupt; output.
9	Vss	Circuit ground potential
10	φ1	Phase 1 timing signal; input.
11	φ2	Phase 2 timing signal; input.
12	Reset	A high resets the processor; setting the program counter to 00; input.
13	Test	Test; the logical state of this input can be examined by the program; input.
14	Vdd	Main supply voltage; normally -15V.
15	Vdd2	Voltage for outpuliffers, may be varied.
16	Sync	Syncronizing signal; sent to ROM and RAM memories to indicate the beginning of the instruction cycle; output.
17-20	CM-RAM0 CM-RAM3	RAM Bank Select; these signals are bank select signals for RAM memory.
21	Vdd1	Supply voltage for the timing signals, normally -15V.
2	CM-ROM0	ROM Bank Select; these signals are the bank
23	CM-ROM1	select signals for ROM or PROM memory.
24	CY	Carry; gives the state of the carry flip-flop.

Parts List for Fig. 4-4.

been designated reset, the system would be in the reset condition when the signal is low.

The 8080 is a second generation microprocessor. The first generation of the same family is the 8008, which is shown in Fig. 4-5. This is a smaller, slower unit, with fewer capabilities than the 8080. The third generation of the same family consists of the 8048 and the 8085, shown in Figs. 4-6 and 4-7 respectively. The 8048 is a true one-chip computer. It contains a microprocessor, 1K of ROM, 64 words of RAM, 27 input/output lines, and all support circuitry required. All that is required to operate the 8048 is 3 capacitors, a crystal, and a 5 volt power supply. Two capacitors and the crystal set the operating frequency. The third capacitor is for power up reset.

The 8085 is a combination of the microprocessor, clock generator, and system controller on one integrated circuit. This is compatible with the instructions used by the 8080, so programs developed using the 8080 can be used with the 8085 without program rewrite. Few of the third generation microprocessors offer this advantage.

The capability of the microprocessor is limited by the number of pins on the package. Most second and third generation units use 40 pin packages. This is presently the largest available package that has found widespread use. With 16 pins for the address bus and 8 pins for the data bus, only 16 pins are left for such other uses as control and power. If it is desirable to add some input/output ports to the microprocessor, there are not enough pins in the standard 40 pin package. This is solved in some systems, such as the 8048 and the 3850 (see Figs. 4-6 and 4-8), by multiplexing the data and address buses. For the 8048, the ALE signal signals that the data on port 0 is the low order 8 address bits, and the high order 4 bits on port 2 is the high order 4 address bits. This gives a total of 12 address lines. Both these ports can be used as data input/output ports during other portions of the instruction cycle. For this type system, all communication to and from the microprocessor is through the ports, under control of the various control signals. This type of microprocessor can be expanded using some of the special new multifunction chips which contain memory and input/output ports, but these chips have not yet been made available for widespread use.

Bit-slice processors are basically small pieces of a microprocessor. These are connected in parallel to make up any size system. For example, six 2-bit slice processors can be connected to form a 12-bit system. Bit slice systems require several chips to make up a system.

They offer the added feature that the instructions are contained in a microprogram memory in the form of microinstructions. These instructions are executed by the microprogram control unit. The bits in the microinstructions are used to set up the control logic to execute the instructions. The instructions can be tailored to suit the specific application, and the execution time is considerably shorter than for the standard microprocessor.

The microprocessor shown in Fig. 4-9 is different from the other systems. This is a 4-bit slice system from which the IMP 8 and IMP 16 systems are built. These are 8- and 16-bit systems, using 2 or 4 of the basic 5750 register and arithmetic units (RALU). A control read only memory (CROM), such as the 5751, is required to

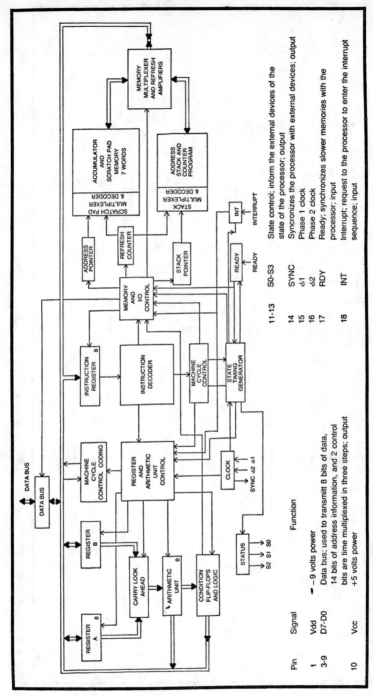

Pin	Signal	Function
1	Vdd	– 9 volts power
3-9	D7-D0	Data bus; used to transmitt 8 bits of data, 14 bits of address information, and 2 control bits are time multiplexed in three steps; output
10	Vcc	+5 volts power
11-13	S0-S3	State control; inform the external devices of the state of the processor; output
14	SYNC	Syncronizes the processor with external devices; output
15	φ1	Phase 1 clock
16	φ2	Phase 2 clock
17	RDY	Ready; synchronizes slower memories with the processor; input
18	INT	Interrupt; request to the processor to enter the interrupt sequence; input

Fig. 4-5. 8008 functional block diagram.

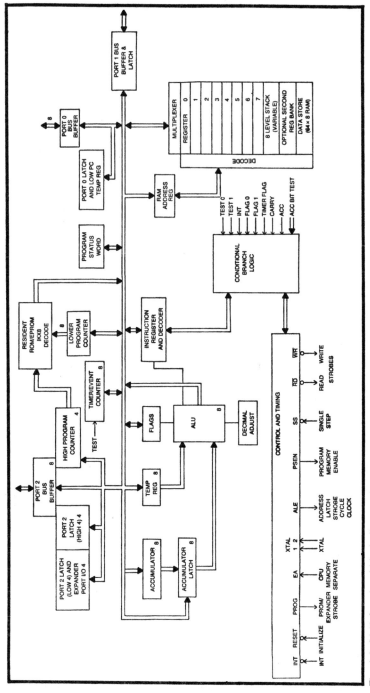

Fig. 4-6. 8048 functional block diagram (see parts list on page 59).

Pin	Signal	Function
1	T0	Test 0-this line can be sampled by the program as a condition input-input.
2	XTAL1	Crystal Input-one side of crystal input for external oscillator-input.
3	XTAL2	Other side of crystal input.
4	RESET	Reset-low initializes the processor
5	SS	Single Step-low enables single stepping the program, one instruction at a time-input.
6	INT	Interrupt-low initiates interrupt sequence if interrupt is enables-input.
7	EA	External Access-forces all program memory fetches to reference external memory-input.
8	RD	Output Strobe-low during a bus read. Used to enable data onto bus from external device-output.
9	PSEN	Program Strobe Enable-low during fetch to external program memory-output.
10	WR	Write-low during write, used as strobe to external memory-output.
11	ALE	Address Latch Enable-occurs once during each cycle-output.
12-19	D0-D7	Bus-bidirectional port which can be written or read by the processor.
20	Vss	Circuit ground potential
21-24 35-38	P20-P27	Port 2-8 bit quasi-bidirectional port
25	PROG	Programming pulse input pin for EPROM version.
26	Vdd	Programming power supply, +25V during programming,
27-34	P10-P17	Port 1-8 bit quasi-bidirectional port
39	T1	Test 1-this line can be sampled by the program as +5V during operation a test condition input.
40	Vcc	Main power supply, +5V.

Parts List for Fig. 4-6.

control the RALU for the execution of the instructions. The CROM generates the control signals for the RALU to execute the instructions. The control signals are stored in ROM memory, and are read by the signals generated by the RALU.

The bit-slice processor gives the advantage that instructions are stored in memory. These instructions are defined by the information stored in the memory of the CROM, and can be tailored to suit the needs of the user. Figure 4-10 shows the basic block diagram for such a system. Figure 4-11 shows the block diagram for a 16-bit processor. These processors offer potential for making systems

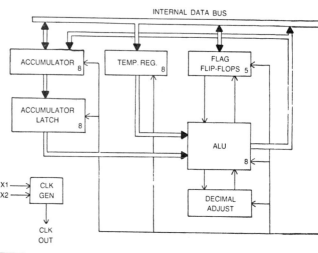

INTERNAL DATA BUS

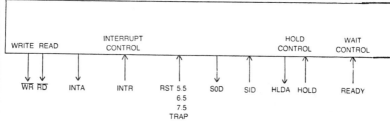

Pin	Signal	Function
1	X1	Crystal
2	X2	Crystal
3	RSOT	Reset out-reset for use by system-output
4	SOD	Serial output data line-set or reset as specified by the program-output
5	SID	Serial input data line-data on this line is loaded into accumulator bit 7 by program-input
6	TRAP	Nonmaskable restart interrupt. This is highest priority of any interrupt-input.
7	RST7.5	Highest priority restart interrupt-input
8	RST6.5	Second priority restart interrupt-input.
9	RST5.5	Lowest-priority restart interrupt-input.
10	INTR	Interrupt request-used as a general purpose interrupt-input.
11	INTA	Interrupt acknowledge-indicates that INTR has been recognized-output.
12-	AD0-	Low order 8 bits of address bus-output
19	AD7	

60

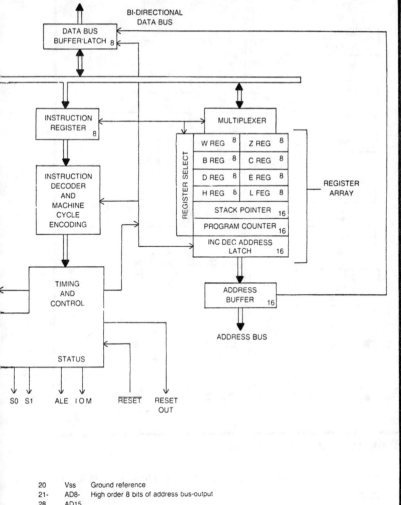

20	Vss	Ground reference
21-	AD8-	High order 8 bits of address bus-output
28	AD15	
29	S0	Bit 0 of data bus status
30	ALE	Address latch enable-occurs when address is on the data bus-output
31	$\overline{WR}$	Write- indicates on data bus is to be written into memory or I O-output 3 state
32	$\overline{RD}$	Read-indicates that the selected memory or I O is to be read-output 3 state
33	S1	Bit 1 of data bus status-output.
34	IO M	Input output memory-indicates whether the read write is to memory or to I O-output 3 state
35	Ready	High indicates that memory or peripheral is ready to send or receive data
36	$\overline{RST\ IN}$	Reset input-resets microprocessor and sets program counter to zero-input
37	CLK	Clock output
38	HLDA	Hold acknowledge-indicates that the CPU has received a hold request-output
39	HOLD	Hold request-request to CPU to cease operation upon completion of the current instruction-input.
40	Vcc	5 Volts

Fig. 4-7. 8085 functional block diagram.

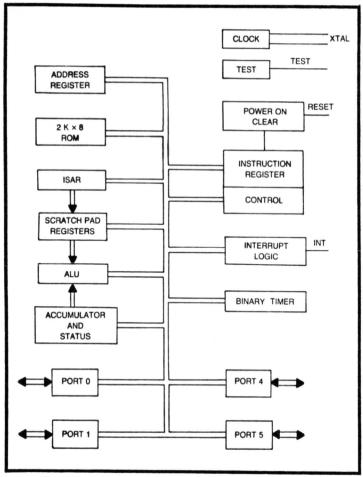

Fig. 4-8. 3850 functional block diagram.

tailored for sophisticated uses, where standard microprocessors are not practical.

BUS DRIVERS

Bus drivers are required wherever the load on a bus can exceed the drive capability of the unit driving the bus. Typical bus drivers have the load capability of 30 to 50 mA, which can drive several circuits at low impedance, giving some noise immunity to the bus.

Since the buses are tri-state, having three states of output, the drivers must also be tri-state. The three states are high (1), low (0), and off (high impedance). The off state turns off the signal, while the high and low states are detectable by the devices connected to the bus.

Figure 4-12 shows a 6-bit bus driver. The DIS 1 and 2 inputs enable the circuit. When either of these signals is high, the circuit is in the off state, with all outputs in the high impedance state. When both of these signals are low, the circuit acts as a buffer for the input. These enabling inputs must be connected to the desired signals

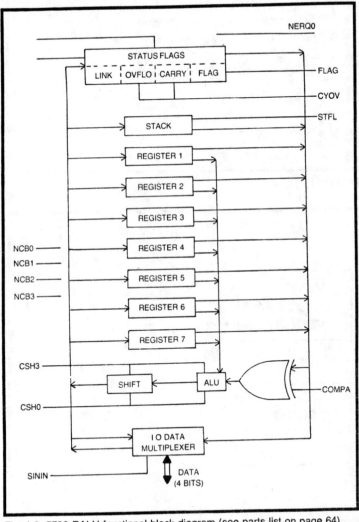

Fig. 4-9. 5790 RALU functional block diagram (see parts list on page 64).

Pin	Signal	Function
1	$\phi2$	Non-overlapping clock inputs
2	$\phi1$	
22	$\phi5$	
23	$\phi7$	
3	STFL	Stack full; indicates that the stack has been loaded with data in all 16 locations; output
4	D_2	Four bit bi-directional data bus
5	D_1	
7	D_3	
17	D_0	
6	NREQ0	Bus equals zero; output
8	V_{11}	Ground
9	SVRST	Save/restore; provides a means of modifying the status flags over the data bus; input
10	SININ	Designates most significant byte of a processor system; input
11	CSH3	Carry output
12	V_{ss}	+ 5 volts
13	Select	Selects either overflow or carry to CYOV-output.
14	CSH0	Carry-input
15	CYOV	Carry or overflow flag-output
16	Flat	Flag status-direct input to status flags.
18	NCB2	Command inputs from CROM
19	NCB1	
20	NCB3	
21	NCB0	
24	V_{gg}	− 12 Volts

Parts List for Fig. 4-9.

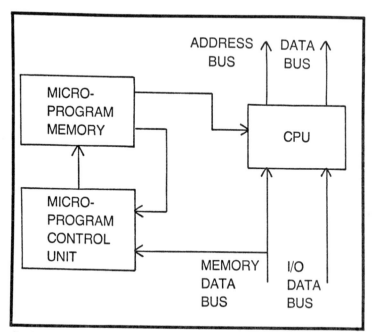

Fig. 4-10. Block diagram for a bit-slice microprocessor.

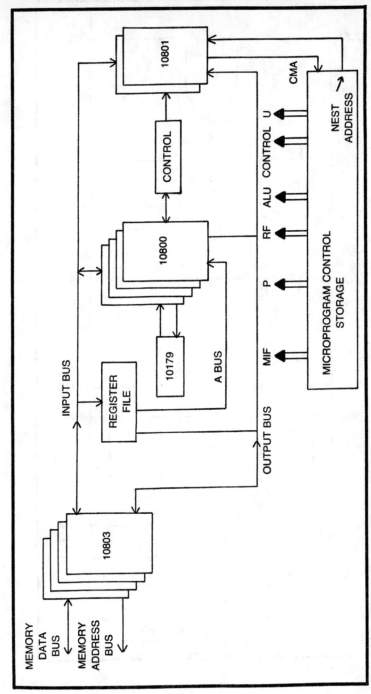

Fig. 4-11. Functional diagram for a bit-slice microprocessor.

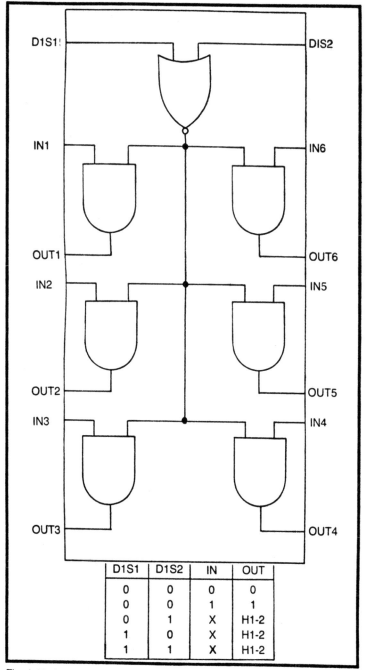

D1S1	D1S2	IN	OUT
0	0	0	0
0	0	1	1
0	1	X	H1-2
1	0	X	H1-2
1	1	X	H1-2

Fig. 4-12. A 6-bit bus driver schematic.

which will turn off the circuit when the bus is off, such as when a HLDA is generated.

Some systems use a multiplexed bus which has the address and data on the same bus, but at different times. For this type of application a latching-type driver is required. Figure 4-13 shows the use of the 8212 type chip for this application. $\overline{DS1}$ and DS2 are used to gate the information into the latch, and MD is used to tri-state the circuit.

These drivers work for data going in one direction, such as on the address bus. Figure 4-14 shows a typical bidirectional bus driver which drives the signal in both directions, with the input and output separated on one side. This provides separate data input and output lines for the processor or any other device. If the separate input and output is not required, these lines can be tied together as shown in Fig. 4-15. The DIEN signal input gates one directional driver or the other to achieve bidirectional data flow. The $\overline{CS}$ input provides a means of putting the outputs in the high impedance state.

Bus drivers are contained in the system controller chip, so data bus drivers are not required if the controller chip is used with the 8080 system.

The control logic to generate the control signals is also included. Figure 4-16 shows the 8228 connected into the system to provide the control signals and the data bus drivers. The $\overline{BUSEN}$ input forces the data bus output buffers and the control signal buffers into their high impedance state, allowing external control of the buses.

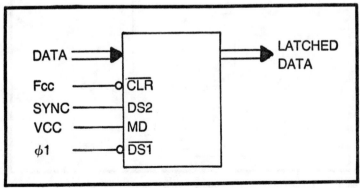

Fig. 4-13. Using the 8212 as a bus driver.

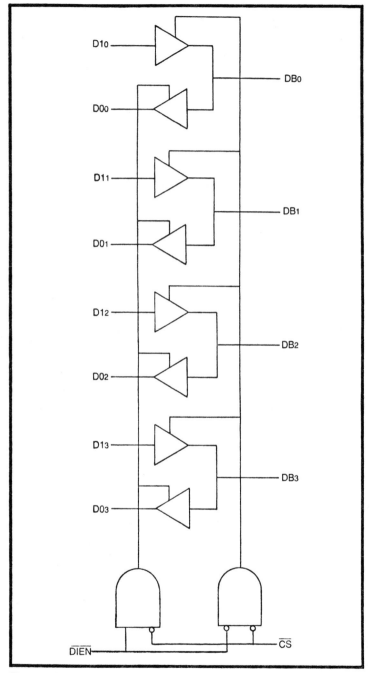

Fig. 4-14. Typical bi-directional bus driver.

SYSTEM CONTROLLER

Some microprocessor families require decoding the control signals from the processor and decoding the data bus to provide the control signals listed below in their proper time relationship:

1. Memory read ($\overline{\text{MEM R}}$)
2. Memory write ($\overline{\text{MEM W}}$)
3. I/O read ($\overline{\text{I/O R}}$)
4. I/O write ($\overline{\text{I/O W}}$)
5. Interrupt acknowledge ($\overline{\text{INTA}}$)

The first 4 signals are generated by gating the outputs of the status latch with DBIN and $\overline{\text{WR}}$. These signals control the memory and I/O devices. The interrupt acknowledge signal is used to enable the interrupt instruction port which holds the RST instruction on the data bus.

These signals for the 8080A system can be generated using an 8212 8-bit gated latch, but this would also require the use of added

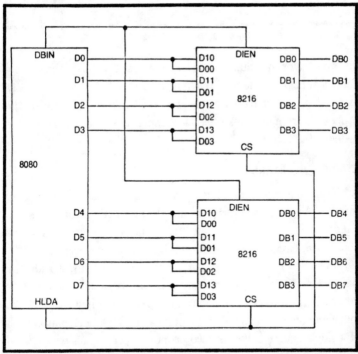

Fig. 4-15. Bi-directional bus driver with common input and a common output.

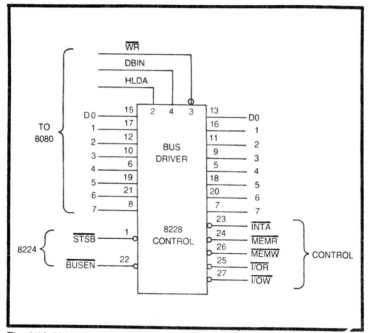

Fig. 4-16. Using the 8228 as a system controller.

bus drivers for the data bus and added gates. The 8228, the system controller chip for the 8080A family, replaces all this circuitry with a single chip. This chip provides bidirectional bus drivers to isolate the processor from the system. This improves noise immunity and reduces the loading.

CLOCK GENERATORS

Timing is required to keep the system operating in the correct manner. A sync pulse is issued when the instruction read starts. Using this pulse as a starting gate, timing pulses are generated by a countdown circuit operating from a basic clock generator.

All microprocessors require a system clock to provide the timing for the processor operations. The frequency of the clock determines the processor operating speed, and is limited by the maximum operating speed of the processor. This clock may consist of a single square wave, or two or more clock signals with a fixed time relationship. These clocks may be generated using a crystal or an RC network.

Some families of microprocessor families require only an RC timing network or crystal, with the actual oscillator inside the microprocessor. Others require a simple square wave generator, while others require complex clock generator circuits. Figure 4-17 gives the clock requirements for the various microprocessor families.

The clock circuits for the 8080A microprocessor must supply two non-overlapping clock signals, plus some control signals that effect the timing. These signals are status strobe, ready, and hold. The status strobe indicates when status information is available on the data bus. This is used to generate the control signals which determine which type of instruction is to be executed. The ready signal is generated in response to the wait request, and allows for reading of slower memories. The hold, generated by the hold request, is used to temporarily stop the processor and place the buses in their high impedance state. This is used by the Direct Memory Access inputs.

Figure 4-18 shows the schematic and waveshapes for a discrete component clock generator. This generates all the clock signals required by the 8080A and the control signals. The clock signals (ϕ1 and ϕ2) are converted from the TTL levels to the high levels required by the microprocessor. All this and an additional function which gives system reset provisions are contained in the clock generator chip (8224).

The frequency of the crystal is nine times the desired processor speed. For 500 ns, the basic crystal frequency is 18 mc. This divide-by-nine is accomplished in the clock generator to generate ϕ1 and ϕ2. When using crystals above 10 mHz, a small capacitance (3pf to 10pf) may be required in series with the crystal to provide trim. If overtone mode crystals are used, an LC network must be connected to the tank connection. This increases the gain to compensate for the

8080A—Two non-overlappling clock pulses.
        Clock period—0.48 to 2 usec.
2650 —Clock frequency DC to 1.25 MHz, TTL oscillator.
6800 —Two non-overlapping clock pulses Clock period—1 to 10 μs.
SC/MP—Internal oscillator. external crystal required. 01. to 4 MHz.

Fig. 4-17. Clock requirements for microprocessor families.

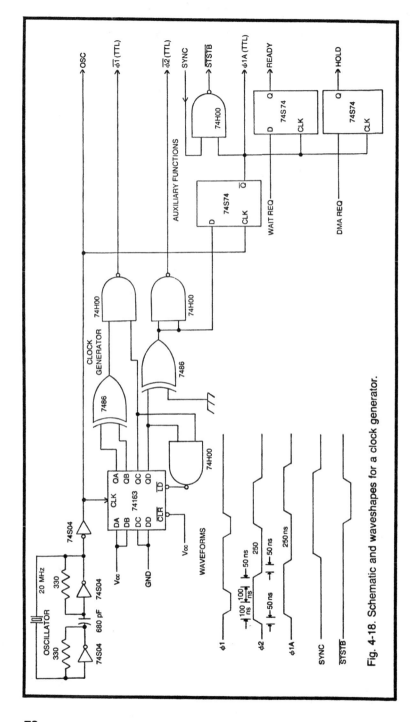

Fig. 4-18. Schematic and waveshapes for a clock generator.

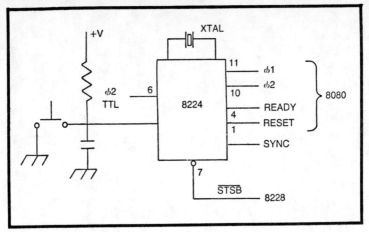

Fig. 4-19. Using the 8224 clock generator.

lower amplitude of this type crystal. The formula for the LC network is:

$$LC = 1/(2\pi F)^2$$

The reset function, $\overline{RESIN}$, incorporates a Schmitt trigger to provide a reset pulse when power is turned on. This input is also used to provide system reset by using a pushbutton switch to ground this input, as shown in Fig. 4-19. This figure also shows pin connections for the 8224.

The RDYIN input provides for an external wait request which places the processor in the wait mode by controlling the ready input to the processor.

Chapter 5

Microprocessor Memories

The memory stores the program and data in addressable memory cells. The information is stored as a series of highs and lows which can be detected by amplifiers when the memory location is read. This chapter will discuss the different types of memory available, and how memory is accessed by the microprocessor.

TYPES OF MEMORIES

There are two basic classifications of memories: Read Only Memories (ROMs) and Random Access Memories (RAMs).

The microprocessor system can read data from the write data into a RAM. This type of memory is normally used for temporary program storage and data storage. Unless special precautions are taken, the data in RAM storage will be lost when power is turned off. When power is applied to a RAM, it may come up with either a 1 or a 0 in any bit cell, and the result will be unpredictable. So if the initial value of a RAM memory is assumed to be zero by the program, it must be initialized that way with the program.

The microprocessor system can only read data from a ROM. ROMs are programmed either at the time of manufacture or by a special programmer. ROMs are used to store permanent programs, and other data that should not be lost when power is removed.

Read Only Memories

There are three types of ROMs: Read Only Memories (ROMs), Programmable Read Only Memories (PROMs), and Erasable Programmable Read Only Memories (EPROMs).

ROMs. The ROM is preprogrammed during the manufacture of the chip. The last step before encapsulation is to coat the entire surface of the chip with a layer of aluminum. This coating is then selectively etched, leaving the desired interconnecting pattern. Since this pattern is made up from the customers program, the cost of the chip is quite high for small quantities, but the charge to make up the mask which generates the pattern is a one time charge, so the cost per chip is low for high volumes. This makes ROM memories the cheapest for high volumes.

ROMs are available with preprogrammed data, which can be used with almost any system. Figure 5-1 lists several of the preprogrammed ROMs. These are available containing programs, look-up tables, or conversion tables. The use of the ROMs can simplify programming since the data is available and does not have to be generated.

Type Number	Number of pins	Voltages	Program
2516N	24	+5,−5,−12	ASCII Characters
MM4220AE MM5220AE	24		ASCII-7 to Hollerith
MM4220AP MM5220AP	24		BCDIC to ASCII
MM4220BL MM5220BL	24		Baudot to ASCII
MM4220BM MM5220BM	24	+12,−12	Sine look up table
MM4220BN MM5220BN	24	+12,−12	Arctangent look up table
MM4220DF MM5220DF	24	+12,−12	'Quick brown fox"
MM4220NP MM4230NN MM4230NO	24	+12,−12	7 × 9 horizontal scan display character generator
MCM6570 MCM6571 MCM6571A MCM6572 to MCM6579	24	+12,+5, −3	Horizontal scan character generators with shifted characters
MCM6580 MCM6581 MCM6583	24	+12, +5,−3	Vertical scan character generator
MCM6591	24	+12,+5,−3	Six different character conversion codes

Fig. 5-1. Preprogrammed ROMs.

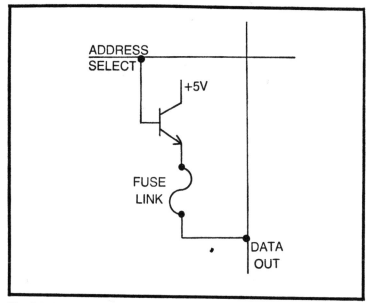

Fig. 5-2. A typical fusible link memory cell.

PROMs. PROMs are Programmable Read Only Memories. These are user-programmable; but, once programmed, they cannot be reprogrammed. These are made with a fusible link which is blown during the programming. Once programmed, the blown fuses cannot be restored, but additional fuses can be blown.

Figure 5-2 shows a typical fusible link cell. This type of memory comes with all locations as a logical 1, with all fuses intact. During programming the selected fuses are blown for the zeros. If the fuse is not blown, the output will be high when it is strobed. If the fuse is blown, or open, the output will be open, which will be detected as a low by the sense amplifiers.

The typical programming procedure for a unit which has all high levels during manufacture is as follows:

1. Apply V_{cc}.
2. Using the address inputs, select the location to be programmed.
3. Apply a logic high (5 volts) to either or all enable inputs.
4. Apply a programming pulse to the outputs where a low level is desired. The voltage and current must be limited to the value given on the specification sheet.

5. Verify that the bit has been programmed by applying a logic zero to the enable inputs, and check for a low level at the output.

6. Advance to the next bit or address, and repeat.

Another version of the fusible link PROM is shown in Fig. 5-3. This PROM comes with all locations as a low, with the fuses intact. When the fuse is blown, the output goes high. Here again, once this unit is programmed, the highs cannot be reprogrammed, but the lows can be made high by blowing additional fuses.

The typical programming procedure for PROM which is shipped with the bits low is as follows:

1. Terminate all device outputs with a 10K resistor to V_{cc}.

2. Select the address to be programmed.

3. Raise V_{cc} to V_{ccp}.

4. After 10 μs delay, apply I_{out} to the output to be programmed. Program only one bit at a time.

5. After 10 μs delay, enable chip select (logic 0 for $\overline{CS}$ and logic 1 for CS) for 1 to 2 ms.

6. After 10 μs delay, remove I_{out} from the programmed output.

7. After 10 μs delay, return V_{cc} to 0 volts.

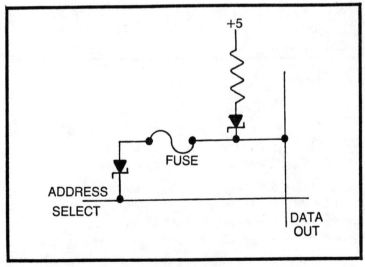

Fig. 5-3. A second type of fusible link memory cell.

Type Number	Number of Pins	Voltage	Organization
74S287	16	5	256 × 4
74S387			
74S470	20	5	256 × 8
74S471			
74S570	16	5	512 × 4
74S571			
72S114	24	5	256 × 8
DM7577	16	5	32 × 8
SN74188	16	5	32 × 8
DM75S222	20	5	256 × 8
82S23	16	5	32 × 8
82S123			
10139	16	5	32 × 8
82S27	16	5	256 × 4
82S126	16	5	256 × 4
82S129			
82S130	16	5	512 × 4
82S131			
82S114	24	5	256 × 8
82S115	24	5	512 × 8
82S136	18	5	1024 × 4
82S137			

Fig. 5-4. Fusible link PROMs.

8. To verify programming, after 50 μs delay apply $V_{cc} = 5$ volts, and enable chip select. The programmed bits should be as programmed.

9. Repeat for all other bits to be programmed.

These are only two of the many typical programming procedures for PROMs. Always consult the specification sheet for the programming requirements. Figure 5-4 lists the characteristics of several PROMs, along with the programming requirements.

Most programming requires pulsing of the writing voltage or current. If the duty cycle of the pulse is too long, the device can be damaged, so most PROM programmers use one-shots to apply the high current.

Figure 5-5 shows a manual programmer for a SN74186 PROM. This is a 64-byte by 8-bit memory. The six address leads must be all held at -5 to -6 VDC (low for programming). This selects address 0. The address switches are opened in a binary order to count up the address. The programming pulse must be less than -7 VCD at 120 to 130 milliamps for at least 700 milliseconds. The one shot provides the relay control to generate this pulse. PROMs with similar programming requirements can be programmed with this unit by chang-

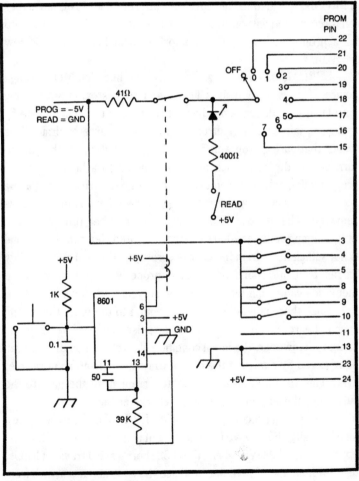

Fig. 5-5. SN74186 programmer.

ing the time constant, voltage levels, and current limiting to those required by the type of PROM used.

Programmers are built which are under program control, and connected to an output port of a microprocessor system. The program sets up the delay time, but external circuitry must be used to set up the voltages and currents required. So different circuits are required for the various voltage and current levels. Care must be taken not to exceed the maximum duty cycle.

EPROMs. Erasable Programmable Read Only Memories (EPROMs) are permanent memories which are erasable and reprogrammable by the user. Although the cost of these is more than that of PROMs, it is justified because they are reusable. Program errors can be corrected without the cost of a new chip, and when the need for a program is over, the memory can be loaded with a new program.

EPROMs use a floating gate avalanche injection MOS storage device. This is essentially a field effect transistor with a floating gate. Operation depends on charge transport to the floating gate by avalanche injection of electrons from either source or drain. This means that during programming, a charge is built up on the gate to turn on the devices which are programmed to a high. Once the programming voltage is removed, there is no discharge path for the accumulated charge on the gate. So it remains, even after power is removed. The electric field in the structure after removal of the programming voltage is due to the accumulated electron charge, and is not sufficient to drain the charge across the thermal oxide energy barrier built up around the gate. If properly programmed, these memories can retain information for 10 years or more.

Since there is no electrical connection to the gate, the charge cannot be removed by an electrical pulse, such as reading the memory. However, the initial condition of no charge on the gate can be restored by exposing the device to radiation from an ultraviolet light. This results in a flow of photocurrent from the gate to the substrate, thereby discharging the charge at the gate.

The erasing procedure for a typical EPROM is as follows: Use a high intensity short-wave ultraviolet light at a wavelength of 2537 A. Examples are the UVS-54 and the S-52 short wave ultraviolet lamps, used without short wave filters. Place the lamp about one inch from

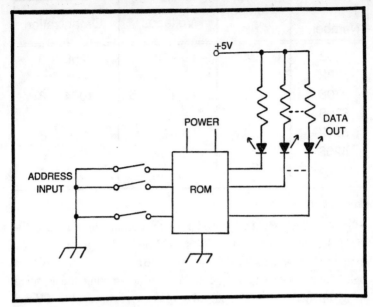

Fig. 5-6. Manual EPROM reader.

the chip. Erasing time is 10 to 20 minutes. The erasing can be checked by reading the EPROM with a system or manual EPROM reader. Figure 5-6 shows one such reader. The addresses are manually selected, and the proper enable signals are applied to the chip. An LED on indicates a 1 in that bit position of the selected address. This device can be built in a small box with the socket, switches, and LEDs mounted on the cover, or it can be built on a small circuit board. To use the reader, plug in the memory being read, apply power and set up the address on the switches. To read, depress the switch and read the LEDs, then release the switch.

Always, when using ultraviolet lamps, take precautions not to look into the lamp, or to expose hands or body to the direct radiation. These lamps give off a faint blue glow, so the operation can be checked by observing the blue glow reflected from the top of the chips.

Figure 5-7 lists several EPROMs and gives some of the programming requirements. Figure 5-8 shows typical programming waveshapes. The object of the programming is to build up a charge on the floating gate, making it a 1. The object of erasing is to neutralize the charge on the floating gate, making the bits all zeros.

Type Number	Number of pins	Voltages	Organization
1702 8702	24	+5,−9	256 × 8
2708 8708	24	+5,+12,−5	1024 × 8
5202	24	+5,−9	256 × 8
4203	24	+5,−12	256 × 8
4204	24	+5,−12	512 × 8

Fig. 5-7. EPROMs.

The following is the procedure for programming a 1702A EP-ROM. During programming, V_{cc} should be held at ground and V_{bb} should be held at +12V. Address levels are approximately -40V for a logic '0' and about 0V for a logic '1.' When programming, the negative going supply (V_{dd}) must be pulsed to -47V. V_{gg} is brought to -9V and the complement of the address to be programmed is applied.

After power is applied for at least 25 microseconds, the address must be returned to its true form. Ten or more microseconds after this, and at least 100 microseconds after turning on power, the 3 millisecond program pulse is applied. During the interval when V_{dd} is applied, data signals are applied to the data output lines. A data level of 0V will result in the bit remaining unchanged, while a level of -47V will program a logic '1.' After the program pulse is turned off. V_{dd} and V_{gg} must be turned off. This turn off should occur from 10 to 100 milliseconds after removal of the program pulse.

For best results, each address should be programmed at least 32 times. The duty cycle for applied power must not exceed 20%. Usually all the addresses are sequenced through 32 times to keep the duty cycle low, and assure complete writing of the programmed bits.

As with PROMs, there are many different programming requirements for the different EPROMs. The procedure is basically the same, but the times, voltages, and currents are different. Programmers are available which can program a limited number of types of EPROMs. Several of these programmers have several 'personality' boards which match the characteristics of the various EPROMs.

Figure 5-9 shows the schematic for a programmer for the 2708 EPROM. This unit is connected to the output port of a microprocessor system, and uses a computer program to program the 1K by 8 memory.

The 2708 is set up for programming by raising the $\overline{CS}$ input to 12 volts. The address is selected in the normal manner, using the address inputs. Data to be programmed is then placed on the data output lines. The logic level of the address and data signals is 5 volts, the same as the system levels. After the address and data are set up, one program pulse is applied to the program pin (P). This pulse must be between 0.1 and 1 millisecond long. Normally all addresses are programmed sequentially, then the programming is repeated until the sum of all the pulse widths for any one address is greater than 100 milliseconds. If the pulse width of the program pulse is 0.5 milliseconds, it will take 200 passes through the pro-

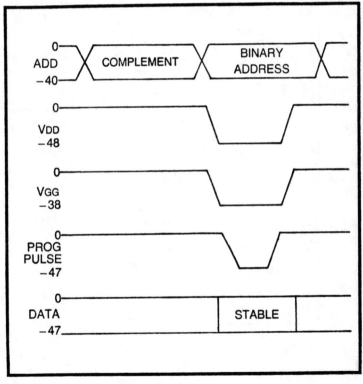

Fig. 5-8. Typical programming waveshapes.

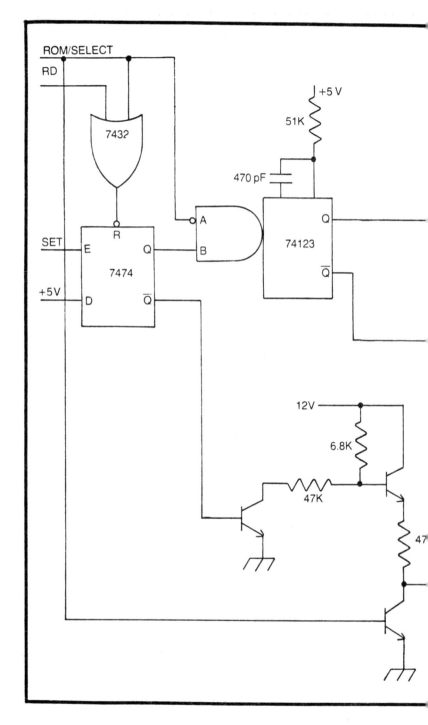

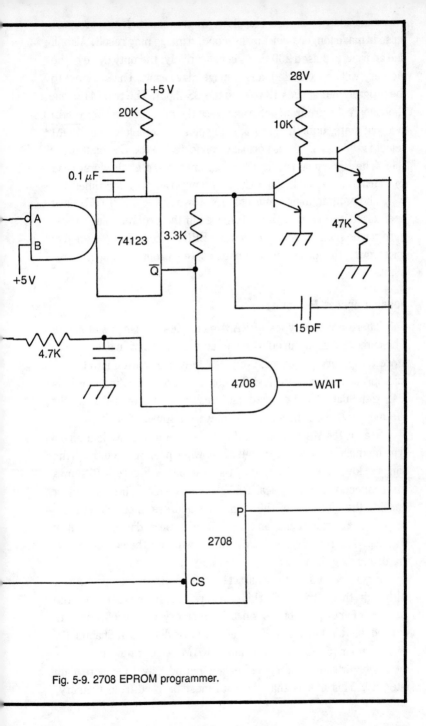

Fig. 5-9. 2708 EPROM programmer.

85

gramming loop to assure complete programming. If the program pulse is made longer than 1 millisecond, damage may result. Also, if one address is pulsed 200 times consecutively, the duty cycle of the memory will be exceeded, and damage may result. The set input to the programmer applies 12 volts to the $\overline{CS}$ input. The two 74123 one shots apply the program pulse and place the microprocessor system in a wait state, until the programming pulse is complete. The $\overline{ROM}$ $\overline{select}$ is the signal that is normally connected to the $\overline{CS}$ input of the chip. The RD signal resets the programmer. To meet worst case specifications, all addresses should be programmed 255 times.

The programming requirements of two types of EPROMs have been discussed so that the differences in the programming procedure can be seen. Carefully check any EPROM to be programmed to make sure the programmer matches the programming requirements.

Random Access Memories

There are two types of RAM memories, dynamic and static. These memories are used to store temporary program data, and to store temporary programs. Normally they are written into by the microprocessor system, and the contents are lost when power is lost. If the data is to be saved, facilities must be provided to power the memory when the system is powered down.

Static RAMs. Static RAM memories are usually field effect type memory cells, which output a high when programmed. Both the high and low states are forced by the read pulse. Figure 5-10 shows the connections to a typical RAM memory chip. The chip select enables the circuitry of the chip. The address lines address the respective memory cells, and the data lines carry data in and out of the chip. The read/write signal controls whether the chip is receiving or sending data.

Figure 5-10 lists the characteristics of several static RAMs. Although these memory chips are relatively inexpensive, the number of bits per chip is small. A memory expansion board to expand the RAM memory of a small system is detailed in Chapter 10.

Dynamic RAMs. Dynamic RAMs are random access memories which must be refreshed periodically to ensure data integrity. This means that the data must be read from memory,

Type Number	Number of Pins	Voltages	Organization
2101	22	+5	256 × 4 Static
8101			
2102	16	+5	1024 × 1 Static
2111	18	+5	256 × 4 Static
6604	16	+12 ,+5,−5	4096 × 1 Dynamic
6605	22	+12, +5,−5	4096 × 1 Dynamic
6616	16		16384 × 1 Dynamic
14505	14	10	64 × 1 Static
14537	16	10	256 × 1 Static
14552	24	10	64 × 4 Static
2601	22	5	256 × 4 Static
2611	18	5	256 × 4 Static
2112	16	5	256 × 4 Static
2612	16	5	256 × 4 Static
2606	16	5	256 × 4 Static
2680	22	5,12,−5	4096 × 1 Dynamic
1101	16	5,−9	256 × 1 Static
4262	22	5,8.5,−15	2048 × 1 Dynamic
5262			
8111	18	5	256 × 4 Static
5101	22	5	256 × 4 Static

Fig. 5-10. Static RAMs.

amplified, and read back into memory. Typically, the memory cells must be reprogrammed every two milliseconds.

Although this requires extra circuitry, a large dynamic memory is cheaper, requires less power, and has higher density of bits per square inch than static RAMs. For large requirements, these chips with supporting circuitry can be cost effective. For example, a 2116 type memory chip is organized as a 16K by 1 memory. So eight of these 16 pin chips, and a refresh circuit are required for a 16K memory, which occupies less than 16 square inches of board space.

Figure 5-11 shows the concept of a dynamic memory cell. It is basically a capacitor with a read and a write switch. During the write operation, the write switch is closed, and the input amplifier charges the capacitor to the required voltage. Then the switch is opened,

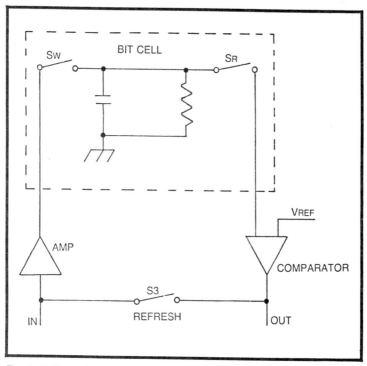

Fig. 5-11. Dynamic memory cell.

and the leakage resistance slowly drains the charge on the capacitor. For the read operation, the read switch is closed, and the capacitor voltage is compared to the reference voltage by the comparator. The output is forced high for a 'one' and low for a 'zero.'

Due to the leakage of the memory cell, the voltage stored in the memory cell will gradually decrease, resulting in all zeros, and the data being lost. To overcome this, the cell is recharged to increase the capacitor voltage for the stored ones. This is the refresh mode, in which the output of the memory is connected to the input to the memory, rewriting or recharging the voltage in the cell. This must be done without interfering with the normal operation of the micro-processor system. The memory cannot be read during the refresh cycle, because addressing may not be the same. That is, one ad-dress may not be addressed while another is being refreshed. Both addresses on the address bus will cause problems. Also, only small sections of the RAM are accessed by the program at a time, so not all addresses may be addressed during the refresh time. The refresh cycle may be under program control, where a subroutine addresses and rewrites all RAM memory locations, but provisions must be made to enter this subroutine often enough to refresh memory before the voltage deteriorates to a level beyond recovery. This can be done with an interrupt and a timer.

Hardware is often used to refresh memory. This circuit consists of a timer and gating circuits. The timer determines when it is time to refresh. The gates place the microprocessor in the wait mode, stopping operation while the outputs are connected to the inputs. Then the address bus is sequenced through the addresses requiring refreshing. For exact refresh requirements and applications consult the specification sheet.

MEMORY ACCESS

A memory can be functionally illustrated as shown in Fig. 5-12. To read this memory takes a memory read pulse and an address on the address bus. The address decoder decodes the address and provides a single line output for each binary word input. For example, to address word 3 requires that address lines 0 and 1 be high (binary 3). The decoder senses this and generates a high on the 03 line, and a low on the other decoder output lines. This high applies a positive to the anodes of the diodes connected to line 03.

When the memory read pulse is present, the sense amplifiers are enabled. If address 0 is being read (address decoder output line 0 high), the top row of switches will be enabled. The input to the sense amplifiers will depend on the position of the switches in the top row. And open switch results in a zero output while a closed switch results in a 1 output. If switch 00 is closed and the remaining switches open, the output will be 0001. If switches 01 and 03 are closed, the output will be 1010. The output will be only when the memory read pulse is present, otherwise the output will be off.

Each of the switches represents a memory cell, capable of storing one bit of information. It takes 8 memory cells to store one 8-bit computer word or byte. When the memory is loaded, or written into, the switches are functionally closed for 1's and left open for 0's. The data is read out in parallel, with all bits for the same word (horizontal row) enabled and read at the same time.

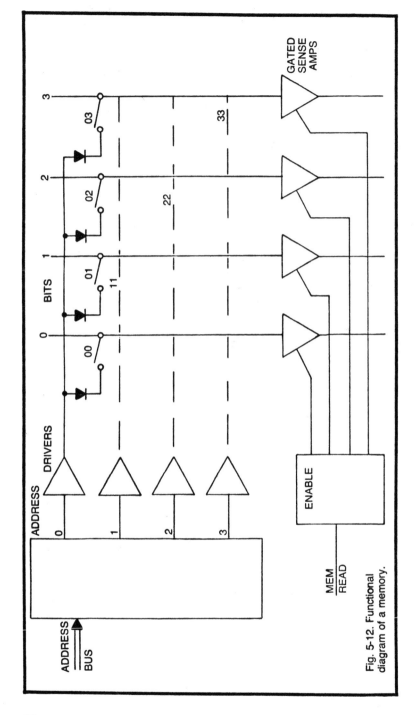

Fig. 5-12. Functional diagram of a memory.

90

Address Decoders

When several memory chips are connected into a system, each chip must be enabled for its particular addresses. For example, for 8 memories, each of 100 (hex) bytes, the addresses of each chip would be as shown below:

Chip	Addresses	Binary Bits				
0	0- FF	0000	0000	0000 - 0000	1111	1111
1	100-1FF	0001	0000	0000 - 0001	1111	1111
2	200-2FF	0010	0000	0000 - 0010	1111	1111
3	300-3FF	0011	0000	0000 - 0011	1111	1111
4	400-4FF	0100	0000	0000 - 0100	1111	1111
5	500-5FF	0101	0000	0000 - 0101	1111	1111
6	600-6FF	0110	0000	0000 - 0110	1111	1111
7	700-7FF	0111	0000	0000 - 0111	1111	1111

Notice that high order four binary bits of each address show a binary progression from one chip to the next. Since the 256 (100 hex) word memory has 8 address input lines, the low order 8 bits are connected to these inputs. A chip select signal enables the memory chip. It is this signal which determines which memory chip is enabled for which addresses. The purpose of the address decoder chips is to decode the binary number, and generate signals for each number. Typically these are 1-of-8 decoders, as shown in Fig. 5-13.

This circuit decodes the three address inputs, A_0, A_1, and A_2, to achieve eight outputs, O_0 thru O_7. The decoded output is low, and all the remaining outputs are high. This corresponds to the active low

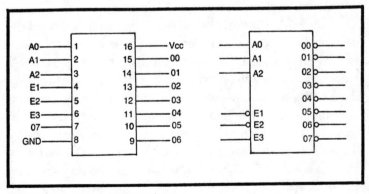

Fig. 5-13. A typical 1-of-8 decoder.

ADDRESS			ENABLE			OUTPUTS							
A0	A1	A2	E1	E2	E3	0	1	2	3	4	5	6	7
L	L	L	L	L	H	L	H	H	H	H	H	H	H
H	L	L	L	L	H	H	L	H	H	H	H	H	H
L	H	L	L	L	H	H	H	L	H	H	H	H	H
H	H	L	L	L	H	H	H	H	L	H	H	H	H
L	L	H	L	L	H	H	H	H	H	L	H	H	H
H	L	H	L	L	H	H	H	H	H	H	L	H	H
L	H	H	L	L	H	H	H	H	H	H	H	L	H
H	H	H	L	L	H	H	H	H	H	H	H	H	L
X	X	X	L	L	L	H	H	H	H	H	H	H	H
X	X	X	H	L	L	H	H	H	H	H	H	H	H
X	X	X	L	H	L	H	H	H	H	H	H	H	H
X	X	X	H	H	L	H	H	H	H	H	H	H	H
X	X	X	H	L	H	H	H	H	H	H	H	H	H
X	X	X	L	H	H	H	H	H	H	H	H	H	H
X	X	X	H	H	H	H	H	H	H	H	H	H	H

Fig. 5-14. Truth table for address decoder.

chip select inputs for most memories. Figure 5-14 gives the truth table for this decoder. Three enable inputs are provided to enable or disable the decoder. Enable 1 and 2 (E_1 and E_2) are active low, so they must be low for the decoder to generate an output. Enable 3 (E_3) is active high, so it must be high to enable the decoder. As shown in the truth table, any other condition of the enable inputs disables the decoder, resulting in all high outputs.

Figure 5-15 shows the use of the enable inputs to connect two decoders to provide the chip select signals to sixteen memory chips, each 256 bytes long. This assumes that address lines 13, 14, and 15 are not used. If they are, provisions will have to be made to prevent the enabling of these decoders when those addresses are used. Since the upper decoder is enabled when A_{11} and A_{12} are low, if A_{13} is high and all other address lines are low, the top decoder will output 0_0. The lower decoder is enabled when A_{11} is high and A_{12} is low, so protection is built in for A_{12} if it is used. To protect against the remaining address lines, connect A_{12}, A_{13}, A_{14}, and A_{15} to an AND gate, and connect the output to the E_2 input.

The 8205 is a 1-of-8 decoder. That is, it decodes the inputs (3 lines), and generates an output on one of eight lines, depending on the binary equivalent of the input. This fits in a standard 16 pin DIP package. Larger decoders can be used for larger memory systems, such as a 1-of-16 decoder. This decodes the four input lines and generates an output on one of 16 lines. Although this takes a 24 pin DIP package, it is equivalent to the two decoders shown, and normally has two active low enable inputs. In fact, almost any of the available decoders can be used for address decoding, providing the voltage levels are compatible and the loading on the address bus is low. For this reason, it is advisable to use CMOS type integrated circuits.

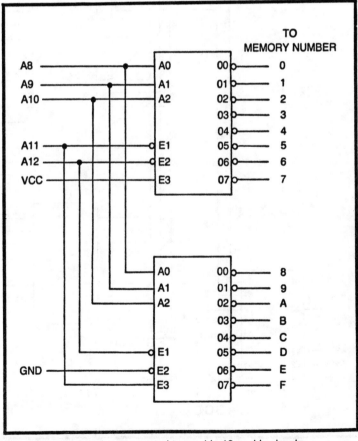

Fig. 5-15. Two decoders connected to provide 16 enable signals.

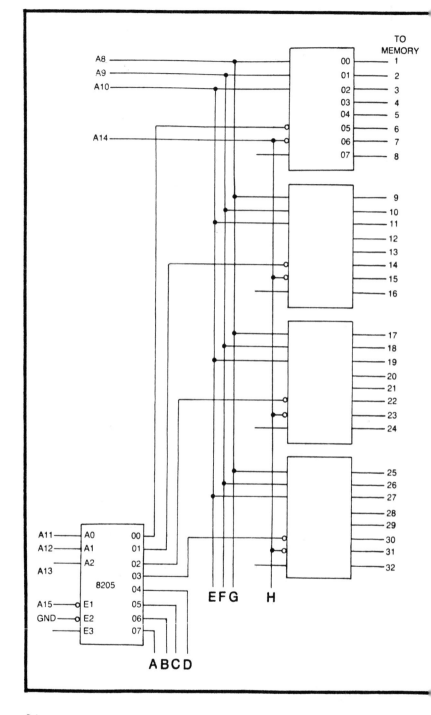

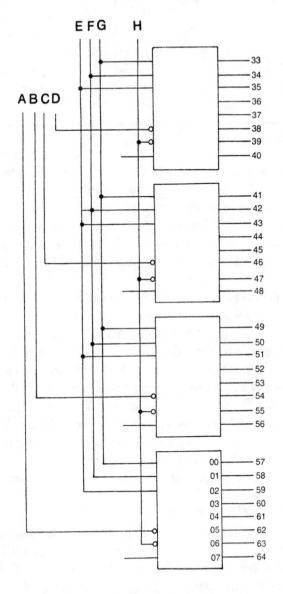

Fig. 5-16. Using decoders to provide 64 chip select signals.

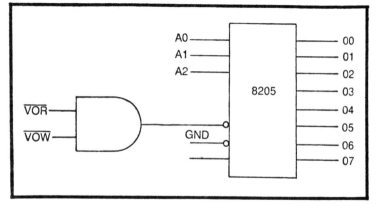

Fig. 5-17. I/O decoder.

For large memory systems, decoders can be pyramided, as shown in Fig. 5-16. This circuit provides 64 chip select signals by using one decoder to provide one of the enable inputs to eight other decoders. This circuit is shown to decode address lines A_8 through A_{13}. A_{14} and A_{15} are connected to other high active enable inputs of the decoders, which disables the decoders if these address lines are used.

Decoders can also be used to enable input or output circuits by connecting the low order address lines to the decoder, as shown in Fig. 5-17. This provides eight enable signals from the lower three address lines. Input/Output (I/O) read and I/O write are OR'd and connected to one of the enable inputs, so the decoders are enabled only for an I/O instruction. This connection requires that the I/O read and I/O write also go to the I/O circuits. To eliminate this, two decoders can be used as shown in Fig. 5-18. One of the decoders is for inputs and the other decoder is for outputs, so only one enable signal is required for each of the input and output circuits.

Figure 5-19 lists some decoders and their characteristics.

Memory Organization

Memory organization refers to how the individual cells in the memory are connected. A 4 by 4 memory is 4 words, each 4 bits long. A 256 bit memory can be 256 by 1, 32 by 8, or 64 by 4. The 256 by 1 means that the memory chip supplies one data bit for 256 different sequential memory addresses. To make up a 256 by 8 memory from these chips requires eight chips, connected as shown in Fig. 5-20. The data lines are stacked, with one data line to each of the eight chips. The addresses are connected in parallel, so that when an address is read, all eight chips are enabled, with one chip supplying data to one data line.

Memory chips have an enable control signal which enables the total chip. Using this enable, the memory chip can be at almost any address, by connecting the address expansion bus to this pin. For example, a 64 word chip requires six address lines, and contains 40 (hex) words. By decoding the next two address lines and using these as the enable signal, a total of 256 (100 hex) words are addressed. Figure 5-21 shows the interconnection for a 256 by 8 memory using 64 by 4 memory chips. The low order six address lines address each

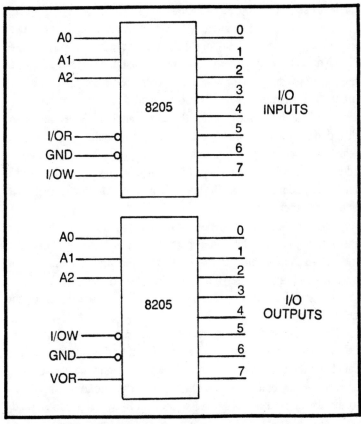

Fig. 5-18. Separate input and output decoders.

8205	1 of 8 decoder	
74138	3 to 8 decoder	
74139	2 to 4 decoder	Fig. 5-19. Address decoders.
74154	4 to 16 decoder	
74155	2 to 4 decoder	
74156	2 to 4 decoder	

memory, and the next two address bits are decoded to enable the selected memories. The left two chips are enabled for addresses 0-63 (0-3F hex), the second two for addresses 64-127 (40-7F hex), the third pair for addresses 128-191 (80-BF hex), and the right pair for addresses 192-255 (C0-FF hex).

The low order data bits (0-3) are stored in the top row of chips, while the high order data bits (4-7) are stored in the lower chips.

Normally, larger memory chips are used. Figure 5-22 shows the functional diagram for connecting four 256 by 8 chips into a 1024 memory. Each memory chip is 100 hex addresses long, and requires eight (0-7) address lines. So for this case, address lines 8 and 9 are decoded to provide the chip enable signals to make up a 400 (hex) word memory. Chip A contains addresses 0-FF and is enabled by address expansion line 0. Chip B contains addresses 100-1FF and is enabled by address expansion line 1. This makes for logical organization of the memory.

Realize that the low order address lines must be connected to the memory chip, and the next higher order lines must be decoded for the expansion bus. If there is only one memory chip in the system, the enable line is not required, so the enable is tied to ground or +V, whichever is required as the active level for the enable input.

Some form of memory read/write is requisite to all memory chips. This tells the memory to read data on to the data bus, or load data from the data bus. For memories which cannot be written into, usually the chip enable input is the signal to the memory to read data to the data bus. For memories which can be written into, a read/write signal, a data in, and a data out signal are used. Sometimes an output disable is used to replace the data in/data out signals.

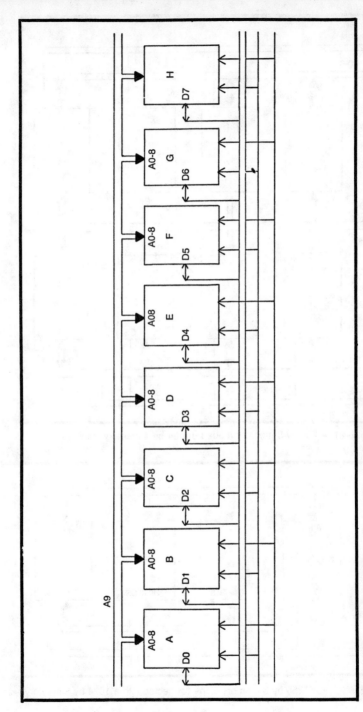

Fig. 5-20. A 256 by 8 memory made from 256 by 1 memory chips.

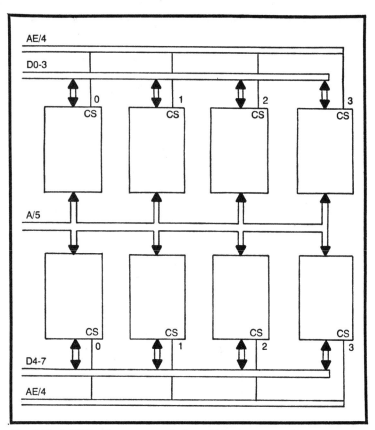

Fig. 5-21. A 256 by 8 memory made from 64 by 4 memory chips.

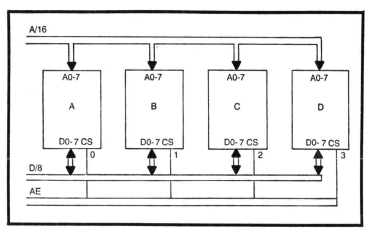

Fig. 5-22. Four 256 by 8 memory chips connected into a 1024 by 8 memory.

100

Direct Memory Access

Direct memory access (DMA) allows the transfer of data directly from an external device to memory without program intervention. The processor is temporarily frozen while the data is transferred under external circuit control.

The use of the DMA capability is beyond the scope of this book. The control circuitry is quite involved, consisting of registers, gates, counters, and address control circuits. Single chip programmable DMA controllers are available which under program control provide complete control for DMA inputs.

Chapter 6
Input/Output Schemes

For a system to communicate with external devices requires some type of interface circuit to get the correct data from the data bus or to the data bus at the correct time. The circuit which does this is called a *port*, either an input port or an output port. Sometimes the port circuitry also contains the input or output device, such as a keyboard or LED display. Other ports connect remote devices, such as printers and terminals, to the system.

There may be several ports connected to the same system, so to differentiate between ports they are numbered. These numbers are the address of the port, and are connected to the address bus. They are addressed when their address appears on the address bus. Input and output ports can have the same address, such as IN 01 and OUT 01. They are kept separate by the I/O read and I/O write signals connected to the select inputs of the ports. To enable a port requires an I/O read signal for input ports or an I/O write signal for output ports, and the port address on the address bus.

There are many input/output schemes, and the choice of which to use depends on the type of information transferred and the device connected to the port. Most applications fit into the normal input/output mode which uses conventional addressing and the instructions for input and output.

INTERFACING

The input and output devices depend on the application. The port, which connects to the data bus, is addressable and must not load the bus. This port may drive other devices to provide the proper response to fulfill the need of the port. When designing the output circuitry, care must be taken to assure that the semiconductors are not overstressed by high voltages or currents.

Handshaking

Some external devices require *handshaking* with the system. Handshaking is where the system and the external device tell each other that data is ready to transfer and that the receiver is ready to receive data. For example, if the system is outputting eight parallel bits to a printer, the system loads the port and then tells the printer that data is ready. The printer reads the port, then tells the system that it is ready for more data. So the system loads the port with the next data word and the process is repeated. Handshaking is accomplished using one bit of an input port and one bit of an output port.

The only handshaking used in this book is to let the system know that data is ready from the keyboards. This handshaking is accomplished by the operator depressing an execute switch.

The devices which require handshaking are those devices which transfer several data words, and/or operate on the data. For example, if a printer did not print the word from the system before the next word appears, some data would be lost. If the printer processed data faster than the system provided the data, the same character might be printed twice.

Buffers

No device which interfaces to the buses must load the bus when the device is active or when it is disabled. For output ports this is particularly important when several output ports are connected to the data bus because the loading is cumulative. For input ports, this is a must; two ports cannot drive the bus without problems. So all input ports which connect to the bus must have tri-state circuits connected to the bus. When the circuit is disabled, it is off, and in the high impedance state. When enabled, the circuit responds to the

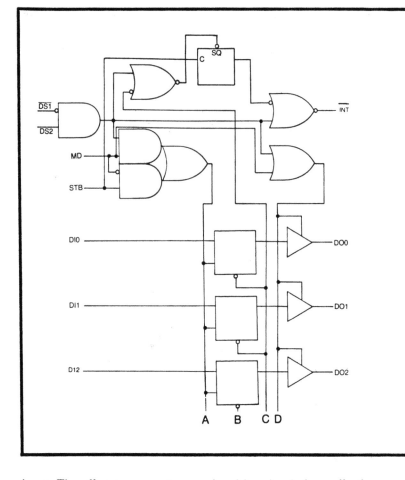

input. The off state prevents opposing drive signals from affecting the bus, because only one circuit is enabled.

All circuits being driven by the bus must have low drive and low idle current, to keep from loading the bus. Several ports connected to the bus may load down the bus because the input is always connected and normally cannot be disabled. The LS series of ICs require low drive current, about 300 microamps, or a fifth of that required by TTL circuits. The CMOS series of ICs is ideal because the drive current is on the order of 10 microamps. This a significant improvement over the 1.6 milliamps required by standard TTL integrated circuits. It is advisable to use the CMOS ICs where required.

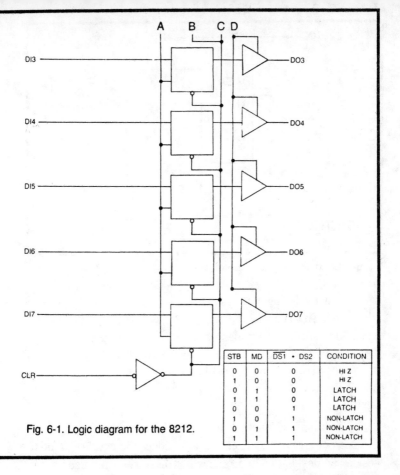

STB	MD	$\overline{DS1} \cdot DS2$	CONDITION
0	0	0	HI Z
1	0	0	HI Z
0	1	0	LATCH
1	1	0	LATCH
0	0	1	LATCH
1	0	1	NON-LATCH
0	1	1	NON-LATCH
1	1	1	NON-LATCH

Fig. 6-1. Logic diagram for the 8212.

Circuits that input to the bus must be tri-state to prevent their loading down the bus. These tri-state circuits usually consist of the tri-state buffers having enable signals to control the buffer. If it is enabled, the output is either in the high or low state. If the circuit is not enabled, the output is off or in the high impedance output state. This prevents loading the bus when the circuit is not enabled.

The output ports can be either latching or non-latching. The latching ports retain the outputs until they are addressed and the information is changed, or until the port is reset by the external signal. This retains the data at the port until it is used by the external device, or until it is programmed to change. This is useful for turning on lights or indicators.

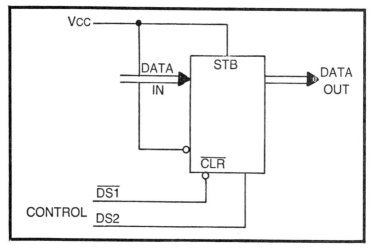

Fig. 6-2. Using the 8212 as a gated buffer.

The non-latching port has the data at the output only when it is addressed. This is useful for input ports, so that the port is on only when addressed. Some types of output ports, such as high speed data transfer ports, require that the data be available only for about a microsecond. This type of port can be non-latching.

Control Chips

Several special function integrated circuits are available for use as input/output circuits. These greatly reduce the effort required to design and develop I/O ports. Two of these chips are used in the discussion later in this chapter, the 8255 and the 8212.

Other functional chips are available but they are for more complex operations. Also, different families have similar chips available under different type numbers. It is advisable to use I/O chips from the same family as the microprocessor to assure that all control signals and the buses are compatible.

The 8212. The logic diagram for the 8212 is shown in Fig. 6-1. This is an 8-bit input/output port which can be used either as a bus driver or as a gated buffer, with the chip addressing supplying the enable signal as shown in Fig. 6-2. When the circuit is enabled, the input is directly transferred to the input. Figure 6-3 shows the truth table for the control signals. From this chart, the requirements to operate this chip as a latching port can be seen. The condition to use for an addressable port is the third data latch condition, STB low, MD low, and $\overline{DS_1}$ · DS₂ high. This means that the circuit is addressed, and the strobe and mode are both low. If single line addressing is desired, attach DS₂ to +5V through a 4.7K to 10K resistor. This gives an active low enable line ($\overline{DS_1}$) and is as shown in Fig. 6-4. If an active high address line is desired, ground $\overline{DS_1}$ and attach DS₂ to the desired address line.

The function of this type chip is defined by the hardware connections. For an output port, the input of the 8212 is connected to the data bus, and the output connects to the external circuitry. For an input port the connections are reversed. The connections to the control inputs define the operating mode of the chip.

The 8255. The 8255 is a programmable, complex, 3-port interface chip with many applications. Figure 6-5 shows the block diagram for this chip. The control functions are defined in the table. This chip can be used to input data on some of the ports, and to output data on other ports. $\overline{CS}$ enables the chip, and is active low. A₁ and A₂ address the port, and are active high. $\overline{RD}$ and $\overline{WR}$ define a read or write operation. These four lines are the control lines which define the function of the individual operations. Figure 6-6 shows the state of the control lines required for the various operations.

A1	A0	$\overline{RD}$	$\overline{WR}$	$\overline{CS}$	OPERATION
0	0	0	1	0	Port A read
0	1	0	1	0	Port B read
1	0	0	1	0	Port C read
0	0	1	0	0	Port A write
0	1	1	0	0	Port B write
1	0	1	0	0	Port C write
1	1	1	0	0	Control word write
X	X	X	X	1	Disable

Fig. 6-3. Truth table for 8212 control signals.

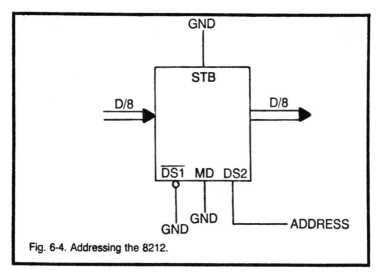

Fig. 6-4. Addressing the 8212.

To define the function of the individual ports, a control word is written into the 8255. The control words required to set up the chip for the conditions shown are given as bits of the control words. Bit 7 will always be high, and the bits not listed will be low. For example,

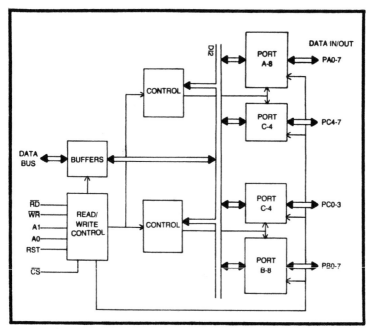

Fig. 6-5. Block diagram for the 8255.

to set up the chip to output on ports A and C and to input on port B requires that a control word, 10000010, be written into the chip by a write command. If A_1 is connected to address line 1 and A_0 is connected to address line 0 the port number is 03. But to turn the chip off requires $\overline{CS}$ going high, so $\overline{CS}$ must be connected to an active low signal, such as 0_4 from an I/O address decoder. The address of the chip becomes 40, 41 and 42, and the control word address is 43. To write in the control word requires outputting the desired control word to port 43.

Notice from Fig. 6-6 that port C can be operated as two individual 4-bit ports, or as one 8-bit port. This table defines the control words to set up the chip for the various combinations of input and output ports.

THE STANDARD I/O METHOD

The programmed input/output method is sometimes called the *standard*, or the isolated I/O method. This is the method most

D4	D3	D1	D0	Port A	Port C Upper 4	Port B	Port C Lower 4
0	0	0	0	output	output	output	output
0	0	0	1	output	output	output	input
0	0	1	0	output	output	input	output
0	0	1	1	output	output	input	input
0	1	0	0	output	input	output	output
0	1	0	1	output	input	output	input
0	1	1	0	output	input	input	output
0	1	1	1	output	input	input	input
1	0	0	0	input	output	output	output
1	0	0	1	input	output	output	input
1	0	1	0	input	output	input	output
1	0	1	1	input	output	input	input
1	1	0	0	input	input	output	output
1	1	0	1	input	input	output	input
1	1	1	0	input	input	input	output
1	1	1	1	input	input	input	input

Bit Format: 1 0 0 D4 D3 0 D1 D0

Fig. 6-6. Control signals for the 8255.

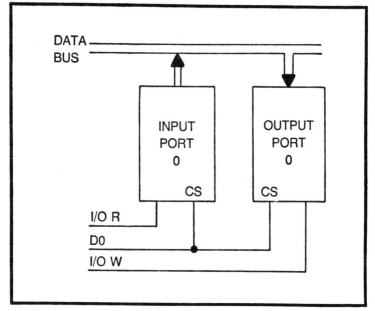

Fig. 6-7. Functional diagram for 1 input and 1 output port connected as port 0.

commonly used, and will be employed throughout this book. The port is designed to respond to the I/O read and write signals, and to be enabled by a select line. This select is usually active low, and is connected to the output of an address decoder. This connection determines the address of the port, or the port number. An input port and an output port can have the same port number, and are separated by the read and write commands. Figure 6-7 shows the functional diagram for one input and one output port connected to the data bus and addressed as port 0 for both.

Using standard method address and control, up to 256 input and 256 output ports can be controlled. Since the addressing is done by the second byte of the instruction, the maximum number is 255 for the 8 bits. Add to this, address 00 and there are 256 possibilities. This is enough input and output for most applications, especially for small systems.

An OUT 00 instruction will write the information in the accumulator to the output port. This instruction places the port number on the address bus and generates an I/O write signal. This is what is required to transfer data to this port, and to enable the port.

If the port is the latching type the data will remain at the output of the port until another OUT 00 instruction is executed.

An IN 00 instruction tranfers the information from the input port to the accumulator by enabling the port to transfer the data to the data bus, and enabling the accumulator to read the data bus. This instruction places the port number on the address bus, and generates and I/O read signal. This instruction does not affect the output port because no I/O write signal has been generated.

Memory Mapped I/O Method

Memory mapped I/O overcomes the limitation of 256 output and input ports by treating the I/O as special memory location. Another convenience of using memory mapped I/O is that the addressing of 15 ports can be achieved using only one address line to each chip. But this will be an active high signal, so the enable must be an active high. This eliminates the need for an address decoder, but severely restricts the number of ports available.

If the system has less than 32K bytes of memory, address line A_{15} is not used in the normal addressing. So, if this line is dedicated to addressing I/O, then up to 32K I/O ports are available. This is enough for any usage and also allows the I/O to use the memory instructions, such as direct and indirect addressing, immediate load, and move, reducing the programming required for I/O operations.

The normal approach to this is shown in Fig. 6-8. The $\overline{MEMR}$ and $\overline{MEMW}$ (memory read not and write not) signals are combined with A_{15} to generate the $\overline{I/O\ R}$ and $\overline{I/O\ W}$ signals. These signals are low only when A_{15} is high (addressed), and a read or write command is generated. These signals are used in place of the I/O read and write signals shown in Fig. 6-7. To address a port, simply add A_{15} to the port address. For example, to move data from the accumulator to output port 03, an STA 80 03 instruction is required. The address of the port is 80 03, so address lines A_{15}, A_1 and A_0 will be high. Lines A_1 and A_0 go the the port while A_{15} selects input/output instead of memory operations.

Another approach to memory mapped I/O is to assign a block of addresses, such as addresses 1000 thru 1100 (hex). Then the I/O is addressed in a fashion similar to addressing memory, using address decoders and buffers. This is convenient when addressing several bits, such as a pegboard. (Fig. 6-9). The pegboard can be divided up

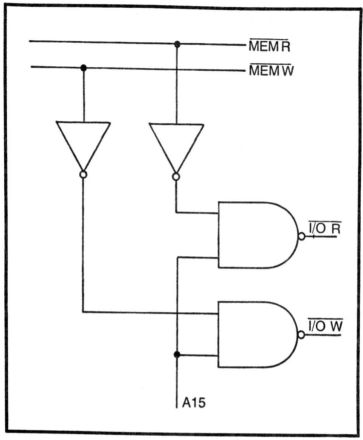

Fig. 6-8. Signal generation for memory mapped I/O.

as an 8 by 256, or a 16 by 128, or any combination which makes an even multiple of 8 bits across, and a submultiple of 256 vertical. The address lines may be any number from 1 to 32K. Using binary digits, such as 1, 2, 4, 8, 16 etc., simplfies the addressing.

Figure 6-10 shows an 8 bit by 256 matrix set up as a pegboard. A shorting pin is inserted in the holes in the board to short the address lines to the bit output lines. Depending on the programming, a peg can be inserted for all the one's required or for all the zero's required.

The address decoder consists of several decoder chips connected as an 8 to 256 decoder, which can be done by pyramiding decoders. The address decoder grounds the address line when that

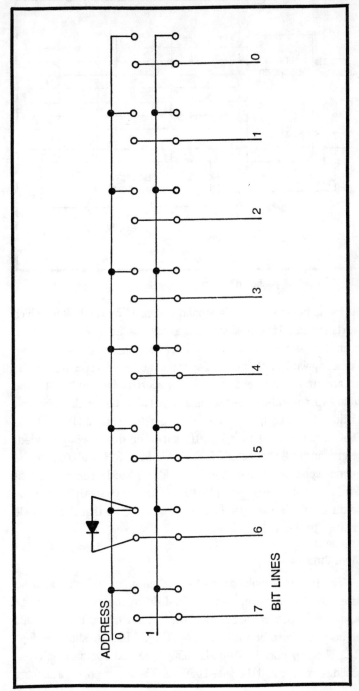

Fig. 6-9. Pegboard and pins.

113

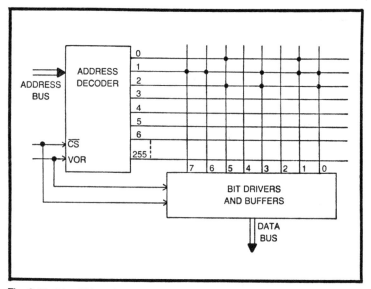

Fig. 6-10. 8 by 256 pegboard.

address is being read. This ground is sensed by the buffer, which inverts the signal and applies it on the data bus. Each bit which has no pin in it is sensed as a low. To prevent one address line from interacting with another one, diodes must be used as the pins. If the pins are straight connections, the low address line can transfer the ground to any other address line that has a pin in the same bit position. For example, in Fig. 6-10 the top row, address 00, is initially programmed as 00100010, but when this line is grounded, the ground will be reflected back to bit lines 7, 6, 3, and 0 due to the common connection on bit line 1, to address line 1. This means that address 00 will be read as 11101011 instead of 00100010. To overcome this, diodes are used as pins, polarized so that the cathode connects to the address line.

Output Circuits

The general requirements for any output circuit are that it be addressable, selectable, and not load down the bus. The input/output chips, such as the 8255 and the 8212, fulfill this requirement. The ports can also be made up from CMOS ICs, as shown in Fig. 6-11. The top port is a non-latching type and contains only the enabling circuitry and the gated buffers. The lower port is a latching port. This circuit contains the enabling circuitry, a reset one shot, the gated buffers, and the latches. The reset one shot issues a reset pulse to the latch when the chip is addressed. This reset pulse must be shorter than the enable pulse, so for a 0.5 microsecond system, this pulse must be about 0.2 microseconds or less. Without the reset

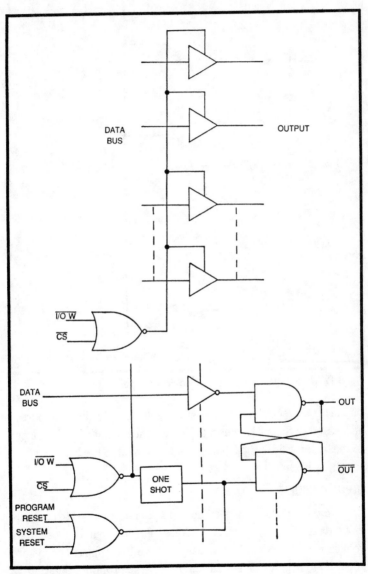

Fig. 6-11. CMOS output ports.

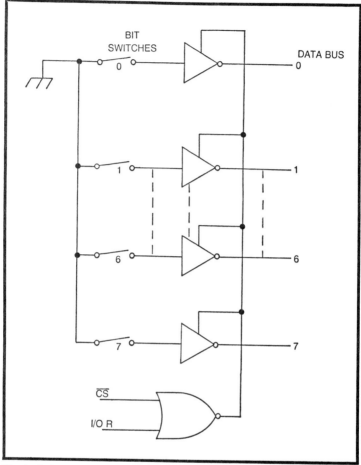

Fig. 6-12. Using toggle switches to drive an input port.

one shot, a reset command must be issued every time the port is addressed so that all latches start in the reset condition. A high input to the buffer will set the latches, but a low input to the buffer will not reset the latches.

INPUT CIRCUITS

Toggle switches and pushbutton switches are used to manually input data. Toggle switches make a simple input because they remain in one state until manually changed. No input latches are required to hold the data until sampled by the program. Figure 6-12 shows eight toggle switches used as inputs to one port. When the switches are open, the input to the gated inverters is high, giving a low to the data bus. When the switches are closed, the input to the data bus is high. The NOR gate provides the enable signal to the gated tri-state inverters. When $\overline{CS}$ and $\overline{I/O\ R}$ are both low, indicating that the port is addressed and to be read, the output of the NOR gate is high, enabling the inverters. If non-inverting buffers are used, turn the switches around so that the switches are closed for a low, and open for a high. Normally the switches are mounted so that 'up' is a one and 'down' is a zero.

Pushbutton Switches

Pushbutton switches are set up in two ways, with latching or non-latching ports. The latching mode is shown in Fig. 6-13. The switch sets a latch which is connected to the tri-state buffer. When the switch is depressed, the respective latch is set. If more than one switch is depressed, more than one latch will be set. When the port is read, the bits, representing the switches depressed, will be high; the remaining bits will be low. However, once a latch is set, it must be reset, or else it will stay in the set condition no matter what the condition of the input. The reset must supply a ground to the reset input of each latch. One simple method of accomplishing this is to provide a reset   pushbutton switch for each port or set of switches. Another method is to use one bit of a non-latching output port to reset the latches. Another, simpler method is to provide a one-shot as shown in Fig. 6-14 to reset the latches. This one-shot fires when the select signal, or enable signal, goes low. This resets the latches after the port has been read.

The non-latching pushbutton switch input port simply replaces the toggle switches of Fig. 6-12 with pushbutton switches. If the switches are the normally open type, shown in Fig. 6-15, the output to the bus will be high for the switches depressed. This is a momentary switch, so the program must read the switch while it is depressed. This usually involves a loop where the port is constantly read until information is received, which places restrictions on the programming and use of this type input.

Keyboards

One of the common data inputs is a keyboard, such as used on calculators. Normally, these are the single switch type, as shown in

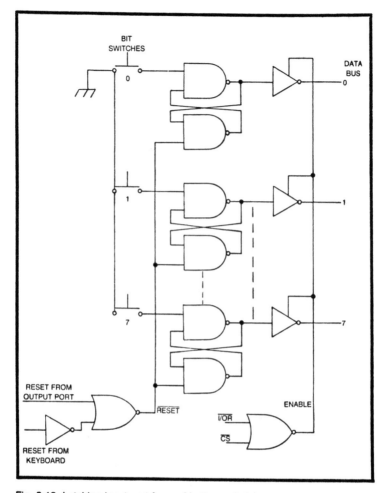

Fig. 6-13. Latching input port for pushbutton switches.

Fig. 6-16, using one bit for each switch, and requiring one input word for each eight keys. A 20 button keyboard takes 2½ input words, and they must be the latching type inputs unless a contrary indication is given when the entry is required. The keyboard, shown in Fig. 6-16, mated with the input shown in Fig. 6-13, and reset as shown in Fig. 6-14, makes a good input. Of the 20 keys, 16 are required for hexadecimal input. The remaining four keys can be used for program control or for hardware control. If four more switches are added, making the total 24 switches, three input ports are available. This will mate to a 8255 as shown in Fig. 6-17.

118

The matrix type keyboard, as shown in Fig. 6-18, is commonly used in the communications area and is finding its way into microcomputers. When a key is depressed, the horizontal and vertical lines connected to that key are connected to a common third line, which is usually ground. This gives two ground inputs to the port for each key. The 20 button keyboard shown is connected into a 4 by 5 matrix, requiring 9 bits for input.

DISPLAYS

Normally, data inputs to the system are displayed on either an LED display or individual indicators. This data can come directly from the input switches as shown in Fig. 6-19, which requires a latching input and displays the input rather than what the system receives. This is called the half-duplex mode. The full-duplex mode is where the system outputs the data received onto an output port, and is used commonly for large systems where the input and the system are separated.

LEDS

LEDs are commonly connected to output ports to serve as bit state indicators. A typical LED requires 5 to 16 milliamps drive

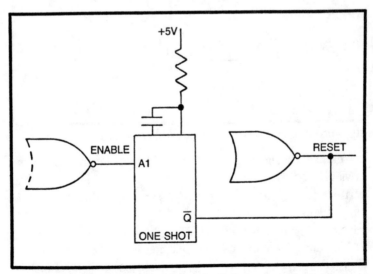

Fig. 6-14. Resetting the latching input port with the port enable signal.

119

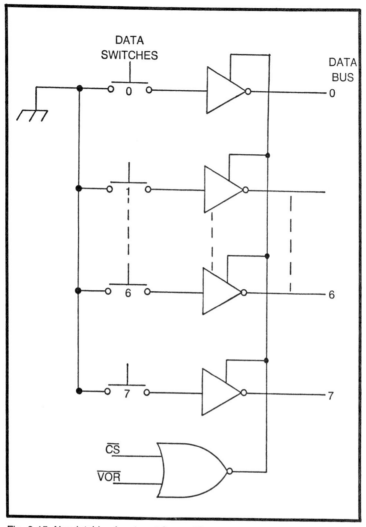

Fig. 6-15. Non-latching input port for pushbutton switches.

current, depending on ambient light conditions. Figure 6-20 shows driving LEDs with the output port. The resistor determines the current, and for the 470 ohm resistors shown, the LED current is about 10mA; so the driver must be capable of supplying this drive current. Most of the standard TTL ICs will supply this, but the CMOS, and most special series, will not. Since the latch does not connect directly to the bus, it can be the standard TTL series ICs, such as the 7400. Some of the special I/O chips, such as the 8212, can supply the required current sink, while other chips, such as the 8255 cannot. When using any of the special chips, always check the data sheet for the current sink limitations.

A typical display for a small system is a seven segment LED display, a unit with seven LEDs arranged as bars, or segments, as shown in Fig. 6-21. These seven-segment displays come in two configurations, the common anode and the common cathode. These names refer to the common connection of the individual LEDs; the internal schematics for both types are shown in Fig. 6-22. To drive

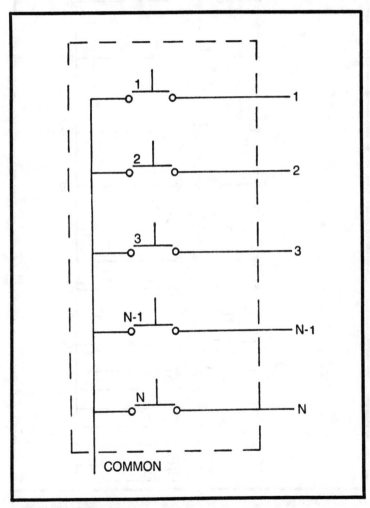

Fig. 6-16. Simple keyboard schematic.

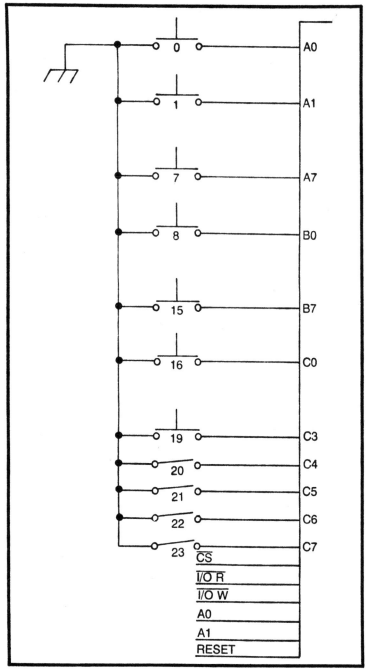

Fig. 6-17. A 20 button keyboard with individual switches mated to an 8255.

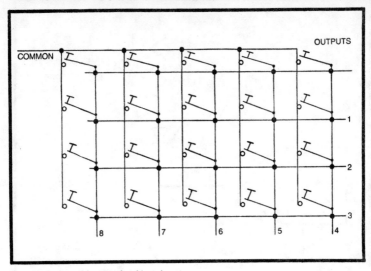

Fig. 6-18. A matrix type keyboard.

the common cathode type requires driver connections between the anode and +5 volts, as shown in Fig. 6-23. This is difficult to accomplish with standard ICs, so the common anode type is normally used. Figure 6-24 shows a common anode type connected to an output port. Segment *a* is driven by bit 1, segment *b* by bit 2, etc., which makes the programming easier. Figure 6-25 gives the segments required for the numbers and letters to use this as a hexadec-

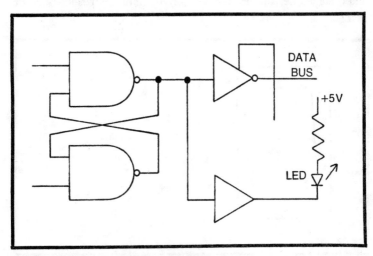

Fig. 6-19. Data input with LED monitoring.

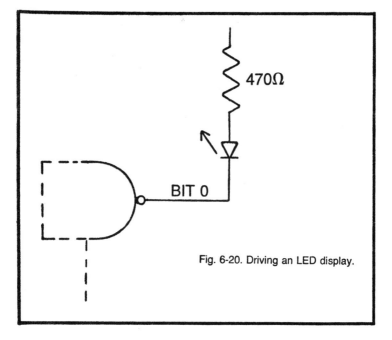

Fig. 6-20. Driving an LED display.

imal display, which requires the numbers 0 thru 9 and the letters A thru F. Lower case B and D are used, and the 6 has a bar across the top to separate it from the lower case B.

To turn on a number, simply place the bit pattern shown in the table on the data bus and address the port. If this is a latching port, and it should be, the display will stay on until it is readdressed or reset.

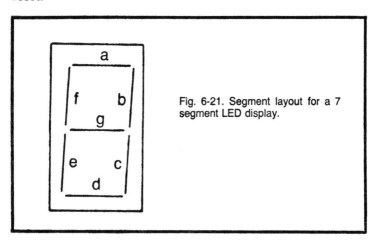

Fig. 6-21. Segment layout for a 7 segment LED display.

LED indicators are usually mounted from panels by mounting rings supplied with LEDs. These rings hold the LED securely, and are easy to use. If the rings are not available, the LEDs can be mounted in rubber grommets, and secured by rubber cement. LEDs can also be mounted from their leads from terminals on the circuit boards. Seven segment displays are mounted in standard 14 pin DIP sockets, either on the circuit board or from the back of the panel by spacers.

The 16 segment alpha-numeric displays can be used, but this takes two ports, and two words to drive it. This makes the display

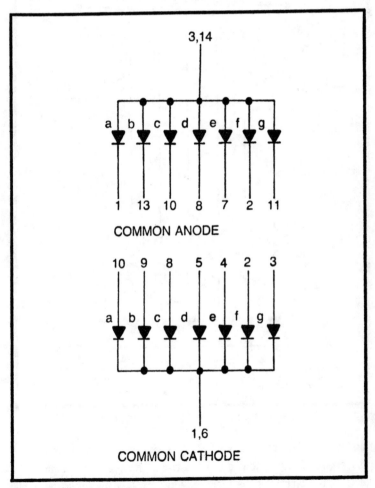

Fig. 6-22. Internal schematics for 7 segment displays.

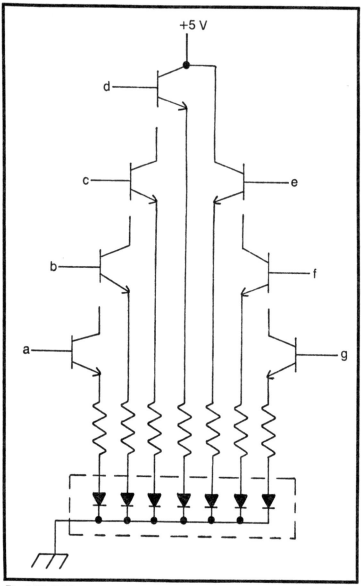

Fig. 6-23. Driving a common cathode 7 segment display.

unduly complex, especially when three or more segments are being driven. Also, the table used to determine the segments required to display the characters is twice as long, 16 bits by 16 words. This requires considerably more program to drive the displays.

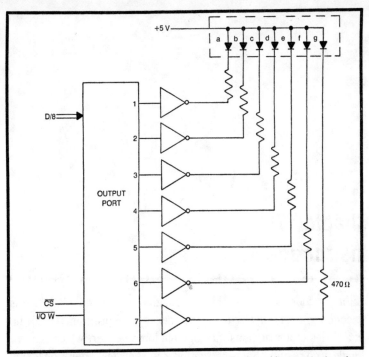

Fig. 6-24. Driving a common anode 7 segment display with an output port.

Liquid Crystal Displays

Liquid crystal displays can be used, but the drive voltage must be generated by an oscillator. For low current systems and portable systems, consider the liquid crystal displays and their low current drive requirements. These displays are used on timers, clocks, and many kinds of portable instrumentation.

Character	Segments	Character	Segments
0	abcdef	8	abcdefg
1	bc	9	abcfg
2	abdeg	A	abcefg
3	abcdg	B	cdefg
4	bcfg	C	adef
5	acdfg	D	bcdeg
6	acdefg	E	adefg
7	abc	F	aefg

Fig. 6-25. Segments required to generate characters on a seven segment display.

Chapter 7
Instructions

An instruction is a unique bit combination of 1's and 0's which is decoded by the hardware to do one operation. A program is made up of a series of instructions, arranged in logical order, which achieve the desired results. Each instruction is the smallest operation that is programmable, and the execution of these operations is done by the hardware.

TYPES OF INSTRUCTIONS

There are four basic types of instructions. These are:

1. Data movement.
2. Data manipulation.
3. Program manipulation.
4. Status management.

Data Movement Instructions

Data movement instructions move data around the computer. They move data from the input circuits to the registers or to memory, from memory to the registers, or from any one place to another place in the system. For the computer program to work, the information that is to be operated on must be in the right place at the right time. These instructions allow the programmer to do that.

Data Manipulation Instructions

Data manipulation instructions, such as add, subtract, AND, OR, operate on the data. These instructions assume that the data is already in a specified place, usually in the registers, the data movement instructions having been used to get the data to that place.

Program Manipulation Instructions

A program consists of a series of instructions stored in sequential addresses in memory. These instructions are also executed sequentially unless the program flow is altered by the program manipulation instructions which interrupt the sequential reading of the memory addresses. Program manipulation instructions can be unconditional transfers or conditional transfers. Unconditional transfers alter the program flow when the instruction is executed. The conditional transfers alter the program flow if a specified condition is met as a result of the execution of the previous instructions.

Status Management Instructions

The state of the conditions is stored in the program status word (PSW). The status management instructions are housekeeping functions which set the individual bits of the PSW. The bits of the PSW are called flags; they are set either high or low depending on the results of the execution of data manipulation instructions, and remain that way until the execution of other data manipulation instructions resets them. These flags are sampled by the conditional program transfers, especially the JUMP CALL and RETURN instructions, allowing the program to make programmed 'decisions' about transferring the program flow.

The instructions which set the flags are typically arithmetic, logic, increment, and rotate instructions. Some instructions affect only some of the flags, while others affect all the flags. The common flags are Zero, Carry, Parity, and Sign flags. Some microprocessor families have other flags, and may define the flags differently, but fundamentally they are the same.

Zero Flag. The zero flag will be set to a high if the result of the instruction is zero, otherwise it will be low. For example, if two equal numbers are subtracted, the zero flag will be set.

Carry Flag. The carry flag is set if the instruction results in a carry (for addition) or a borrow (for subtraction), and is zero for all other conditions. For example, if a large number is subtracted from a smaller number, the carry flag will be set because the operation results in a borrow. If two large numbers are added so that the answer exceeds the data handling capacity of the microprocessor, this flag will be set because the addition results in a high order carry.

Some microprocessors have an auxiliary carry flag. This flag is set high if the instruction caused a carry out of bit 3 into bit 4 of the resulting value This flag is used in the decimal adjust instruction.

Parity Flag. The parity bit is set if there is an even number of 'one' bits (even parity) in the results of the execution of the instruction. This flag will be zero if the number of 'one' bits is odd (odd parity). For example, if the result is 10110001 the parity bit will be high, and if the result is 11110001 the parity bit will be low.

Sign Flag. The sign bit is set if the most significant bit of the result of the execution of the instruction is a one. Otherwise this flag is zero. This flag indicates a negative number for a subtraction.

INTERFACING SIGNALS

The instruction and control section of the CPU controls the decoding and execution of the instruction. It does this by generating enable signals to the various circuits required in the execution. During the instruction fetch, the first byte of the instruction is transferred into the 8-bit instruction register. This is decoded by the instruction decoder and combined with various timing signals to provide the control signals for the register array, ALU, and data buffer blocks. In addition, the outputs from the decoder and external control signals feed the timing and state control section which generates the state and cycle timing signals. The phase 1 and phase 2 ($\phi1$ & $\phi2$) clock inputs are from the clock generator circuit. These two clocks are used to generate the internal timing for the execution of the instructions.

An instruction cycle is defined as the time required to fetch and execute an instruction. During the fetch, the instruction is read from memory and deposited in the instruction register via the data bus. During the execution phase, the instruction is decoded and translated into specific processor activities.

Every instruction cycle consists of one to five machine cycles. A machine cycle is required every time the CPU accesses memory or an I/O port. The fetch portion of an instruction cycle requires one machine cycle for each byte to be fetched. So a 3-byte instruction requires three machine cycles for the fetch portion. The execution portion of some instructions requires no additional machine cycles because the execution is done during the latter part of the fetch machine cycle. Other instructions, such as those which read or write memory, require additional machine cycles for the execution portion.

Each machine cycle consists of three to five states. A *state* is the smallest unit of processing activity and is defined as the interval between two successive positive going transitions of the $\phi 1$ clock pulse. The sync pulse is triggered by the low to high transition of $\phi 2$, as shown in Fig. 7-1. This signal identifies the beginning of every machine cycle.

The interface signals between the microprocessor and the system connect the components together to make the system work. Some or all of these signals may be required for any given system, as determined by the application and the requirements of the external components. Some signals for the 8080 microprocessor are explained below.

DBIN (output), (data bus in): indicates to the external circuits that the data bus is in the input mode. This signal is used by the system controller to generate the memory read and the I/O input signals.

READY (input): indicates to the microprocessor that valid memory or input data is on the data bus. This signal synchronizes the CPU with slower memory or I/O devices. If after sending an address out on the address bus, the CPU does not receive a READY input, the microprocessor will enter a WAIT state for as long as the READY line is low. READY can also be used to single step the CPU.

WAIT (output): acknowledges that the CPU is in a WAIT state. The WAIT state is a 'do nothing' state where the microprocessor marks time for as long as the ready line is low. This WAIT state is between the second and third states of each machine cycle.

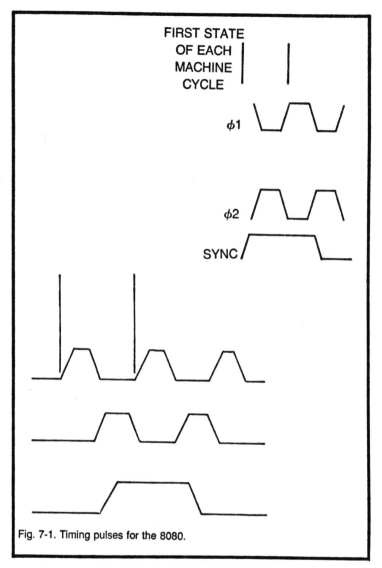

Fig. 7-1. Timing pulses for the 8080.

By connecting the READY and WAIT lines together, one WAIT state will be entered every time memory is read. This allows 1.0 microsecond memories to be used with a CPU operating at 0.5 microseconds.

WR (output), (WRITE): indicates a memory write or an I/O output. This signal is used by the system controller to generate the memory and I/O signals.

HOLD (input): requests that the CPU enter the HOLD state. This forces the CPU into the HALT condition, and places all the buses in their high impedance state. This allows an external device to gain control of the address and data bus. The current machine cycle is completed before entering this state.

HLDA (output), (HOLD ACKNOWLEDGE): appears in response to the HOLD signal and indicates that the data and address bus will go to the high impedance state.

INTE (output), (INTERRUPT ENABLE): indicates the content of the internal interrupt enable flip/flop. This flip/flop may be set or reset by the Enable and Disable Interrupt instructions and inhibits interrupts from being accepted when it is reset.

INT (input), (INTERRUPT REQUEST): is the input to the CPU for interrupts. A signal on this line forces the CPU into the interrupt routine, unless the CPU is in a HOLD state or if the Interrupt Enable flip/flop is reset.

RESET (input): clears the program counter and resets the INTE and HLDA flip/flops. After reset, the program starts at location 0 in memory.

INSTRUCTION FORMAT

A thorough understanding of the instructions for the system to be used is required to effectively use that system. All microprocessors have several standard instructions, and some families have special instructions. The instructions for the 8080 family of microprocessors is explained in this chapter. These are representative of the standard instructions, and have a few special instructions.

Figure 7-2 gives the individual instructions for the 8080, as discussed here, by mnemonic code. Also given is the number of bytes, the operational code, and the flags affected. For each general instruction there may be many actual instructions. For instance, there are eight ADD instructions, each of which details the register or memory location which is to be added to the accumulator, including adding the accumulator to itself, which doubles the value contained in the accumulator.

Study the instructions and visualize how they are used. Start with the simple ones, such as the MOV instructions. For these instructions, the first letter after the MOV is the destination and the

Mnemonic	OP Code	Number of Bytes	Flags Affected
ACI	CE	2	All
ADC A	8F	1	All
ADC B	88	1	All
ADC C	89	1	All
ADC D	8A	1	All
ADC E	8B	1	All
ADC H	8C	1	All
ADC L	8D	1	All
ADC M	8E	1	All
ADD A	87	1	All
ADD B	80	1	All
ADD C	81	1	All
ADD D	82	1	All
ADD E	83	1	All
ADD H	84	1	All
ADD L	85	1	All
ADD M	86	1	All
ADI	C6	2	All
ANA A	A7	1	All
ANA B	A0	1	All
ANA C	A1	1	All
ANA D	A2	1	All
ANA E	A3	1	All
ANA H	A4	1	All
ANA L	A5	1	All
ANA M	A6	1	All
ANI	E6	2	All
CALL	CD	3	None
CC	DC	3	None
CM	FC	3	None
CMA	2F	1	None
CMC	3F	1	Carry
CMP A	BF	1	All
CMP B	B8	1	All
CMP C	B9	1	All
CMP D	BA	1	All
CMP E	BB	1	All
CMP H	BC	1	All
CMP L	BD	1	All
CMP M	BE	1	All
CNC	D4	3	None
CNZ	C4	3	None
CP	F4	3	None
CPE	EC	3	None
CPI	FE	2	All
CPO	E4	3	None
CZ	CC	3	None
DAA	27	1	All
DAD B	09	1	Carry
DAD D	19	1	Carry
DAD H	29	1	Carry
DAD SP	39	1	Carry
DCR A	3D	1	All except carry
DCR B	05	1	All except carry
DCR C	0D	1	All except carry
DCR D	15	1	All except carry

Fig. 7-2. The instruction set for the 8080 microprocessor (continued on next four pages).

Mnemonic	OP Code	Number of Bytes	Flags Affected
DCR E	1D	1	All except carry
DCR H	25	1	All except carry
DCR L	2D	1	All except carry
DCR M	35	1	All except carry
DCX B	0B	1	None
DCX D	1B	1	None
DCX H	2B	1	None
DCX SP	3B	1	None
DI	F3	1	None
EI	FB	1	None
HLT	76	1	None
IN	DB	2	None
INR A	3C	1	All except carry
INR B	04	1	All except carry
INR C	0C	1	All except carry
INR D	14	1	All except carry
INR E	1C	1	All except carry
INR H	24	1	All except carry
INR L	2C	1	All except carry
INR M	34	1	All except carry
INX B	03	1	None
INX D	13	1	None
INX H	23	1	None
INX SP	33	1	None
JC	DA	3	None
JM	FA	3	None
JMP	C3	3	None
JNC	D2	3	None
JNZ	C2	3	None
JP	F2	3	None
JPE	EA	3	None
JPO	E2	3	None
JZ	CA	3	None
LDA	3A	3	None
LDAX B	0A	1	None
LDAX D	1A	1	None
LHLD	2A	3	None
LXI B	01	3	None
LXI D	11	3	None
LXI H	21	3	None
LXI SP	31	3	None
MVI A	3E	2	None
MVI B	96	2	None
MVI C	0E	2	None
MVI D	16	2	None
MVI E	1E	2	None
MVI H	26	2	None
MVI L	2E	2	None
MVI M	36	2	None
MOV A,A	7F	1	None
MOV A,B	78	1	None
MOV A,C	79	1	None
MOV A,D	7A	1	None
MOV A,E	7B	1	None
MOV A,H	7C	1	None
MOV A,L	7D	1	None

Fig. 7-2. (continued).

		Number of Bytes	Flags Affected
MOV A,M	7E	1	None
MOV B,A	47	1	None
MOV B,B	40	1	None
MOV B,C	41	1	None
MOV B,D	42	1	None
MOV B,E	43	1	None
MOV B,H	44	1	None
MOV B,L	45	1	None
MOV B,M	46	1	None
MOV C,A	4F	1	None
MOV C,B	48	1	None
MOV C,C	49	1	None
MOV C,D	4A	1	None
MOV C,E	4B	1	None
MOV C,H	4C	1	None
MOV C,L	4D	1	None
MOV C,M	4E	1	None
MOV D,A	57	1	None
MOV D,B	50	1	None
MOV D,C	51	1	None
MOV D,D	52	1	None
MOV D,E	53	1	None
MOV D,H	54	1	None
MOV D,L	55	1	None
MOV D,M	56	1	None
MOV E,A	5F	1	None
MOV E,B	58	1	None
MOV E,C	59	1	None
MOV E,D	5A	1	None
MOV E,E	5B	1	None
MOV E,H	5C	1	None
MOV E,L	5D	1	None
MOV E,M	5E	1	None
MOV H,A	67	1	None
MOV H,B	60	1	None
MOV H,C	61	1	None
MOV H,D	62	1	None
MOV H,E	63	1	None
MOV H,H	64	1	None
MOV H,L	65	1	None
MOV H,M	66	1	None
MOV L,A	6F	1	None
MOV L,B	68	1	None
MOV L,C	69	1	None
MOV L,D	6A	1	None
MOV L,E	6B	1	None
MOV L,H	6C	1	None
MOV L,L	6D	1	None
MOV L,M	6E	1	None
MOV M,A	77	1	None
MOV M,B	70	1	None
MOV M,C	71	1	None
MOV M,D	72	1	None
MOV M,E	73	1	None
MOV M,H	74	1	None
MOV M,L	75	1	None

Fig. 7-2. (continued).

Mnemonic	OP Code	Number of Bytes	Flags Affected
NOP	76	1	None
ORA A	B7	1	All
ORA B	B0	1	All
ORA C	B1	1	All
ORA D	B2	1	All
ORA E	B3	1	All
ORA H	B4	1	All
ORA L	B5	1	All
ORA M	B6	1	All
ORI	F6	2	All
OUT	D3	2	None
PCHL	E9	1	None
POP B	C1	1	None
POP D	D1	1	None
POP H	E1	1	None
POP PSW	F1	1	All
PUSH B	C5	1	None
PUSH D	D5	1	None
PUSH H	E5	1	None
PUSH PSW	F5	1	None
RAL	17	1	Carry
RAR	1F	1	Carry
RET	C9	1	None
RLC	07	1	Carry
RM	F8	1	None
RNC	D0	1	None
RNZ	C0	1	None
RP	F0	1	None
RPE	E8	1	None
RPO	E0	1	None
RRC	0F	1	Carry
RST 0	C7	1	None
RST 1	CF	1	None
RST 2	D7	1	None
RST 3	DF	1	None
RST 4	E7	1	None
RST 5	EF	1	None
RST 6	F7	1	None
RST 7	FF	1	None
RZ	C8	1	None
SBB A	9F	1	All
SBB B	98	1	All
SBB C	99	1	All
SBB D	9A	1	All
SBB E	9B	1	All
SBB H	9C	1	All
SBB L	9D	1	All
SBB M	9E	1	All
SBI	DE	2	All
SHLD	22	3	None
SPHL	F9	1	None
STA	32	3	None
STAX B	02	1	None
STAX D	12	1	None
STC	37	1	Carry
SUB A	97	1	All

Fig. 7-2. (continued).

Mnemonic	OP Code	Number of Bytes	Flags Affected
SUB B	90	1	All
SUB C	91	1	All
SUB D	92	1	All
SUB E	93	1	All
SUB H	94	1	All
SUB L	95	1	All
SUB M	96	1	All
SUI	D6	2	All
XCHG	EB	1	None
XRA A	AF	1	All
XRA B	A8	1	All
XRA C	A9	1	All
XRA D	AA	1	All
XRA E	AB	1	All
XRA H	AC	1	All
XRA L	AD	1	All
XRA M	AE	1	All
XRI	EE	2	All
XTHL	E3	1	None

Fig. 7-2. (continued).

second letter is the source. For example, MOV A,C moves the contents of the C register to the A register. For these MOV instructions, the contents of the data is still there.

There are many instructions, such as MOV A,A, which in reality do nothing except use time and take up an instruction. These instructions are available because of the coding and the internal connections in the microprocessor; it is easier to make them available than it is to restrict them internally. Some of these instructions, such as the SUB A and the XRA A which gives a one byte instruction to zero the accumulator in place of the two byte MVI A instruction, are used for this purpose.

Learn the mnemonics, and what instructions they represent. Most of the programs in the following chapters are given in mnemonics with no op code assigned. To be effective in using and programming a microprocessor system, the instructions must be fully understood. One starting method is to use mnemonics in place of op codes when discussing programs and not to assign the op codes and addresses until the actual program is written.

Each instruction has a mnemonic and a 2-digit hex number associated with it. The mnemonic is an abbreviation for the name of the instruction. For example, JMP is the mnemonic for jump, INR for increment, and ANA for AND logical. The 2-digit hex number is the hex equivalent of the binary number for the instruction. It is the binary number that is actually loaded into the computer, and that the microprocessor decodes for the instruction. For example:

Mnemonic	Hex	Binary		Instruction
JUMP	C3	1100	0011	Jump
INR, B	04	0000	0100	Increment B register
ANA, B	A0	1010	0000	Logical AND with B register

Several of the instructions affect a register or memory in addition to the accumulator or in place of the accumulator. If this is the case, the register or memory is referenced in the mnemonic. For example, the INR can affect any register or memory, and, as such, the affected location must be referenced. In the above example, the B in the INR B means that the B register is affected. INR M means that the memory location specified is incremented.

The move instructions move data from one location to another in the system. This can be from one register to another register, from memory to a register, or from a register to memory. This is designated as MOV D, S, where D is the destination and S is the source. For example, MOV A,B moves the contents of the B register to the accumulator (the A register).

Some instructions are 2-byte instructions. This means that it takes two consecutive memory locations to store the instruction. These instructions are typically immediate instructions which load a constant into the program. These are referenced as:

ADI

F3

Where ADI is the mnemonic of the instruction, and F3 is the data. This data can be any desired 2-digit hex number, for an 8-bit system.

For a 16-bit system this data can be any 4-digit hex word. The transfer instructions and some of the immediate instructions are 3-byte instructions. These take three consecutive memory locations to store the instruction. These are referenced as:

JMP

05

1F

Where JMP is the mnemonic, and the hex number for this instruction is stored in the first location. The second location contains the low order two digits of the jump to address, 05, and the next location contains the high order two digits of the jump to address, 1F. All the consecutive memory locations must be used, even if they are filled with zeros, for 2- and 3-byte locations. If they are not, the next instruction is loaded into the location, and the microprocessor will interpret this new instruction as data, and not as an instruction causing the program to go astray and give erroneous results.

DATA MOVEMENT INSTRUCTIONS

Data is moved between registers and between a register and memory by the move (MOV) instructions. These are identified as MOV D,S where D is the destination of the data, or where it is to move to, and S is the source of the data, or where it is to move from. MOV B,M will move the contents of the memory location specified by the contents of the H and L register to the B register. C,L will move the contents of the L register to the C register. Normally, these move instructions do not affect the flags.

Several of the instructions operate on or with data from memory. For most microprocessors, one register pair is devoted to memory addressing for data, not to be confused with addressing instructions. This register pair (a register pair because the normal register is eight bits long, and the address needs sixteen bits), denoted H and L for the 8080 family, does not effect instruction addressing. When memory (M) is designated as the source or designation in the instruction mnemonic, the H and L register must be set up beforehand with the memory address. There are several methods setting up these registers, but one common method is the load and move immediate instruction. The load immediate (LXI rp) loads the register pair with the data in bytes 2 and 3 of the instruction. The move immediate (MVI r) loads the designated register with the data in byte 2 of the instruction.

For example:

                    LXI H
                     00
                     01

will load the H register with 01 and the L register with 00, so memory address 100 is set up. If the next instruction is a ADD M, the contents of memory location 100 will be added to the accumulator.

The LXI and MVI instructions can be used to load any register, register pair, or memory by changing the mnemonic. For example LXI B loads the B register pair (the B and C registers) with the data in bytes 2 and 3. The LXI SP instruction is to load the stack pointer (SP) with the address of the stack.

The XTHL instruction exchanges the last two entries on the stack with the H and L register pair. The last entry in the stack is exchanged with the L register and the next to last entry is exchanged with the H register. This is one method of reading or writing into the stack without changing the stack pointer. The XCHG instruction exchanges the contents of the H and L register pair with the contents of the D and E register pair.

The DAD *rp* instruction adds the contents of the designated register pair (*rp*) to the contents of the H and L register pair. The results are placed in the H and L register. Only the carry flag is affected. This instruction gives the microprocessor the ability to add two 16-bit numbers, or to indirectly address memory by adding a variable to the contents of the H and L register.

The SPHL instruction moves the contents of the H and L register pair to the stack pointer. This instruction is used in some exotic programs as a conditional jump to one of many locations based on the outcome of given operations. The result of the operations is the address of the starting point to be executed in the program. A CALL instruction reads the locations defined by the stack pointer for the address to jump to, so loading the stack pointer with the address of a pointer affects the jump.

There is a group of direct load and read memory instructions which do not use the H and L register. These are:

LDAX rp: The contents of the memory location specified by the contents of the specified register pair (rp) are moved to the accumulator.

LHLD: The contents of the memory address specified by byte 2 (low order) and byte 3 (high order) of the instruction are moved to the L register, and the contents of the next memory address is moved to the H register.

LDA: The contents of the memory address specified by bytes 2 and 3 of this instruction are moved to the accumulator.

STAX rp: The contents of the accumulator are moved to the memory address specified by the contents of register pair *rp*.

SHLD: Moves the contents of the L register to the memory location specified by bytes 2 and 3 of the instruction. The contents of the H register are moved to the next memory location.

STA: The contents of the accumulator are moved to the memory location specified by bytes 2 and 3 of the instruction.

The LDA and STA instructions provide a means for directly transferring data between the accumulator and memory. By using these instructions it can be done in three bytes instead of in the four bytes required to set up the H and L registers (LXI H) and moving data from or to memory. Figure 7-3 shows both methods for reading address 32F0 into the accumulator. If the data is to end up in some other register, the number of bytes will be the same.

The CMA instruction complements the contents of the accumulator, setting no flags. All ones are replaced by zeros and all zeros are replaced by ones.

The rotate instructions shift the contents of the accumulator one place to the left or right. These instructions are:

RLC: Rotates the contents of the accumulator one bit to the left. The low order bit and the carry flag are both set to the bit shifted out of the high order bit.

RRC: Rotates the contents of the accumulator one bit to the right. The high order bit and the carry flag are both set to the value shifted out of the low order bit.

LDA	LXI H
FO	FO
32	32
	MOV A,M

Fig. 7-3. Two methods to load the accumulator from memory.

RAL: Rotates the contents of the accumulator one bit to the left through the carry flag. The low order bit is set equal to the carry flag, and the carry flag is set to the bit shifted out of the high order bit.

RAR: Rotates the data in the accumulator one bit to the right through the carry flag. The high order bit is set equal to the carry flag, and the carry flag is set to the bit shifted out of the low order bit.

Other immediate instructions introduce a constant (byte 2) into the program. These logic and arithmetic immediate instructions are:

ADI: Adds byte 2 of the instruction to the accumulator.

ACI: Adds, with carry, byte 2 of the instruction to the accumulator.

SUI: Subtracts byte 2 of the instruction from the accumulator.

SBI: Subtracts byte 2 and carry from the accumulator.

ANI: Logical AND byte 2 with the accumulator.

XRI: Exclusive OR byte 2 with the accumulator.

ORI: Inclusive OR byte 2 with the accumulator.

CPI: Compares byte 2 with the accumulator. Byte 2 is subtracted from the accumulator, and the flags are set.

All the immediate instructions, except the LXI and the MVI, set the condition flags. The results of the execution of the logic and arithmetic instructions, except the CPI, are placed in the accumulator. The CPI instruction just sets the condition flags.

The input and output devices are assigned port numbers, which numbers are the addresses of the device, and specified by the contents of byte 2 of the instruction. These instructions are:

IN: The input port specified by byte 2 is read. The data is placed on the data bus and loaded into the accumulator.

OUT: The contents of the accumulator are placed on the data bus to go to the output port specified by byte 2 of the instruction.

Since eight bits (byte 2) are used for specifying the port, it is possible to have up to 256 input and 256 output ports. The function (input or output) and port number is defined by the connections of the functional blocks. These instructions are used for programmed input and output schemes.

Data Manipulation Instructions

The arithmetic and logic instructions operate on the data in the accumulator with data from one of the registers or memory. These instructions normally set the flags as a result of the execution of the instruction. The typical instructions are:

ADD s: Adds the contents of the accumulator to the contents of the source, S (register or memory).

ADC s: Adds the contents of the source with the contents of the accumulator and the carry flag.

SUB s: The contents of the source are subtracted from the contents of the accumulator.

SBB s: The contents of the source and the carry flag are both subtracted from the contents of the accumulator.

ANA s: The contents of the source are logically AND'ed with the contents of the accumulator.

XRA s: The contents of the source are exclusively OR'ed with the contents of the accumulator.

ORA s: The contents of the source are inclusively OR'ed with the contents of the accumulator.

CMP s: The contents of the source are subtracted from the contents of the accumulator, and the accumulator remains unchanged. This instruction is used to set the condition flags without affecting the data.

The results of the execution of the above instructions, except the CMP, are placed in the accumulator, and the source remains unchanged. Each of these instructions represents a family of different mnemonic codes, with the S replaced by the register designation or by M for memory. For example ADD B adds the contents of the B register to the contents of the accumulator. An XRA A zeroes the accumulator because an exclusive OR of two identical numbers results in zero. This is often used to zero the accumulator. ADD A is used to double the value of the accumulator.

The DAA instruction is used for decimal addition. If one 2-digit BCD number is to be added to another 2-digit BCD number, the ADD instruction would be followed by a DAA which would make the answer a 2-digit BCD number.

The logical instructions operate on the individual binary bits which make up the data. A logical AND instruction results in a one in every bit location where both numbers have a one. For example:

$$\begin{array}{r} 10111010 \\ \text{AND} \quad \underline{01101110} \\ 00101010 \end{array}$$

The logical inclusive OR results in a one in every bit location where either or both numbers have a one. For example:

$$\begin{array}{r} 10001010 \\ \text{OR} \quad \underline{01001100} \\ 11001110 \end{array}$$

The logical exclusive OR results in a one in every bit location where only one of the numbers has a one. For example:

$$\begin{array}{r} 10001011 \\ \text{XOR} \quad \underline{11001110} \\ 01000101 \end{array}$$

These logical instructions can be used to mask bits, to detect certain bits, and to add bits to data. For example, if it is desired to see if bit 3 is set high, a logical AND with 08 (bit 3 high) will result in a zero if bit 3 is low. A JNZ following this will transfer the program if bit 3 is set, and a JZ will transfer the program if bit 3 is not set.

STATUS MANAGEMENT INSTRUCTIONS

The program status word (PSW) contains the flags. These flags are defined as follows:

Bit	Flag
0	Carry
2	Parity
4	Aux. carry
6	Zero
7	Sign

Bits 1, 3, and 5 are not used. The PUSH PSW instruction puts the program status word as the lower eight bits, and the accumulator as the upper eight bits, on the stack.

The STC instruction sets the carry flag to one while affecting no other flags, and the CMC instruction complements the carry flag. If the carry flag is a zero, the CNC instruction sets it to a one, and vice versa. This can be used to set up the carry flag to indicate one pass through a loop after the carry flag has been set.

PROGRAM MANIPULATION INSTRUCTIONS

The program is a sequential list of instructions which are read and executed in sequential order unless a program transfer is executed. The program counter keeps track of the address of the instruction to be executed next. This counter is incremented when one type of an instruction is read from memory into the instruction register. Some instructions affect the program counter; the program transfer instructions interrupt the normal sequential order of execution, and transfer the program to some other, preassigned point in the program.

For example, if the program flow is from address 100 and a program transfer is in location 205 which transfers the program to 500, the program execution will be from address 100 to 205, then to address 500 and on from there. Remember that the program is executed in sequential order, unless this sequential order is interrupted by a program transfer.

For the 8080 family of microprocessors all program transfer instructions (except return) are 3-byte instructions. Byte 1 is the instruction, byte 2 is the low order two digits of the address, and byte 3 is the high order two digits of the address. Some families of microprocessors use page addressing, where a 2-byte instruction is used to jump to any address in the block of addresses with the same high order two digits (256 memory locations).

The conditional program transfer instruction gives the computer the ability to "think." A conditional program transfer instruction is executed only if a condition is met. This condition is based on the results of the execution of previous instructions which have affected the flags. Normally there are four or more conditional flags, each representing a different condition. These conditions can be sampled as either set or reset (on or off).

For example, if the condition for a program transfer is that the zero flag should be set, and the flag is set, then the program will transfer. If the flag is not set, the program will not transfer but will flow to the next sequential instruction. If the condition is that the zero flag should not be set, the program will only transfer if the flag is off.

These conditional program transfer instructions give the program the ability to make decisions by transferring the program flow based in the input information. For example, if it is required to output one set of data if the input data is more than 200, and another set of data if the input data is 200, and a third set of data if the input data is less than 200, the zero and minus flag will give the proper conditions. The steps required are:

Input data
Subtract 200
Check zero flag, output second set of data if set.
Check minus flag, output third set of data if set.
Output first set of data.

The program to carry out these steps must make three decisions, that is, which of the three sets of data to output. This is accomplished by the two conditional program transfers.

The Stack

The stack, a very useful tool for the programmer, is a storage area in which program addresses are temporarily stored by some instructions. It is loaded by the CALL instruction and read by the RETURN instruction.

The top address of the stack is initialized early in any program using the stack by executing a LXI SP with the address assigned to the top of the stack (usually the last address in RAM) as bytes 2 and 3. When an instruction is executed which puts information on the stack, the pointer moves down one and stores the high order eight bits. Then the pointer moves down again and stores the low order eight bits. This process is repeated whenever new information is to be placed on the stack, but the process is reversed for stack read instructions, such as RETURN.

When the stack is loaded, it can contain addresses from previous CALL instructions. In this case, the contents of the stack are 'pushed down one' or moved down one address to make room for the

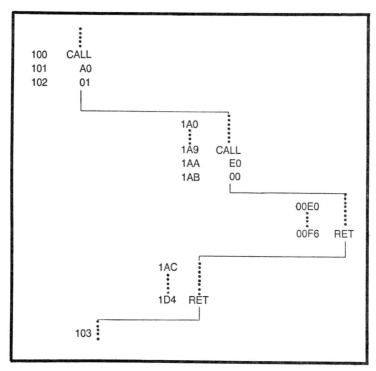

Fig. 7-4. Nesting CALL commands and subroutines.

added address. When one RETURN instruction is executed, the last entry to the stack is read and the stack is then 'popped' by moving the SP up by one address in the stack so that the next location contains the return address for the next level of subroutines. In this manner subroutines can be "nested," i.e., called from subroutines as illustrated in Fig. 7-4. This program will execute the first CALL instruction and transfer to 1A0. When 1A9 is executed, the program will transfer to address E0. When address F6 (RTN) is executed, the program transfers back to address 1AC. When the next RE-TURN is executed, the program transfers back to address 103. This illustrates two levels of CALL instructions: many more can be used if required. Some microprocessor families have a limited number of levels because of the limited size of the stack.

A subroutine is a small piece of a program that is repeatedly used in the main program or in other subroutines. By treating them as a subroutine, the same set of instructions can be used many times while requiring only a 3-byte CALL instruction to be entered. This CALL instruction places the address of the next instruction on the stack. When the subroutine executes the RETURN instruction at the end of the subroutine, the program is transferred back to the next instruction after the CALL instruction. This is done by placing the two stack locations, the location that the pointer is pointing to and the next higher location, in the program counter. Since the program counter contains the address of the next instruction to be executed, the RETURN transfer is effected.

JUMP Instructions

The jump instruction changes the normal program flow to the specified address instead of the next address by changing the program counter.

Figure 7-5 illustrates a program which will proceed until the jump command is decoded; the program counter will then be loaded with bytes 2 (low order) and 3 (high order) of the instruction. The next instruction executed will be the instruction at memory address 205. This is an *unconditional* jump; that is, every time the instruction is executed, the program jumps. There are also several conditional jumps, which sample the program flags and jump only if the flag is high or only if it is low. The common conditional jumps are:

ADDRESS	MNEMONIC	
100	⋮	PROGRAM
101	⋮	
102	⋮	
103	JMP	JUMP COMMAND
104	05	
105	02	
205	⋮	CONTINUE
206	⋮	PROGRAM

Fig. 7-5. Illustrating the use of the JUMP instruction.

```
ADDRESS          MNEMONIC

  100             DCR B
  101             JNZ
  102              00
  103              01
  104              ⋮          CONTINUE
  105              ⋮          PROGRAM
```

Fig. 7-6. Illustrating the use of the JNZ instruction in a count down loop.

JZ: Jump if the zero flag is set high
JNZ: Jump if the zero flag is not set high
JC: Jump if the carry flag is set high
JNC: Jump if the carry flag is not set high
JPE: Jump if parity flag is set high
JPO: Jump if parity flag is not set high
JM: Jump if the sign flag is set high
JP: Jump if the sign flag is not set high

Care must be taken to insure that the instruction on which the conditional jump is keyed does indeed set the flag, and that the flag is not affected by subsequent instructions. An illustration of the use of the JNZ instruction is shown in Fig. 7-6. If the B register is preloaded with a number, when the program executes address 100, the B register will be decremented by one. The JNZ instruction samples the zero flag, and if it is not set (the B register is not zero), the program will jump to the specified address (100). The B register will again be decremented, and the zero flag sampled. The program will continue looping between addresses 100 and 103 until the B register is counted down to zero. Then the zero flag will be set, and the program will not jump; instead, it will execute the next sequential instruction (address 104). If the B register is zero when the program reaches address 100, the B register will be all 'ones' with the first decrement, and then count down to zero. This loop forms a program delay which holds the system in status quo for a short duration of time. These loops are built into some programs to stop the program execution in order to allow other things to happen or indications to be observed.

CALL and RETURN Instructions

The unconditional call instruction (CD) is used to call the subroutines when the instruction is executed. The unconditional return (RET) returns the program control to the address last stored in the stack. Figure 7-7 shows the use of the unconditional call and return instruction in a simple executor type program, where the main program is used to tie several subroutines together.

When the program reads address B0, the call is decoded; address B3, the contents of the program counter after reading the 3 bytes of the first call instruction, is loaded into the stack. The program jumps to address 200 and executes the program starting at that address. When the program reads address 265, the contents of the last entry of the stack are transferred to the program counter and the program control transfers to address B3. From B3, the program will transfer to address 300 by virtue of the call instruction. This program as shown will sequence through the three subroutines in

ADDRESS	MNEMONIC	ADDRESS	MNEMONIC
B0	CALL		
B1	00	200	⋮
B2	02	265	RET
B3	CALL		
B4	00	300	⋮
B5	03		⋮
B6	CALL	32A	RET
B7	00		
B8	04	400	⋮
B9	CALL		⋮
BA	00	416	RET
BB	02		
BC	CALL		
BD	00		
BE	04		
BF	JMP		
C0	B0		
C1	00		

Fig. 7-7. Using the CALL and RET instructions in an executor type program.

```
        ⋮           SUBROUTINE
       RZ           RETURN IF ZERO FLAG SET
       OUT          OUTPUT DESIRED DATA ON
       XX           OUTPUT XX
       RET          UNCONDITIONAL RETURN
```

Fig. 7-8. Conditional exit from a subroutine using the conditional return instructions.

the order shown (address 200, 300, 400, 200, 400, then repeat) until the program is stopped.

In this manner, the same subroutine can be used in several places in the main program without keeping track of the return address in the program. All return addresses are specified by the call instructions.

In addition to the unconditional call and return instructions, there are several conditional call and return instructions. As with the conditional jump instructions, the execution of these instructions is dependent on the condition of the specified flag. These instructions are:

CALL   RETURN

CZ   RZ   Call and return if zero flag is set
CNZ   RNZ   Call and return if zero flag is not set
CC   RC   Call and return if carry flat is set
CNC   RNC   Call and return if carry flag not set
CPE   RPE   Call and return if parity flag is set
CPO   RPO   Call and return if parity flag not set
CM   RM   Call and return if sign flag is set
CP   RP   Call and return if sign flag not set

These instructions do not have to be used together. That is, a CZ may call a subroutine and its corresponding return may be a RM. There may be several different exits from a subroutine, all returning to the same point in the program—but under different conditions. For example, if the results of a given subroutine are zero the subroutine must be exited; and, if the results are not zero, an output must be energized and the subroutine must then be exited. This is illustrated in Fig. 7-8, using a RZ instruction to exit the subroutine if

152

the results are zero, and an RET after the output portion of the subroutine. If the output is made a subroutine, a CNZ can be used as shown if Fig. 7-9. This transfers the program to the output subroutine if the zero flag is not set. If the zero flag is set, the RET instruction returns the program to the main program. The return from the output subroutine will be to this RET instruction, which will return the program to the main program. Care must be taken when using call instructions to include a return instruction for every call instruction. If this is not done, and the stack is not adjusted, the program can end up at some undesirable place because it did not return to the next level of the program.

Remember that a return will load the program counter with the last or top address in the stack. Normally this is the address of the first instruction after the last call instruction, which is the normal desired program transfer point. Under certain conditions it may be desirable to eliminate the top address in the stack in order to bypass one level of return. The POP instruction does this by transferring the top address of the stack to a register, and moving the stack up one level, eliminating the current return address. The PUSH instruction moves the contents of a designated register pair to the top of the stack, pushing the contents of the stack down one address. This can be used to add a return address to the top of the stack.

The PCHL instruction moves the contents of the H and L registers to the program counter. So the program jumps to the address specified by the H and L registers.

Other Instructions

The increment (INR) and decrement (DCR) instructions add (INR) or subtract (DCR) one from the specified register, memory,

```
        :          SUBROUTINE
        .
       CNZ         CALL OUTPUT SUBROUTINE AT
        XX         ADDRESS YYXX IS ZERO FLAG
        YY         NOT SET
       RET         UNCONDITIONAL RETURN
```

Fig. 7-9. Using the conditional CALL instruction to call a subroutine.

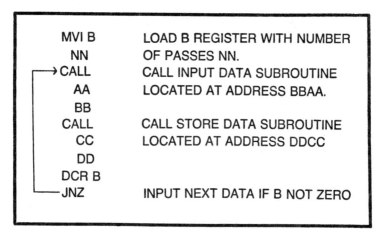

MVI B	LOAD B REGISTER WITH NUMBER
NN	OF PASSES NN.
→CALL	CALL INPUT DATA SUBROUTINE
AA	LOCATED AT ADDRESS BBAA.
BB	
CALL	CALL STORE DATA SUBROUTINE
CC	LOCATED AT ADDRESS DDCC
DD	
DCR B	
JNZ	INPUT NEXT DATA IF B NOT ZERO

Fig. 7-10. Inputting and storing data using subroutines.

or stack pointer. The INX and DCX are increment and decrement *extended*, meaning that a 16-bit register pair is affected instead of an 8-bit single register or memory. These extended instructions add one or subtract one from the specified register pair or the stack pointer. The DCR and INR set the flags, while the DCX and ICX normally do not affect the flags.

These instructions are used to pass a program through a loop a specified number of times, then exit through a conditional jump or transfer. Figure 7-10 shows the use of the decrement in a loop. It is desired to read a data input fifteen times and store this data for each pass. The MVI B loads the B register with 15 (F hex). The two call instructions input the data and store it by use of subroutines. The B register is then decremented. If the B register is not zero, the program jumps back to the two call instructions and continues to loop until the B register is counted down to zero; the zero flag is then set and the program does not jump on the JNZ instruction.

The disable interrupt (DI) instruction turns off the interrupt circuitry in the microprocessor so that no interrupts will be recognized until the enable interrupt (EI) instruction has been executed. For an interrupt to be acknowledged the external hardware must put a restart n (RST n) instruction on the data bus. This instruction is a single-byte call instruction which transfers the program control to the address of eight times n, where n is zero through seven. These locations can contain a short interrupt service routine, or a jump to another service routine. Since the RST *n* is a call instruction, the address of the next instruction to be executed in the main program is stored in the stack. An RET at the end of the service routine restores the program to the point where it left for the interrupt.

The halt (HLT) instruction stops the program and is used in the event problems arise. It takes a hardware reset or an interrupt to resume the program.

The NOP instruction is a dummy instruction, which changes nothing except the program counter. If there is an extra instruction in the program which must be removed, change it to a NOP; this effectively removes it, yet saves rewriting the program or reassigning addresses.

INTERRUPTS

An interrupt is an external request to the microprocessor which demands immediate attention. Usually it indicates that some external device has data for the system or needs data from the system, or else it is a command to the system to do something. The interrupt results in a special subroutine call instruction which stops the current program execution at the end of the current instruction and transfers control to a special interrupt service subroutine.

Three types of interrupts are used with the different microprocessor families. These are:

1. **Single line interrupt:** tells the unit that an interrupt has been requested. The program must query all the possible sources to determine the souce of the interrupt.
2. **Vectored interrupt:** tells the unit that an interrupt address or number is on the data bus. The microprocessor looks at the data bus to determine the source of the interrupt, and enters the designated interrupt service routine. The external hardware must put the required information on the data bus.
3. **Multi-line interrupt:** more than one interrupt line conveys the information to the processor. This may be in binary code, or a straight one line for one interrupt.

Most second generation microprocessors, such as the 8080, use the vectored interrupt. Some third generation units use multiline interrupts.

INTERRUPT NUMBER	DECIMAL ADDRESS	HEX ADDRESS
0	0	0
1	8	8
2	16	10
3	24	18
4	32	20
5	40	28
6	48	30
7	56	38

Fig. 7-11. Interrupt addressing.

When an interrupt is acknowledged, the program control transfers to preassigned memory locations. These are usually located in the first 64 words of memory, so they do not have space enough for service routines. Usually jump commands are placed in these locations to transfer the program to longer service routines.

The RST instruction for the 8080 family is the interrupt instruction. The bit pattern for the op code of this instruction is 11NNN111, where NNN is the interrupt number. This system has the capability for eight interrupts, numbers 0 thru 7. The RST instruction, which is generated externally, transfers program control to an address which is eight times the interrupt number. Figure 7-11 gives the interrupt numbers and the respective addresses in both decimal and hex.

Figure 7-12 shows a simple interrupt port. If there are some which have priority over others, a priority interrupt scheme must be used. This means that unless the interrupts are disabled, the highest priority interrupt must be serviced first. The circuit shown in Fig. 7-13 will do this. The highest order interrupt is interrupt 0, and the lowest order is interrupt 7.

The binary equivalent of the interrupt number is obtained by the 8 to 3 encoder. This is the 3 inputs to the 8 bit latch; all other bits are high to generate the RST instruction. When the INTA signal is received, the information in the data latches is gated onto the data bus, generating the vectored interrupt.

156

There is an enable interrupt instruction and a disable interrupt instruction. The enable interrupt instruction enables the interrupt circuitry in the processor. This allows the processor to receive and acknowledge interrupts. The disable instruction turns off the interrupt recognition circuitry so that no interrupts will be acknowledged. When an interrupt is acknowledged, no other interrupts will be acknowledged until an enable interrupt instruction has been executed.

Since an interrupt may occur at any point in the program, the contents of all the registers and the program status word must be saved to assure that the program returns to the same condition as before the interrupt. The PSW and all the registers can be put on the stack at the start of the service routine by the appropriate PUSH instructions. The accumulator is loaded on the stack as the high order eight bits of the PSW. At the end of the service routine, just before the return instruction, these registers must be restored by the appropriate POP instructions.

There is nothing to prevent one interrupt from interrupting another as long as the enable interrupt instruction is executed. If this capability is included, only the higher priority interrupts must be

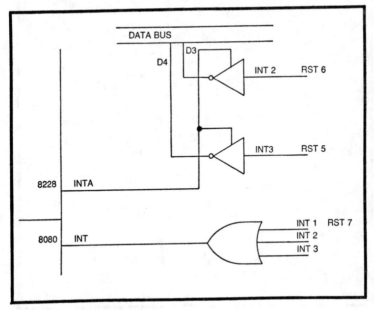

Fig. 7-12. A simple interrupt port.

recognized; otherwise, there may be several interrupts being serviced at the same time. Normally the interrupt service routine is short enough so that this capability is not needed. If several interrupts occur at the same time, they will be serviced in order of their priority.

A typical use for interrupts is when there are several I/O devices connected to a system, such as safety monitors, displays, keyboards, and sensors. Some of these supply information only when they demand attention, and others transfer data at a slow rate. Without interrupts, the common method of servicing these devices is by polling each device in turn to see if it needs servicing, which can take up a large amount of program space. The interrupts allow the processor to run the main program and do other work until an interrupt is received; the program then services the interrupt and goes back to the main program.

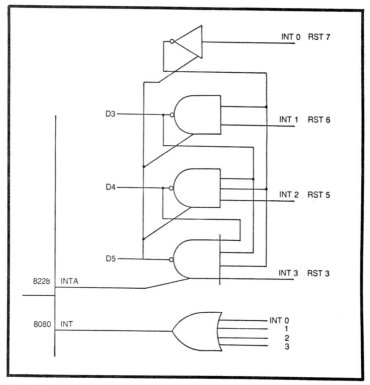

Fig. 7-13. Priority interrupt.

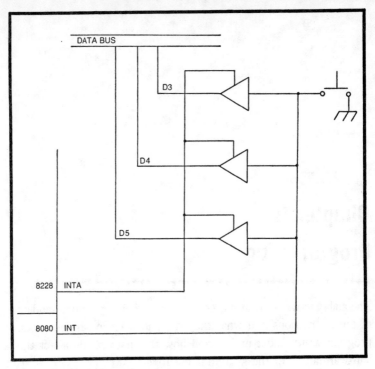

Fig. 7-14. Using interrupt 0 as system reset.

Another use of interrupts is for a monitoring type sensor, such as a low voltage sensor or a fire detector. The system may be servicing other programs, such as temperature control, until the sensor is tripped. This sends an interrupt to the system, and the service routine generates the corrective action.

For most small general purpose systems, interrupts are not neeced. The number of I/O devices is limited, and they are not usually set up as monitors or controls. Several of the systems do use interrupt 0 as system reset, which restarts the program at address 0. Figure 7-14 shows using this interrupt as the system reset.

Programmable controllers are available which simplify the use of interrupts.

Chapter 8
Programming

◆◆

The ability to write programs comes from a thorough understanding of the instructions and what they do, and from experience. The program writer must understand how the instructions affect the hardware and how the system is put together.

The object of this chapter is to program the simple system shown in Fig. 8-1. This system has 512 bytes of EPROM, 256 bytes of RAM, three 8-bit output ports, and three 8-bit input ports. One of the input ports is connected to a 16-button keyboard, and one is used for special, user-designated switches. Part of the third input port is used for data ready signals, and interrupts. Two of the output ports are connected to single LED indicators, and the third is for commanded outputs.

THE BASIC STEPS

The steps used and the order in which they are used depend on the size and complexity of the program and the experience of the programmer.

1. Define the objective of the program.
2. Break the objective up into logical parts. Visualize how each of these areas will be accomplished.
3. From this, draw up a simplified flow diagram.

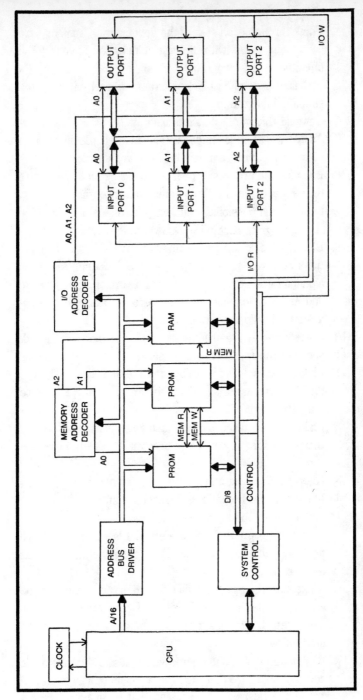

Fig. 8-1. Functional diagram for simple system used in this chapter.

4. Think through each step of the flow diagram, making sure each block works with the other blocks to accomplish the objective of the program.
5. Visualize a detailed block diagram for each block of the simplified diagram.
6. Compile this into a detailed diagram.
7. Assign words consisting of an alphanumeric designation to address and program variables not yet determined.
8. Examine the program, one block at a time, and investigate the effects of the different variables and program transfers. Look for the possibility of getting into undesirable loops or of the program recognizing unwanted conditions.
9. Block by block, assign the mnemonic codes for the instructions required to complete the blocks. Either assign an alphanumeric code for the program variables and jump to addresses or leave a dash for reference. Mark these variables in the flow diagram.
10. Make sure each instruction works in the manner desired, and that the results are as desired.
11. Make sure each flag is set by the conditions desired before the flags are used, and that they are not changed before they are used.
12. Make sure each call instruction has a return instruction, or that provisions are made to account for the required return.
13. Keep track of the initialization requirements.
14. Make sure each conditional transfer instruction transfers only on the conditions desired.
15. Talk the program through several times, setting up all possible conditions, to verify that the program works as desired.
16. Make sure the program will exit as desired. It must not be left to wander around aimlessly. Either loop it back on itself, return it to look for new commands, or give it a halt instruction.
17. Assign addresses and operational codes to the mnemonic codes. Make sure that the program can get into the memory in the desired manner, and that all instructions are

loaded sequentially, except for the instructions entered from a program transfer instruction.

18. Determine the initialization requirements. Make sure that the stack pointer and all required conditions and all program variables are initialized to the proper conditions.

The rest of this chapter is an explanation and elaboration of these steps.

DATA TRANSFER

Remember that there are four basic types of instructions: data manipulation, data movement, program manipulation, and status management. The data manipulation operates on data in the accumulator with data located as specified in the instruction. These are the arithmetic and logic instructions, and the data may be in a register, memory, or second byte of the instruction.

It is important to keep track of the location of the data, to make sure it is where it is required at the time required by the program. If the data is in a register, care must be taken to keep the data intact, and not to use the register for another purpose before the data is used. If the data is from memory, some form of memory addressing must be used before it is required, usually in the previous instruction. For these instructions, memory is addressed by the H and L register pair, so both these registers must be set up previously by the program. This is done for most applications by the LXI H instruction, where bytes 2 and 3 are the memory address. For example, the following series of instructions will add the contents of memory address 16AF to the contents of the accumulator:

LXI H

AF

16

ADD M

Remember that all data and addressing are in the hexadecimal number system covered in the appendix.

If the source of the two data words to be added are the B register and memory address 16AF, the following series of instructions could apply:

MOV A,B
LXI H
AF
16
ADD M

This takes five program locations. A simpler method is to use the
LDA instruction as follows:

LDA
AF
16
ADD B

This loads the accumulator with the contents of the memory location, then adds the B register, saving one program step.

Data is transferred to the output ports by the output instruction, where the second byte defines the output port. This instruction
transfers the contents of the accumulator to the referenced output
port by the data bus, with the address bus defining the port. The data
must be placed in the accumulator prior to the output command, and
care must be taken not to alter this data before it is used. For our
system, to output 55 to ports 0 and 1 (to turn on every other LED),
the following instructions can be used:

MVI A
55
OUT
00
OUT
01

The MVI A instruction loads the accumulator with the desired
output (55). The output instructions send this data to ports 0 and 1. If
the output ports are of the latching type (that is, if the outputs remain
until the port is addressed again), the LEDs will stay on. For this
case, to turn off the LEDs replace the 55 with 00 in the above
example. To output the contents of register B to port 0 and register
C to port 1, the following instructions can be used.

```
MOV A,B
OUT
00
MOV A,C
OUT
01
```

Notice that for both outputs, the data was moved to the accumulator before the output command.

The input instruction transfers the data from the designated input port to the accumulator. Here again the port is identified by the second byte of the instruction. The data bus carries the data and the address bus carries the port number during the addressing of the port.

To input the keyboard and determine if a key has been depressed, the following instructions can be used.

```
IN
00
ORA A
JNZ
00
01
```

This inputs port 0 to the accumulator, does an ORA A to set the flag (which does not change the accumulator contents), and then does a jump non zero to address 100. So, the program will transfer to address 100 if a key has been depressed. Replacing the JNZ with a CNZ (call non zero) will enable the program to return to the next instruction. If no key has been depressed, the program will continue to the next sequential instruction. If it is desired to wait in the loop looking for a key depressed before proceeding, change the JNZ to a JZ to the IN instruction. This will lock the program in the short loop until a key is depressed. Be careful when using this type of loop, because the time the program is hung in this loop could be spent doing other things with the program, such as looking at the other input ports, or commanding an output port.

For the type of input port shown for port 0, a reset is required to set the port to 0. This can be done two ways: by a program reset using one of the commanded outputs, or by a hardware reset, where port is reset when a key is depressed. This system uses both, so that the port can be reset when the program is started, and only the last key depressed will be read. The program reset is required to assure that the first read command reads a key depression and not extraneous data from the power-up of the system. If bit 0 of output port 2 is connected to the reset, the following instructions will provide the reset pulse:

```
MVI A
  01   (bit 0 high)
OUT
  02
MVI A
  00   (bit 0 low)
OUT
  02
```

The first MVI A and OUT instructions turn on the reset pulse, while the second MVI A and OUT turn off the reset pulse. If the pulse is not turned off, no data will enter the input port. If the other bits are used to display data in this output port, and if this data must be preserved, the following series of instructions can be used:

```
LDA
 XX
 YY
ORI
 01
OUT
 02
ANI
 FE
OUT
 02
```

Address YYXX is the address of the memory location used to store the output word for port 2. Most programs which use individual bits of an output word to represent different things compile this output word in a memory location or in a register. The ORI instruction adds bit 0 to this word to turn on the reset pulse. The ANI

FE logically AND's the last output with all bits except 0, turning off the reset pulse. Care must be taken not to turn off some of the bits when they are supposed to be on.

When using conditional transfers, always make sure that the proper condition flag is affected by the desired instruction, and that there is no instruction which affects the flag until it is sampled. Consult the instruction list if there is any doubt about which flags are affected. It is always advisable to place the conditional transfer as close as possible to the instruction that the transfer is keyed on.

Timing keeps the instructions separated from the data. Both can appear on the data bus, but at different times during the instruction cycle. An instruction cycle is the time-sequence of steps required to read and execute one instruction. The first step is the instruction fetch, where the memory location defined by the program counter is read. During this time the information of the data bus is the instruction. After the CPU has decoded the instruction, the commands required for the execution of the instruction are issued, during the next cycle time. So data appearing on the data bus during this time is data, or the second byte of the instruction. The CPU keeps track of this, and if the program is correct and there are no noise transients, the CPU will keep everything running properly. If byte 2 of a 2-byte instruction is left out the program will read the next instruction as byte 2, which causes program errors. If a transient affects some of the address lines, the wrong address will be read, again throwing the program off. Always make sure that the proper number of bytes are used for each instruction.

FLOW DIAGRAMMING

The first step in writing any program is to define the objective of the program completely. What is the program supposed to do? What are its inputs and outputs? What conditions will the program be working under? The next step is to break this objective down into the generalized steps required to complete the assigned task, with the inputs, outputs, and conditions. From this a flow diagram is drawn, a 'picture' of the program, giving blocks for the steps, with the definition of the steps inside.

Figure 8-2A gives the flow diagram for a portion of a program. The objective of this portion is to check if bit 0 in memory location

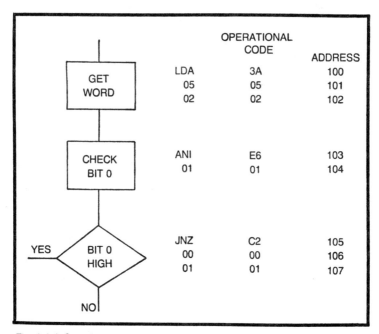

Fig. 8-2.A Completed flow diagram.

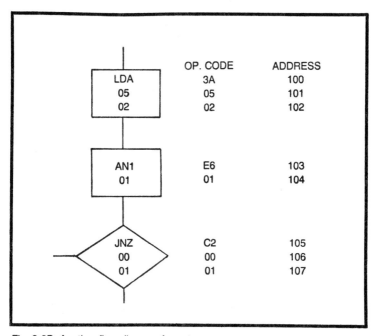

Fig. 8-2B. Another flow diagram format.

205 is set, and to jump to program address 10D if it is. Otherwise, the program is to continue. This program is to start at address 100. The first block is to get the word so that it can be checked. The second block checks for bit 0 set, and the third block transfers the program if this bit is set. The flow diagram can be simplified by eliminating the second block and changing the third block to bit 0 set, with the two branches. All conditional transfers are shown as diamonds with two outputs, one for the transfer condition and one for the non-transfer condition.

It is advisable to break the flow diagram down into as small functions as possible, at least in the beginning. This will make the next step easier; but, before going on to the next step, always check the flow diagram to make sure that nothing has been left out.

The next step is to assign instruction to each block of the flow chart. This is done using the mnemonic code for the instructions, as shown next to the flowchart in Fig. 8-2A. To assign the instructions, visualize the instruction steps required to complete the block. For example, the first block, 'get word,' requires that the word in memory location 205 be transferred to the accumulator so that it can be checked. The LDA instruction loads the accumulator with the contents of the memory location specified by bytes 2 and 3, so this instruction is used. The MOV A,M instruction can be used, but it requires an extra instruction. To check to see if bit 0 is set, the ANI (AND immediate) instruction is used, where byte 2 is the data. If bit 0 of the accumulator is set, the results of the AND with 01 will be 01, and the zero flag will be low. If this bit is not set, the result will be 0, with the zero flag set. To sample the zero flag, and fulfill the objective, the JNZ transfers the program to address 10D if the flag is not set.

The remaining step is to add the hexadecimal code for the instructions, and to assign memory addresses. This is shown in the next column of Fig. 8-2A. The operational code is the information to be stored as binary numbers in the memory locations in the address column. For example 00111010 is stored in the eight bits (0 thru 7) in address 100.

Figure 8-2A is but one of many formats for flow charts. Figure 8-2B shows another format, where the mnemonic code is listed inside the block, and the operational code and addresses are listed outside. This type of flow chart effectively eliminates the second step of breaking down the program requirements into generalized steps. Where the program cannot be visualized this can cause problems, so it is more advisable to use the format of Fig. 8-2A. Another common method is to write the flow chart and program separately, on different sheets of paper. Although this makes for a clean-appearing flow chart, both papers must be consulted when working with the program. Usually, line numbers are added to this type of program listing, to aid in correlating the various parts of the program. This type of flow chart and program listing is used wherever the program is punched on cards or tape by a keypunch operator rather than by the machine operator.

Some operational programs are made up mostly of subroutines, while others have few or none. The subroutines give the ability to use the same small routine several places in program. These are set off from the main program, usually at the end, and are entered by the call instruction.

Data is carried to and from the subroutine by the registers, and by storing in a data memory location. Since the call instruction affects none of the registers, any of the registers can be used, even the accumulator. In the subroutine, care must be taken not to alter any of the registers which contain data used later in the main program. This can be done by adding notes to the flow chart which indicate which registers are used, and what for. An alternative is to store all the registers either in the stack or in the RAM memory upon entering the subroutine, and restoring the registers just before exiting.

The normal exit for a subroutine is the RET instruction, which returns the program to the instruction after the last call instruction. As shown in Chapter 7, subroutines can be "nested," that is, a subroutine can be called from another subroutine. Several levels of nesting can be used if required, but care must be taken to have either a RET instruction or a POP instruction for each call instruction. If this is not done, the program will end up at the wrong place when returning from a nested subroutine.

An executor is a control routine which controls the execution of the program through the use of subroutines. Not all programs can be logically broken up into this format, but when possible, it should be done to allow subroutines to be developed as small programs, then combined into the operational program by an executor. Also the order of execution can be changed by changing a few instructions in the executor, instead of changing complete sections of the program. Several levels of subroutines can be used, without worrying about the return address.

Figure 8-3 gives the flow chart for the executor portion of an operational program. This program uses several subroutines which are called up in the order desired by the executor. The program runs through the program completely, then loops through the last two subroutines until the system is reset. The first step is to initialize the program; this sets all the program variables to their desired value, and resets all the input and output ports. Most programs must be initialized to assure that the program starts in a known condition. In this example, two of the data words represent conditions which are important to the program, and the individual bits are set as required by the program. If these words are not set initially to zero, the program can interpret them as conditions which do not exist, causing program errors. When power is removed from RAM memory, the contents are lost, and when power is applied, the contents are unpredictable; therefore, those RAM locations used as data words and as program temporary storage must be set to zero or the desired starting value.

This program is set up to allow the development of the program by sections, and to allow some of the subroutines to be called both from the executor and from other subroutines. The first subroutine allows entering of a test mode, where some of the subroutines are called in a different order, and some of the program variables are forced and not determined.

Figure 8-4 shows the flow diagram to place the keyboard on the LEDs of output port 0. Each switch is represented by a bit for the row and a bit for the column, with the row being the low order four bits and the column being the high order four bits. The first task is to break down the objective of the program into generalized steps. The first step is to reset the keyboard so that any data will be meaningful. The next step is to read the switches and check to see if the input word contains any bits, representing a switch which has been de-

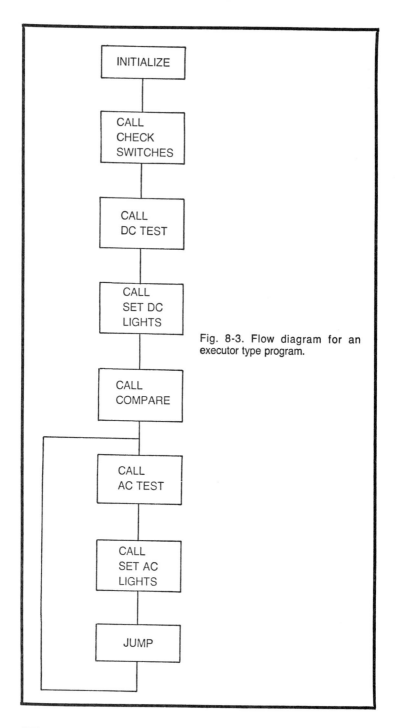

Fig. 8-3. Flow diagram for an executor type program.

pressed. Then it is a matter of outputting the input word, and jumping back to look for the next switch depression.

To assign mnemonic codes to each block, take each block and visualize what the block is to accomplish. The first block is to reset the system. The reset pulse must be applied to the keyboard circuitry (bit 0 of output 02), and all the LEDs must be turned off. The first two steps apply the reset pulse to the keyboard circuitry,

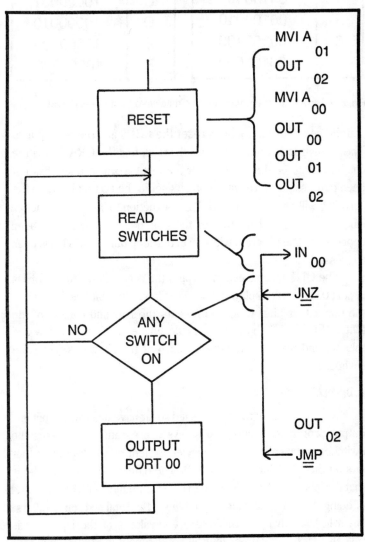

Fig. 8-4. Flow diagram for keyboard program.

KEY	DATA WORD	KEY	DATA WORD
0	00010001	8	01000001
1	00010010	9	01000010
2	00010100	A	01000100
3	00011000	B	01001000
4	00100001	C	10000001
5	00100010	D	10000010
6	00100100	E	10000100
7	00101000	F	10001000

Fig. 8-5. Hexadecimal equivalent of the data word from the keyboard.

and the next four instructions reset the LEDs and the reset pulse. The IN instruction reads the switch word, and the ORA A sets the condition flag for the condition of the input word. If a key has not been depressed, there will be no bits set in the accumulator, so the zero flag will be set by the ORA A instruction. The JNZ instruction jumps the program back to read the switches if no switch has been depressed. The program will stay in this loop until a switch has been depressed.

The OUT 00 instruction outputs the accumulator to the LEDs of port 0. This will display one bit in the lower four bits, and one bit in the upper four bits, which represents the row and column of the switch. Figure 8-5 shows the hexadecimal equivalent, the row and column, and the data word in for each of the sixteen keys of the keyboard.

A DISPLAY PROGRAM

Most of the programs discussed so far have dealt with input and output programs. Figure 8-6 shows a program which reads the switches and displays their binary equivalent on the low order four bits on the LEDs of output port 0. The difference from Fig. 8-4 is that the input word is converted to its binary equivalent. One method of doing this is to use a look-up table for the total sixteen numbers, but a little studying of the binary equivalents of the input words reveals that the low order four bits of the input word determine the low order two bits of the binary equivalent, and the high order four bits determine the high order two bits of the binary equivalent. The relationship is:

Input word	Binary equivalent
0001	00
0010	01
0100	10
1000	11

So a short, 4-place look-up table can be used to determine the equivalents.

However, a little more studying will reveal that if the input word is shifted right until the bit shifts out, and the number of shifts required is counted, except the last one, the binary equivalent will be obtained. The following list of instructions will accomplish this:

RAR

JC

INR r

JMP

The RAR instruction rotates the contents of the accumulator right one place. If a bit is shifted out of the lower bit position the carry flag is set, so the JC will exit the loop when this happens. The INR r increments the chosen reigster by one to count the number of times the bit is shifted. The JMP transfers the program back to the RAR instruction to pass through the loop again. The binary equivalent will end up in the chosen register r.

This loop must be passed through twice, or else two similar loops must be used, one for the low order four bits of the input word, and one for the high order four bits. The flow chart given in Fig. 8-6 shows two loops. The reset block, read block, and the JNZ are the same as in Fig. 8-4.

The MOV instruction is to save the input data for use in the second half of the program. The ANI OF instruction masks out the high order four bits, because only the lower four bits are used. The LXI B loads the B register with zero. These three instructions initialize the program. The following instructions comprise the part detailed above. The MOV D,B saves this count in the D register. The next three instructions initialize the program for the second loop, to determine the equivalent of the upper four bits. The loop can be made the same, but that requires shifting the initial data right four places to align the upper four bits of the input word to be shifted right. Instead, shifting the upper four bits left, and counting down the number of shifts is required. For this reason, the B register is preloaded with 03, and decremented for each pass through the loop. When the binary equivalent for the upper four bits is determined, it is shifted left two places to make it the higher order two bits of the results. These bits are ORed with the low order two bits from the D register to obtain the binary equivalent of the input word. This is transferred to the output port to light the appropriate LEDs by the OUT 00 instruction. From this the program loops back to look for the next input. If another key is not depressed, the same word will be decoded, because the keyboard electronics have not reset.

If just one pass through this subroutine is required, then the program is to be exited by replacing the last JMP with an RET instruction. It may be advantageous to move this data to a register before exiting to clear the accumulator for later use without destroying the information.

To complete the program shown in Fig. 8-6, the operational codes and the addresses must be added, and the program transfer addresses must be determined and added. These locations in the mnemonic listing are shown by the dashes. The lines on the left side of the mnemonic listing show where the jumps transfer to. This keeps track of the jump to addresses, and makes it easy to fill them in when the addresses are assigned.

GENERATING A SUBROUTINE

So far, only portions of subroutines, or representative programs have been generated. Next, let us try to generate a full operational subroutine from scratch. The objective of this subroutine is to load addresses in RAM memory from data from the keyboard. Input 01, bit 3 commands input to this subroutine, bit 4 commands the data entered as the address to load. Bit 5 commands the data to be loaded into the address. Exit from the subroutine is by system reset.

The first objective is to enter the subroutine when bit 3 of input 01 is on, indicating that the proper switch is depressed. This can be

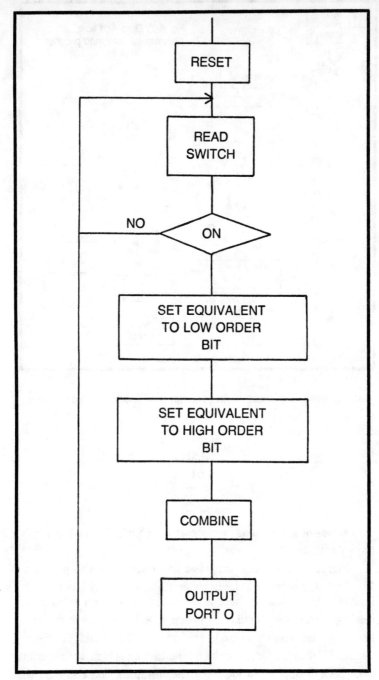

Fig. 8-6. Binary conversion flow diagram.

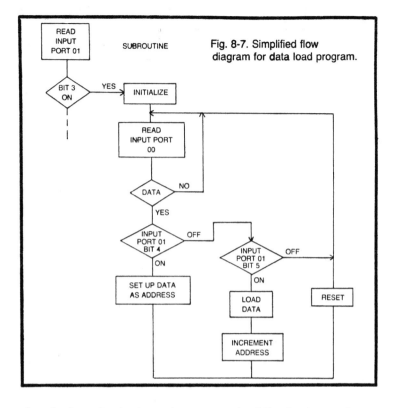

Fig. 8-7. Simplified flow diagram for data load program.

done by inserting in the main program the following instructions:

$$IN$$
$$01$$
$$ANI$$
$$04$$
$$CNZ$$
$$--$$

This series of instructions inputs port 01, checks for bit 3 and calls the subroutine if bit 3 is set.

Figure 8-7 shows the simplified flow diagram for this program. The first step is to read the keyboard, and see if any bits are set, indicating input data. If there is no data, the program loops back, reading the keyboard until a key is depressed. This indicates data is inputted. The next step is to check input 01, bits 4 and 5 to determine if this data is address or data. If neither bit is high, the program loops back through again, looking at the bits again. This also gives the operator the chance to change the data input, because the keyboard electronics is reset every time a new switch is depressed. If bit 4 is set, the data input is set up as the first address to be loaded with the following data. If bit 5 is set, the information from the switches is loaded as the data to be entered into the address.

Now we must further define the objective, because some things were left out in the original definition. These are listed below:

1. Can address all addresses possible in the system.
2. Can insert all 16 bits of data.
3. Can overwrite address errors by continuing to enter data. The address consists of the last four switches depressed.
4. The data is the last two switches depressed.
5. Bits 4 and 5 do not have to be depressed after each switch depression.
6. Data is entered in consecutive addresses, unless bit 4 is high again.
7. The information is displayed on output ports 0 and 1.

The requirement for the additional definitions is a result of examining the simplified flow chart. This illustrates the requirement of fully defining the objective of the program, covering all variables. If the program listing was started before these were defined, the program would end up as shown in the flow chart of Fig. 8-6. This program will work, but a little studying will show that it requires depressing of the switch for bit 4 or bit 5 of input port 1 after each key is depressed. This can be confusing, and can lead to entry errors, with no way of checking the data going in.

Figure 8-8 shows the new flow diagram for this program. The main difference is that the data is compiled as the information is read in, then it is handled when it has been determined whether the information is data or address. The keyboard is read; when information is obtained, the keyboard is reset and the data is compiled. Then bits 4 and 5 are checked, and if they are off, the next bit is looked for, or the bits are checked again to see if they are high. Notice that the program does not just cycle through the read keyboard block until data is presented, as in Fig. 8-6. A little thought will reveal that if bit 4 and bit 5 are not set during the pass through the loop that the keyboard was read, the program will lock up in the read keyboard

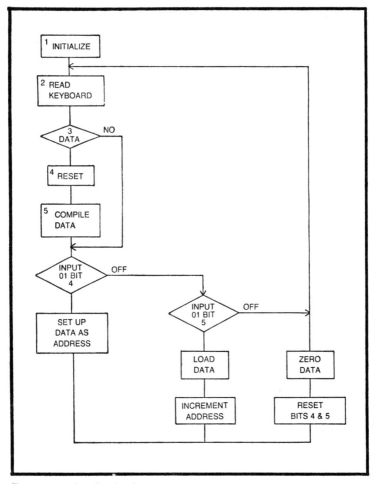

Fig. 8-8. Another data load program.

loop with no exit until the keyboard transmits data again. Then the first bit of the data will be lost, and so will the second bit if bits 4 and 5 are low during the current pass through the loop. Eliminating the reset loop will overcome this problem, but it will introduce a new problem. That is, once a key is depressed, the program will compile the first bit as data. Then if bits 4 and 5 are low during this pass, the same keys will be read as the second bit of data, and so on until bits 4 and 5 are high. This is why the program is set up to check bits 4 and 5 every pass through the loop, and the keyboard is reset once information is obtained from the keyboard.

Bit 4 and bit 5 of input 01 is supplied by operator actuated pushbutton switches. The input circuitry sets the bits high when the switch is released, so that the length of time the bit is high is under program control. If the switch was monitored directly, and the bit set high when the switch was depressed, several passes could occur while the switch was depressed, loading the same data into several consecutive addresses. Since bit 0 of output 02 resets the keyboard, let's assign bit 1 of output port 02 to reset bits 4 and 5 of input port 01.

Figure 8-9 shows a detailed flow diagram for the blocks numbered 2, 3, 4, and 5 in Fig. 8-8. This inputs the data, moves it to the D register for saving, checks for data, sets and resets the reset pulse, and compiles the data. The data is compiled by shifting the B C register pair right four places and moving the data in from the binary conversion subroutine into the low order four bits. The binary conversion subroutine is as shown in the program listing of Fig. 8-6, blocks 4 and 5, and enclosed by the dotted lines, except the E register is used in place of the B register and the D register is used in place of the C register. The binary equivalent is compiled in the low order four bits of the C register. This will compile up to four bits of data, by shifting the data left four places in the B and C register pair. Previous data is not affected because it is shifted out of the way. The D register is zeroed after it is used so that it will be ready for the next pass containing data. The contents of the B and C register pair is displayed on the LEDs to give the operator a visual indication of the data to be entered.

To set the data up as address, just move the contents of the B and C register to the H and L register. To set up the information as data, simply move the data from the C register to memory.

Figure 8-10 shows the completed detailed flow diagram, along with the subroutine to determine the binary equivalent of the input. What is left is to determine the instructions for each block and list the mnemonic codes. Then the operational codes and the addresses can be assigned.

The initialization is the last block that the mnemonic code is determined because the total initialization requirements may not be known at the start. Sometimes it is convenient to assign four place codes to constants, addresses, and flow diagram points to assist in

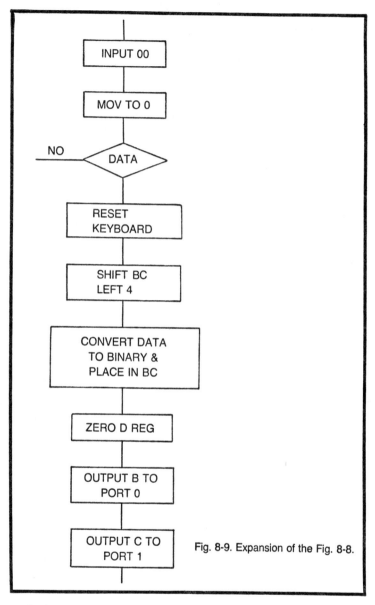

Fig. 8-9. Expansion of the Fig. 8-8.

assigning addresses. This gives a mnemonic code for every address required, except the numerical constants. This is used in this example.

The first several blocks are as discussed previously, and will not be repeated here. The word for output 2 is assigned 02WD, or output 2 word. The information that is current for output port 2 is stored in the address assigned to this word. In this manner, any information that is currently being outputted is stored in this location. When any output is meant for this port, this word is modified and outputted. In this manner, no previously determined information is lost.

To shift any data stored in another register, the information must be moved to the accumulator, shifted, and moved back to the original register. To shift a register pair requires shifting one bit, incorporating any carry in the high order register shift, then shifting the low order register again. The codes assigned to the SHIFT B , C, left 4, does this in a short loop. This can be done serially, but that will take at least three times as many instructions. The remaining parts of the program are straightforward.

By studying the program listing, the initialization requirements can be determined. The keyboard electronics must be reset, so that any previous data in the keyboard is not recognized as input data. Also, bits 4 and 5 must be reset to prevent undesired recognition of these bits. The B and C registers must be zeroed so that only meaningful and desired data is entered. The display must be zeroed so that the indication displayed is the true data. These requirements set up the program for the first few passes.

The first pass through the program, if no keys have been depressed, is through blocks 1, 2, 3, 4, 13, 14, 16, and back to block 2. The program will remain in this loop until a key is depressed or the address or data switches are depressed. When a key is depressed, the program will pass through blocks 2, 3, 4, 5, 6, 7, 8, 9, 10, 11, 12, 13, 14, 16 and back to block 2. If this is the first key depression, the data read in is in the low order for bits of the C register. The program will now pass through blocks 2, 3, 4, 13, 14, and 16 because the keyboard has been reset in block 5 of the previous pass. When another key is depressed, the program will take the yes pass from block 4, recognizing the data. The binary equivalent is loaded into the low order four bits of the C reigster. The data loaded previously is shifted to the high order four bits of the C register.

When the address switch is depressed, the contents of the B and C registers is loaded into the H and L registers. Then the switches are reset and the B and C register is zeroed. The keys are depressed again to load the data to be entered at the designated addresses into the C register. When the data switch is depressed, the C register is loaded by the MOV M, C instruction. Then the H and L registers are incremented so that the next data will be loaded into the next sequential address. Then the switches are reset and the C register is zeroed to condition the program to receive data. If four bits are entered, and the address switch is depressed, the new address will be set up. This must be done to load non-sequential data.

DEBUGGING

It is advisable to check the program over many times to look for program bugs. Program *bugs* are hidden problems in the program, such as the possibility of getting erroneous data into the program, or the program going off on its own. For example, if the B and C registers are not zeroed in the initialization of the program of Fig. 8-10, there would be no problem, as long as the program was entered with these registers at zero, or the address were a 4-digit hex number. However, if these conditions were not met, there could be a problem. If the registers contain data, say FFFF, and a 2-digit address is loaded in, the H and L register will be loaded with FF in the H register and the keyed in address in the L register, which will set up the wrong address to be loaded. This will happen only occasionally.

The method used to find program errors depends on the hardware and software capabilities of the system. If a single step function is built into the hardware, this can be used. If not, break-points can be put into the program to give a positive indication when the program passes a monitored point. Normally these display some data and halt the system. For example, if the following instructions are inserted in place of block 5 in Fig. 8-10, the program will display the data in, and halt, when the program recognizes data from input port 0.

MOV A,D
OUT
00
HLT

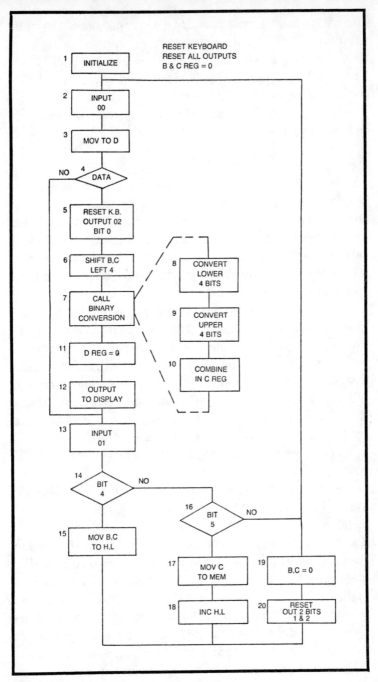

Fig. 8-10. Completed flow diagram for data load.

This will indicate the input data, and the operator can determine if this data is in error. But this will also halt the program the first pass through; so, to look at the data loaded into the memory, block 17 can be replaced with a similar series of instructions, replacing the D register callout with the C register.

To find program problems that are not apparent takes patience, ingenuity, and determination, but they can be found.

Monitors

Monitors are programs which give the operator assistance in developing and running other programs. These include the capability to load memory, read memory, start a program at any location, and even run a program for a given number of operations and stop. Many other capabilities, such as the ability to stop a program, examine what is going on, and resume the program at the point it stopped, are included in some monitor programs.

For a dedicated system, there is usually no monitor type program because there is only one program to be run, and no need to provide the capabilities of the monitor. However, it is advisable to have some monitor type capability in any small general purpose system. The monitor will be loaded into EPROM memory where it will control the programming and operation of the system. This is done in Chapter 11, where some of the programs are given for a small monitor. This is how the programs are loaded into RAM memory for development, and how the program to be executed is selected.

A monitor may reside in the microprocessor memory while the system is in operation running other programs. These are resident monitors, and usually have a short executive type control program. The capabilities of the monitor are utilized by giving a command to the program, such as a switch actuation or a keyboard input. For these programs, the monitor controls what is going on, and all entries into other programs are made with the monitor. When the system is reset, the program enters the monitor routine and waits for a command. For a general purpose system, this is convenient because it gives the operator a way of entering and executing one program from the many which may reside in memory.

Some monitors are loadable or commandable monitors. They may or may not reside in memory, and are not always in control of the program. A loadable monitor is loaded into RAM memory, and some means is provided for entry into it, such as an interrupt. If the monitor is assigned interrupt 01, then the hardware must be capable of providing the proper restart (RST) signal at the correct time. The monitor pointer (the jump to address and jump command) is stored in the proper memory locations. For an interrupt 01, and a monitor program loaded in at address 200 (hex) and above, the following list of commands provides the correct entry:

Instruction	Address
Jump	0008
00	0009
02	000A

This is loaded into the memory starting at address 0008 because the interrupt 01 (RST 1) transfers the program to this address.

The monitor program may have several different commands, each of which comprises a subroutine called by the program when the command is decoded. These are not operational type programs, but are only assistance type programs meant to assist the operator during the development and running of other programs.

Compilers & Assemblers

The use of compilers and assemblers is beyond the scope of this book. They are both powerful tools, and are useful for larger programs. Both assemblers and compilers are designed for a specific computer or microprocessor family, such as the 8080.

While monitors are development tools for the operator, assemblers are development tools for developing the program. The assembler provides the capability of writing the program in mnemonic codes only. For short programs, it is almost as easy to assemble the program by hand in machine langauge, but for long programs the assembly is quite convenient and saves a lot of headaches when writing a program.

Compilers are programs for higher level languages, such as Fortran and PLM. These compilers understand the meaning of such statements as IF, AND, and DO. Each language has its own words and symbols that it recognizes, and the compiler takes these and translates them into the instructions required to accomplish the intent of the statement. Compilers require more memory space than is normally available in the smaller systems, so they must be run on the larger computers.

Chapter 9
Putting the Blocks Together

++

To make a working system, the functional blocks must be connected in such a manner that they work together to accomplish the desired results.

DESIGNING A SYSTEM

The first task is to visualize what the system is to do, and the general capabilities required. At this point the program may or may not be defined. For specialized systems, the program and hardware development must be concurrent because one defines the other, and they both are defined by the purpose of the system. Normally, general purpose programs are developed independently of the hardware development, or after the hardware is built.

The next task is to fully define the system, and the system capabilities. Some of these requirements are defined below:

1. Type of system: dedicated or general purpose.
2. Memory: size; RAM: ROM: PROM: and /or EPROM.
3. Inputs: number and type.
4. Outputs: number and type.
5. Memory and/or I/O expansion capabilities.
6. Manual program controls.
7. Operational monitors of the program.

8. Is speed essential?
9. Self test capabilities.
10. Manual program capabilities such as single step, data load, or PROM or EPROM programming facilities.
11. Is direct load of RAM required?
12. Family of microprocessor circuits to use.

Family

Deciding which family of microprocessors to use is a basic decision which must be made early. This choice is up to the builder and is based on several considerations, as listed below:

1. Experience with a given microprocessor family.
2. Support chips available.
3. Is a microprocessor available?
4. Cost.
5. Available vendor supplied documentation.
6. Available instruction set.
7. Capability.
8. Power required.

Memory

To decide what type, and how much memory to use, a feel of what the program is to do is required. The overview of the program indicates the approximate length. If the system is expandable, the amount of memory is not as critical as with a closed system, but enough memory must be put on the CPU board to allow use as a simple system.

Memory Size. One hundred (hex) or 256 (decimal) words of RAM are enough for program data storage and some manually loaded programs. If the system is a general-purpose expandable, this size RAM will normally suffice.

Usually 512 (200 hex) words PROM or EPROM memory are enough for a simple operational program, but for complex, general purpose systems, several thousand words may be required. Remember that an 8-bit system with 16 address lines can address up to 64K of memory. Twelve address lines can address up to 4K of memory.

For our simple system, let us use 256 words of RAM and 512 words of EPROM. In addition, let us add the facilities for expanding the memory. This gives us a small system for simple applications, and the capability of expanding the system for additional applications. Figure 9-1 shows the system so far. To facilitate expansion, an address decoder is used, with the unused outputs available for additional memory addressing.

Memory Maps. The next requirement is to determine what addresses to assign the memory blocks. Since the 8080 family starts at address 00 upon reset, the program starts at this point. Note that other families may start the program at other addresses. Since the program is loaded in EPROM, let us assign the first 200 (hex) memory words as EPROM. RAM can be assigned any of the remaining locations, but as a starting point, let us assign it as 200 to 2FF.

From this, a memory map is started. A memory map is a composite listing of the memories, their functions, and their purpose and is useful during programming, troubleshooting, and operation. It helps the programmer to keep from overwriting some memory locations, and from using the same memory location twice. The programs are identified, data words are listed, and the stack is identified in the completed map. Figure 9-2 shows the memory map so far. Figure 9-3 shows a memory map for an operational system. Notice that the data words are defined, and, where important, the individual bits of the data word are defined. Also notice that the input and output ports are assigned memory addresses for this system. This map was generated during the hardware design and the programming.

Figure 9-1 shows the functional diagram for the system so far. The addressing is detailed so that the memories respond to the required addresses. Also shown are the control signals required for the memory, the memory read and the memory write signals, which are generated by the system controller from signals from the microprocessor.

The system controller drives the data bus and decodes the control signals to generate the system control functions. These signals can be generated using logic circuits; but this costs more and is more difficult to implement.

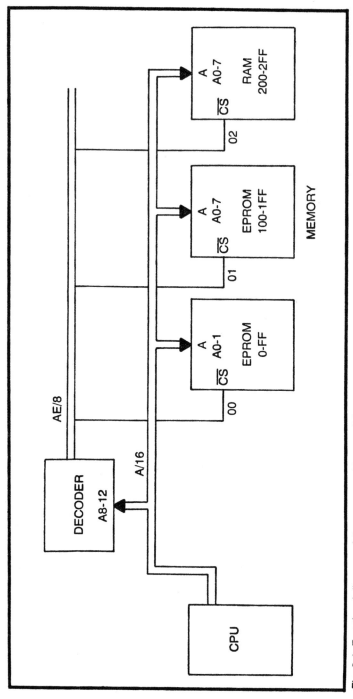

Fig. 9-1. Functional diagram of the system, with control lines.

192

The output circuitry depends upon the application. The object of the output circuit is to get the proper signal to the desired point at the correct time.

Output and Input Circuits

For specialized systems, the output circuitry is arrived at by starting with the device to be driven. Then the drive requirements are determined, and the circuitry to accomplish the drive from the address and data bus is designed. If possible, standard circuits are used.

Inputs for a general purpose system are usually keyboard and individual switches. Here again, various other interface circuits are available on more sophisticated systems. For our simple system, the inputs are a 20-button keyboard and seven toggle switches. In addition, there are other switches for hardware control. The outputs are three 7-segment LED displays and seven individual LEDs. There are also some hardware indicators.

Figure 9-4 shows the keyboard schematic. The 20 keys are connected in a 4 × 5 matrix, with each line connected as one bit to an input port. The first four vertical lines, and all four horizontal lines are connected to port 0. These sixteen keys are for the data entry from the keyboard. Remember that all data, including addresses, must be entered in hex numbers, so this takes sixteen keys. The

ADDRESSES	TYPE	REMARKS
0 FF	EPROM	
100 1FF	EPROM	
200 2FF	RAM	2FF-Stack

Fig. 9-2. Memory map.

193

ADDRESSES	TYPE	REMARKS
00 FF	EPROM	00-15 INITIALIZE PROGRAM 16-33 EXECUTOR 34-AB DC TEST AC-FF RFW
100 1FF	EPROM	100-104 RFW 105-111 DELAY 112-127 TURN ON LIGHTS 128-186 AC TEST 187-1AA COMPARE 1AB-1FE TEST-SELF

200
 	
	RAM	200 RFW WORD DATA WORDS
		201 CWF WORD
		202 BIT 0-RESET TO AC TEST
		           1-CRF FLAG
		           2-CWF FLAG
		           3-NO AC TEST RESPONSE
		           4-OPEN
		           5-NO REFERENCE
		           6-SHORT
		204 DC0
		205 AC0
		206 ACG

Fig. 9-3. Memory map for an operational system.

remaining four keys are for four commands to the program, such as enter, address data, step, or any desired program commands.

Since the keyboard makes only momentary contact, a buffer is loaded from the keyboard. This consists of latches, which are set by the keys and reset by the program. The I/O read and the address are ANDed to enable the 3-state output circuits. The reset bit is one bit of an output port which must be commanded to reset the buffers. If the reset bit is used to trigger a one-shot, then setting the bit momentarily will reset the buffers. The bit can be commanded high when reset is desired, then commanded low anytime before the next reset is needed. Also, one of the keys, column 5 row 4, is used as a manual keyboard reset by use of the OR gate. Both inputs to the OR gate are low when this key is depressed, giving a low out. This low resets the latches in the buffer circuits.

The toggle switches are connected to the input port 1 as shown in Fig. 9-5. Each switch is connected as one bit of the input port.

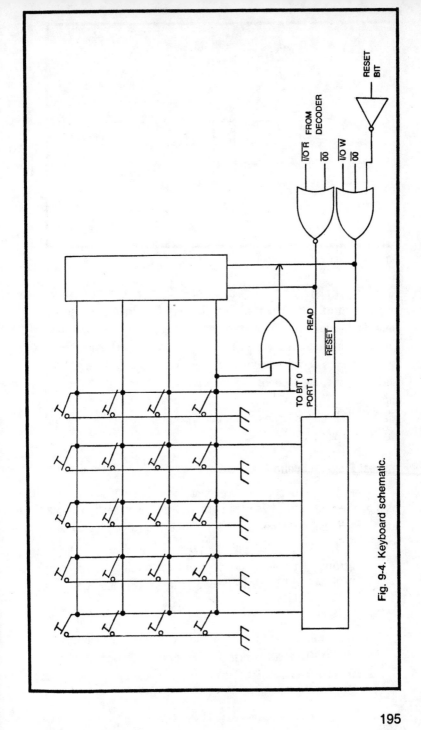

Fig. 9-4. Keyboard schematic.

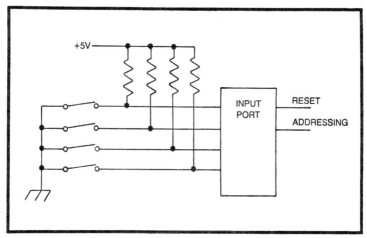

Fig. 9-5. Toggle switches connected to input port.

LED displays are covered in Chapter 6. To drive three displays requires three output ports, with the bits 0-6 driving the seven individual segments. Figure 9-6 shows the circuitry to drive one display, using individual gates. The address for the port is generated by an address decoder connected to address lines 0, 1, and 2, as shown. This same decoder can generate the address signals for the input ports. Figure 9-7 shows an 8255 type output chip driving the display. This chip supplies three output ports, drastically reducing the parts count.

Manual Program Controls

Manual program controls are single-bit inputs which are sampled by the program. These are normally used as a condition input for a conditional program transfer to force the program into subroutines or portions of the program. Typical program controls are:

Program: To select the program subroutine to program PROMS or EPROMS through a special output circuit tailored for the type memory used.

Read: To read any memory address under program control by inputting the address on the keyboard and depressing Enter. The data is displayed on two of the LED displays.

Load: To load RAM by using the keyboard to set up the address and data.

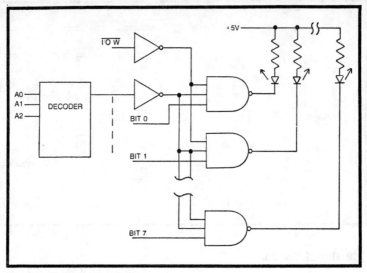

Fig. 9-6. Display drive circuitry.

These controls are the toggle switch inputs for general type use which have been defined by the program. The remaining input switches are also manual program controls, but they are defined by the user and are dependent on the program being run. These can be used for such things as selecting special programs, providing a start indication, and giving a program command.

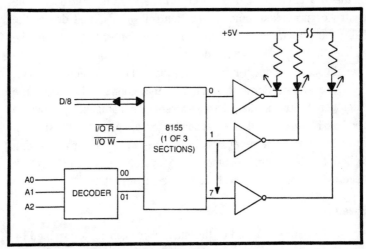

Fig. 9-7. Driving displays with an 8255 chip.

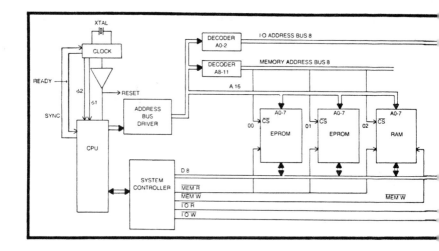

Operational Monitors

The operational monitors are the individual LED outputs; they indicate selected program conditions, as defined by the program. For example, if it is desired to know which branch the program takes at a given conditional transfer, a monitor can be used. At each of the monitored program branches, instructions are included to set the desired monitor, indicating that the program passed that point.

Figure 9-8 shows the completed system, complete with the system controller, data bus, and clock generator. The data bus goes to the I/O circuits, memory, and to the system controller. The controller provides some of the control signals, and drives the bidirectional data bus. To allow for expansion of the system, the address bus, the data bus, and some of the control signals must be brought out to a connector for connection to the expansion circuitry.

A reset amplifier is shown in Fig. 9-8, connected between the clock generator and the microprocessor. This amplifier provides a good solid reset, and the capability for an external reset from another source. The reset switch, which is a pushbutton or a spring loaded toggle switch, provides the system reset to the clock generator chip, one of the hardware control switches.

Speed

The operating speed of the microprocessor is determined by the system clocks. The maximum operating speed is determined by

198

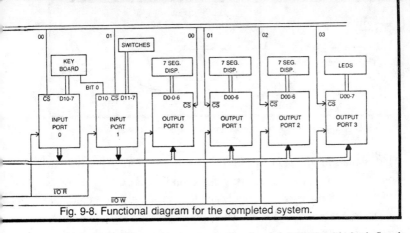

Fig. 9-8. Functional diagram for the completed system.

the maximum speed of the processor; for the 8080A, this is defined as the clock period, the time between ϕ_1 clock pulses. For the 8080A, the operating range is from 500 nanoseconds to 2 microseconds, and is controlled by the crystal or RC network connected to the clock generator.

If the system is operating at a speed faster than the memories are capable of, the system will go haywire because some bits may not be properly read. To overcome this, two things can be done; slow down the processor cycle, or cause the processor to take two cycles to read memory. A simple way to extend the processor cycle during the memory read is to connect the wait and ready lines together; if the memory line is low after sending an address on the address bus, the processor will enter the wait state. When the processor enters the wait state, the wait output goes high, though at other times it is low. So, the wait output is low when the processor looks for a high ready input, which forces the processor into the wait state for one clock cycle. After this clock cycle, the processor again looks at the ready input, which has gone high because the processor is in the wait state and the wait output is high. The processor resumes normal processing after a delay of one clock period. This has the advantage of not slowing down all the operations by lengthening all the clock cycles, but only the clock cycles during the memory read.

If only some of the memories are slow, requiring the double memory read cycle, a gate can be used as shown in Fig. 9-9. The chip

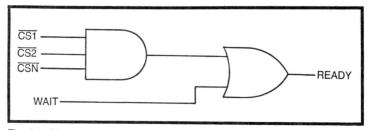

Fig. 9-9. Slowing down the microprocessor for flow memories.

select signals for the slow memories are OR'ed to form a low output when one of these memories is enabled. This is OR'ed with the wait signal to provide a low on the ready input if one of the slow memories is enabled, and the wait is low. This approach may save a few clock cycles if some of the memories are high speed and other memories are slower, but it should be used only if time is critical.

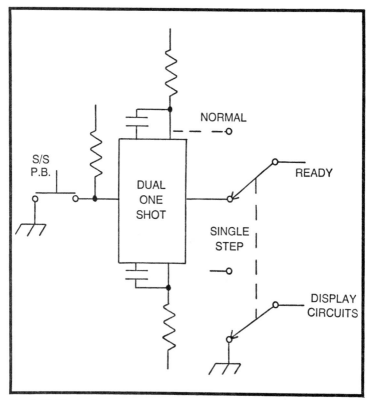

Fig. 9-10. Single step.

Single Step

During the troubleshooting of a system and the development of programs, single step is a convenient and valuable tool for the operator. The single step allows the user to step through the program, one instruction at a time. This is typically done by pulsing the ready input to the processor with a circuit as shown in Fig. 9-10. The pushbutton switch must be a no-bounce switch, or else the debouncing circuit shown must be used. This debounce circuit delays the firing of the one-shot until the switch has quit bouncing (typically 10 to 15 milliseconds). Figure 9-11 shows a typical switch contact closure. In reality, this switch opens and closes several times. This action is more pronounced for low currents and voltages.

The pulse out of the delayed one-shot is fed into a latch circuit. The latch is reset by the timing pulse, so that when the switch is depressed the microprocessor will operate until the memory is addressed again. The steps may be full instructions if the instruction is a single-byte instruction not accessing memory. Otherwise, the steps will be from memory access to memory access.

It is convenient to display the address and data during the single step mode. This can be indicated using individual LED indicators connected to the busses through buffers. They can cycle constantly during the operation, or they can be enabled using the single step switch.

If the data and address indicators are each replaced by eight individual LEDs, as shown in Fig. 9-12, the same LEDs can be used to display the single step information, as shown. The inverter must be a CMOS gated inverter to reduce the loading on the buses. A CMOS NAND gate can be used if desired. The output of the port must be disabled when in the single step mode, to prevent two

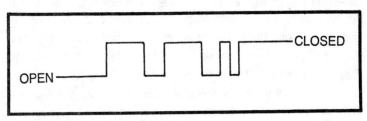

Fig. 9-11. Switch contact bounce.

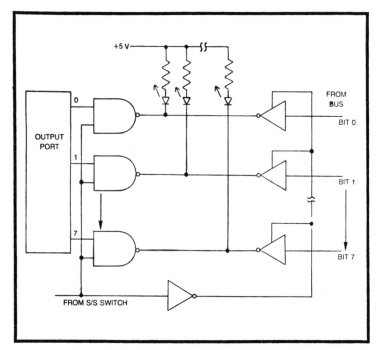

Fig. 9-12. Using individual LED's as displays.

signals trying to drive the LED at the same time. This can be done using either a CMOS gated inverter or a CMOS NAND gate, enabled by the single step signal. This signal is generated by inverting the single step signal. This signal is derived from the switch which places the hardware in the single step mode, the toggle switch for which is shown in Fig. 9-10.

Data Load to RAM

Data can be manually loaded into RAM memory either by the program or by hardware. The hardware load places the machine in the hold state, and manually forces the address and data buses by switches. During the hold, the buses are in their high impedance state, so highs and lows are loaded onto the buses to correspond to the desired address. The data bus is set up with the data switches, and the memory write signal is generated. This loads the data into the selected memory location.

The circuitry for the hardware load can be combined with the data input circuitry, or it can be made completely separate. Figure 9-13 shows the circuitry for a separate hardware load. This consists of 24 switches, resistors, and 3-state inverters. The inverters are gated, or placed in one of the active states, by the load signal which is generated from the load switch, as shown. This goes to the hold input of the CPU. A pushbutton is used to generate the $\overline{\text{MEM W}}$ signal, which goes low to allow writing the data in the memory.

Figure 9-14 shows the functional diagram for the combination method, which uses the same switches for hardware load and stan-

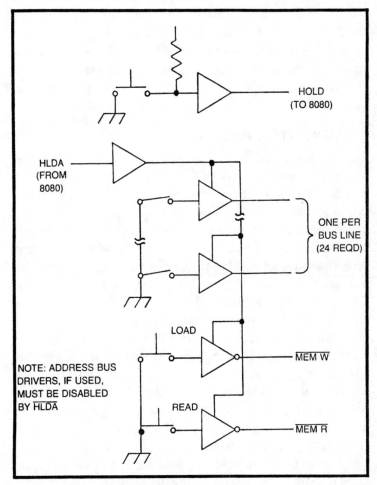

Fig. 9-13. Hardware load circuit.

dard input. This circuit becomes complex when using a keyboard as the input. Because it is complex, it is advisable not to use this method when starting the first system. The separate load facilities can be set up as an expansion of the system, connected to the buses through a connector.

Self Test Capabilities

A self test program is usually included in most systems to test the system for operation and to exercise most of the interface circuits. Some type of small test program is included in the monitor program to run a RAM memory test, and some other tests are designed for when the system is powered up. Other test programs are under manual program control, so that to enter them requires throwing a switch. These programs usually give some visual indica- tion, and may require the operator to exercise some input circuits in a given manner.

A SYSTEM IN OPERATION

Now let us go through some instruction and data flow around the system shown in Fig. 9-8. This will aid in the understanding of how the system works, and how the individual pieces work together.

When power is applied to the system, a reset pulse is generated by the clock circuit. This reset pulse resets the input/output circuits and the program counter in the CPU. Since the program counter is zero (reset), the address bus reads all zeros when the reset pulse goes low. A sync pulse is generated by the CPU, synchronizing the CPU and the clock generator. The clock pulses (ϕ_1 and ϕ_2) provide the timing for the microprocessor. The instruction fetch cycle is initiated by generating a memory read pulse. Since the address bus is all zeros, this will read memory location zero. The contents of this address are placed on the data bus and gated into the instruction register of the microprocessor. This information is decoded as an instruction by the instruction decoder. If this instruction is a jump instruction, which is three bytes long, the program counter is in- cremented and the next memory location (0001) is read. This loca- tion contains the lower eight bits of the jump to address, which is gated to the data bus and into the register array. Then the program counter is incremented again, and the high order eight bits of the

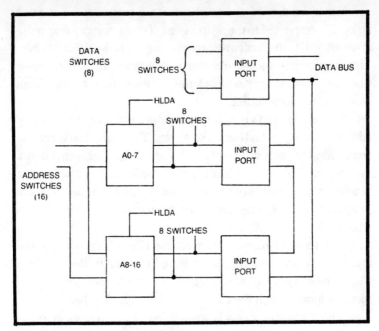

Fig. 9-14. Functional diagram for combination method.

jump to address are placed in the register array. Then the program counter is loaded with the sixteen bits from the register array. The next memory location which is read will be the jump to address, which is now in the program counter. This executes the jump.

If the instruction is a conditional jump, the condition is checked during the first instruction cycle. If the condition is met, the next two bytes are read and the program counter is loaded as for the jump instruction. If the conditions for the jump are not met, the program counter is incremented twice and the next instruction in the normal program sequence is read and executed.

For a memory read instruction, such as a load accumulator from memory instruction, memory is addressed to read the data by connecting the register array to the address bus. The first byte of the instruction is read into the instruction register by placing the program counter on the address bus and generating a memory read pulse. This instruction is decoded, and the second and third bytes are placed in the register array. The second and third bytes of this instruction contain the memory address whose contents are to be transferred to the accumulator.

205

When the second and third bytes are read into the register array, it is connected to the address bus. Then a memory read pulse is issued, gating the contents of the memory location to the data bus. This is gated into the accumulator by the internal microprocessor circuitry. Thus the contents of the memory location have been moved to the accumulator.

For a move from a register to memory instruction, the memory address is set up in the H and L registers. The instruction is read by connecting the program counter to the address bus and generating a memory read pulse. This loads the instruction into the instruction register, where it is decoded. After each instruction is decoded, the program counter is incremented to get ready for the next instruction fetch cycle.

This move instruction connects the H and L registers to the address bus, and connects the selected register to the data bus. Then a memory write pulse is generated which loads the selected memory location with the contents of the register. These last two instructions show how data is transferred to and from memory, as opposed to how instructions are read from memory.

A move immediate instruction, such as a MVI A, loads the specified register, the accumulator in this case, with the contents of byte 2 of the instruction. The instruction fetch portion of this instruction, as with all instructions, proceeds in the manner described above. The differences in the instructions comes from the manner in which they are executed. When this instruction is decoded, the program counter is incremented and the second byte is read. At this time, the specified register (accumulator) is connected to the data bus, and when the memory read pulse is generated, the contents of the second byte of the instruction are transferred from the memory to the specified register (accumulator).

During memory addressing for both instruction and data read and write operation, the memory address decoder enables the proper memory for the address being read. For example, when address 0000 is read, address bits 8 through 11 are low, so output O_0 from the memory address decoder is low and the remaining outputs are high. Since the chip select signal to the memory is active low, the memory connected to O_0 is enabled; so, the left hand EPROM is read. If location 100 is being read, A_8 is high and the remaining address lines are low; so, output O_1 is low, enabling the other EPROM memory. When A_9 is high, and the remaining address bits are low, address 200 is selected, and output O_2 is low, which enables the RAM memory.

An input or output instruction is a 2-byte instruction, with the second byte containing the port number. For an input instruction, the first byte is read and placed in the instruction register. The second byte is read and placed in the register array. Then the register array is connected to the address bus, and an I/O read pulse is generated by the system controller. If port 0 is being read, the address bus will be all zeros, so the output O_0 of the I/O address decoder will be low, and the remaining will be high. This, with the

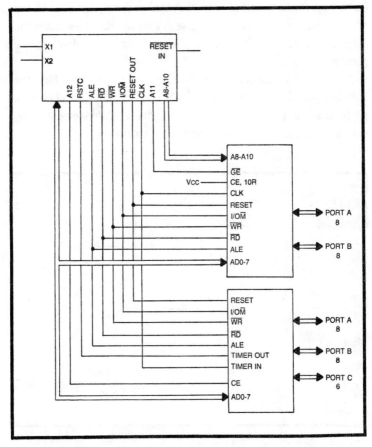

Fig. 9-15. 8085 three chip system.

memory read pulse, enables port 0, and the information is placed on the data bus. Since all input data is read into the accumulator, the accumulator is connected to the data bus and the information from the port is transferred to the accumulator.

O_0 from the I/O decoder also goes to output port 0, but this port will not be enabled because no I/O write pulse is generated. Also, output O_0 of the memory address decoder will be low; but no memory read pulse is generated, so memory is not enabled. This is why ports can be given the same address as memory locations, and why input ports and output ports can have the same address.

An output instruction sends the contents of the accumulator to the specified output port. When the instruction is decoded, the second byte is read into the register array. Then the accumulator is connected to the data bus, the register array is connected to the address bus, and the I/O write pulse is generated. This enables the output port and transfers the contents of the accumulator to the specified output port.

To expand a system requires access to the address bus, the data bus, and the control signals. By proper design, a small general purpose system can grow into a large general purpose system by expanding memory and the input/output capability.

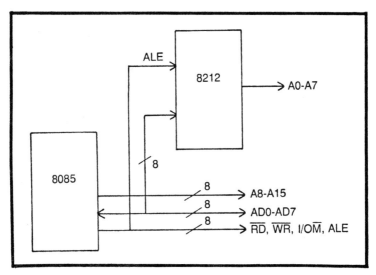

Fig. 9-16. Demultiplexing the address.

The microprocessors that multiplex the address and data buses onto the same output lines require special consideration. For example, the 8085 system shown in Fig. 9-15 uses the same lines (AD_{0-7}) for data and for the low order eight address bits. The circuits shown in Fig. 9-15 take care of keeping the address and data separate by the internal circuitry. To use this 8085 with the standard memories and other standard circuits requiring a separate address and data bus, the address portion of the bus can be de-multiplexed using the circuit shown in Fig. 9-16. The ALE signal latches the address data into the 8212 chip, generating the address bus. The data is on the data bus when the read and write signals are generated, so these signals are used to gate the information to and from the data bus.

Chapter 10
Building a Simple System

++

In the form presented, this simple, basic system serves as an introduction to microprocessor systems and their use. When proficiency is achieved with the simple system, it can be expanded to a more complex system with minimum effort. Any of the mounting methods can be used in assembling the system, including printed circuit boards.

As the system is being assembled and developed, collect the individual functional diagrams, wire lists, and schematics into one folder. Keep the spec sheets of the individual chips and components in this folder. This gives one place for all the hardware information, which is convenient when changing or troubleshooting the system. This folder becomes the system manual, and keeps track of the configuration and hardware capabilities of the system.

The **system** definition is as follows:

- 512 bytes of EPROM
- 256 RAM
- Expandable
- 16 button keyboard for data entry
- 10 button keyboard for program control
- 5 hardware control toggle switches
- EPROM programmer
- Hardware RAM load

- Hardware memory read
- Single step
- Self test
- Individual LEDs for readout
    a. 8 LEDs for data readout
    b. 16 LEDs for address readout
    c. 6 command bits to LEDs.

This definition may be modified, expanded, or simplified by the user to fit his individual needs.

MOUNTING

Give a lot of thought to what to mount the components on, and to the packaging for the system. Plug-in bread boards are more expensive than any of the other types, but are well worth the investment because the chips can be directly plugged in. Interconnecting wires are plugged into pin sockets, so no soldering is required to make reliable connections. Changes can be made very simply, just by pulling out the wires to be changed and sticking them into the proper holes.

It is advisable to breadboard any of the non-standard circuits, and the discrete circuits, to make sure they work. In fact, the total system can be put up on breadboards, and operated that way for a while. If the system is to be expandable, it is advisable to build the circuits up on general purpose plug-in boards, and to mount the connectors on a chassis. This chassis can contain the power supplies, the input devices, and the output devices. The input and output circuits are mounted on plug-in boards.

The system can also be built up on a chassis board, such as vectorboard. This limits the amount of expansion, but it can suffice for limited expansion. Another packaging method is to build up the system on a small piece of vectorboard, and to mount it in a small cabinet.

The circuits can be mounted on vectorboard plug-in boards or on circuit packs with vectorboard mounted in the cut out center of the board. The integrated circuits are mounted in sockets, and the components are mounted on solder terminals. The wiring is point to point, with some effort given to keep the wiring from becoming a

QUANTITY	PART #	FUNCTION
1	8224	Clock generator
1	808A	Microprocessor
1	8228	System controller
2	8212	Address bus drivers (other drivers can be used)
2	1702A	EPROM
2	8111-2	RAM
1	8205	Address bus decoder
2	10K	Resistors
1	30 μF	Solid electrolyte capacitors
3	1000 pF	Filter capacitors
3	20 μF	Solid electrolyte filter capacitors
1	30 pF	Mica capacitor
1	18 MHz	Fundamental crystal (may be 6 MHz to 18 MHz)
1		General purpose, high frequency NPN transistor
1	7404	Inverter
1	39K	Resistor

Fig. 10-1. Parts list for CPU.

rat's nest. Augut pin sockets are often used, but any sockets with leads long enough to allow attachment of the wires will work. Wire wrap sockets work the best because of the long pins which protrude from the back of the board. Cut off the excess length of the pins after the board has been wired and checked out. The circuit packs used by the author were 4½ inches by 7½ inches, with vectorboard glued into the center cutout.

The parts list for this board is given in Fig. 10-1. The type of sockets used is up to the builder, but the size is listed. With the sockets and the circuit board, construction can start. Take time wiring the circuit, and follow the wire list.

WIRING THE BOARD

Always take care when choosing parts, and building a system. Take pride in the finished product because it works, not because there are so many problems getting the system running. The parts can be obtained from many places: electronic hobby stores, parts distributors, or from advertisements in a magazine. Use only good parts, from reputable dealers. Substitutions can be made for the memories and input/output circuits. Use the specified parts for the clock generator and the system controller, or use equivalent circuits.

Using the proper tools makes the assembly of any electronic project easier. For this project, all tools should be of the small size. The wire is small, the spacing on the sockets is 0.1 inch, and the tools have to work within this confined space.

The wire should be size 18 or 20, solid, and well insulated. The plastic type insulations usually give a good clean cut with the wire strippers. Use wire strippers that are adjusted for the size of wire being cut. They must cut the insulation without nicking the wire. This may take a slight rotational motion of the strippers around the wire. If the conductor is nicked, the wire may break at the nick at some later time when the system is in operation.

Most importantly, do not rush the soldering job. It is time consuming, but a little care taken to make sure of a good soldering job will pay for itself. Bad soldering can cause the most time consuming and exasperating problems, which are usually intermittent, and showing up only after the system has been operating for a while.

Use only small, 60/40 rosin core solder, not over 0.032 size, for anything larger will cause problems when soldering. The soldering iron must not be larger than 37.5 watts, preferably with temperature control. If there is no temperature control, cool the iron occasionally with a damp rag.

When soldering, touch the tip to the joint being soldered, and apply solder to the joint but not to the soldering iron tip. Apply only enough solder to make a good connection, and keep the solder from running down the pin to the circuit board. Do not hold the iron on any connection for more than four seconds, which should be plenty of time to make a good connection. If the connection is not good, reheat the joint to remelt the solder.

Always keep the tip tinned well, but solder must not form a glob on the tip. Brush the tip on a damp rag every time the iron is picked up, and at times when several connections are being soldered. If the iron is too hot, the solder will ball on the tip, and not wet the connection properly. In addition, the flux will burn and turn black. Burnt flux can cause bad connections by not flowing out from between the solder and the connection.

Always keep a solder sucker handy, in case too much solder is accidentally applied. A wooden stick, a small dowel with the ends

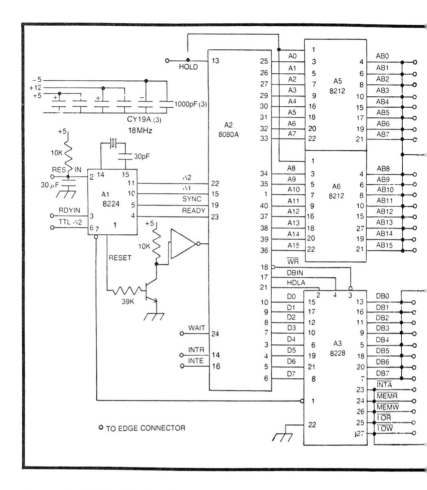

flattened, aids in soldering by holding the wires and keeping solder from flowing between pins.

When wiring the board, do not excessively strip insulation, and leave no bare wire protuding from the terminal. Be careful when soldering not to burn the insulation on close wires. When in doubt, move any close wires with the wooden stick. Do not grip the wire by the insulation with the long nose pliers when soldering. The heat will soften the insulation, and the pliers may expose bare wire. Use the wooden stick.

Remember that most of the integrated circuits used in micro-processor systems are CMOS type and can be damaged by a build up of static electricity. Never touch the pins of the chips without

214

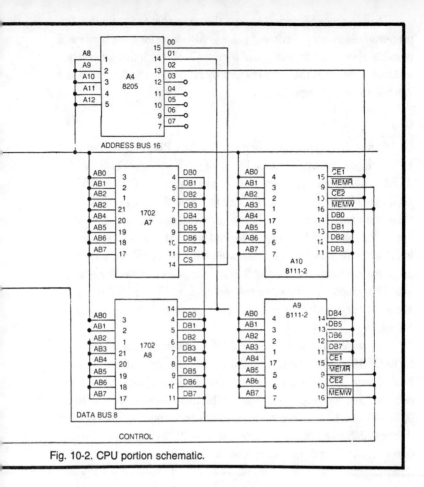

Fig. 10-2. CPU portion schematic.

grounding yourself first. When handling the chips, work on a piece of aluminum foil which is grounded. When soldering when chips are mounted on the board, use only a grounded tip type soldering iron. Most irons with the 3-prong plug are of this variety. It is best not to solder with chips mounted in the sockets being soldered on.

Always inspect each solder joint, either after it is done or all on one circuit at once. Use a magnifying glass and a strong light, and look for loose solder connections, connections that did not wet properly, and cold solder joints. Look for a smooth flow of solder around both parts of the connection, with no sign of flux inclusions. Using the soldering aid, move all connections that do not look right. Touch any suspect connections with the iron to reflow the solder.

Double check all wiring against the wiring list to insure that the proper wires go to the correct places. Also look for bare wires and possible shorts. Eliminate those found. Go through the schematics and make sure that they are correct by reviewing the functions and what is to be accomplished.

CPU

Figure 10-2 gives the schematic for the CPU portion. The 1702 EPROMs are 256 by 8-bit (256 byte) memories. The 8111-2 RAM is a 256 by 4-bit memory. Two of these are stacked to form a 256 by 8 (256 byte) RAM memory. This circuit takes about 70 terminals on the circuit pack connector. These terminals are used to provide a versatile, expandable system, for not all of them are used in the initial system. The arrows designated with an A or B and a number are these connections. The table gives the power connections to the individual chips, and the edge connector pins. Figure 10-3 gives the wire list for this board. Figure 10-4 gives one suggested parts layout.

The wire list defines the EPROM A7 as addresses 00 thru FF, EPROM A8 as 100 thru 1FF, and the RAM (A9 and A10) as 200 thru 2FF. These are determined by the connections of A4, the address decoder, and the chip select lines of the memories. Address bits 8, 9, 10, 11 and 12 are connected to the decoder inputs. This gives a total capability of 800 (hex) addresses, or 2K bytes, using the one decoder. Additional decoders can be used on memory expander boards.

POWER SUPPLIES

Power supplies used for microprocessor systems must be well protected from noise transients. The 8080 system takes four power supplies: +5V, +12V, −9V and −5V. The +5 power supply is the main system power, and must be capable of 1.5 amps. The remaining power sources supply under 100 mA each, and are used to drive the clock and bias circuits. These power supplies can be the module plug-in type, or be built up from voltage regulator chips. Figure 10-5 shows the schematic for these power supplies. They must be well filtered with the small and large capacitors, to reduce both slow and fast transients. On each board, also include a 30 microfarad and a

.001 microfarad capacitor, to provide on-board filtering. Always observe polarity on electrolytic capacitors, and do not use anything but the solid electrolyte type.

KEYBOARDS

Figure 10-6 shows the schematic for the sixteen button keyboard. This keyboard is the type which has two isolated lines to each key. When a key is depressed, the two lines are connected to a third common line. For the circuit shown, this third line is ground. When no keys are depressed, all the data lines are high, representing a zero or low input to the data bus. When a key is depressed, the two lines connected to that key are grounded, representing a high or a one.

The tri-state inverters connect the latch outputs to the data bus. These gates are enabled by the $\overline{I/O \text{ read}}$ and $\overline{O_0}$ signals. When these two signals are present, the port is being read. When the port is not addressed or enabled, the output is in the high impedance state.

The latches are reset by the NOR gate and inverter, or by the one-shot. If the commanded reset goes high, or the switch reset goes low, the output of the NOR gate goes low and resets the latches. The commanded reset is a program command to reset the keyboards. This is connected to a bit of output port 3. The switch reset is from one of the keys on the other keyboard, and it resets both keyboards. The one-shot fires after the enable signal goes low to reset the keyboard after the data has been read.

Figure 10-7 shows the connections for using the 8212 and the 8255 interface chips in place of the latches and inverters. The 8255 is a bidirectional, programmable, three-port chip. Both input ports and one output port can be connected to one chip. But this chip must be programmed with a control word to define the operation. Using interface chips greatly simplifies design and construction of the input and output circuits.

Figure 10-8 shows the schematic for the other keyboard. Of the ten switched, eight are connected as program inputs and two are momentarily hardware inputs. The hardware inputs are keyboard reset and system reset. The keyboard reset clears the keyboard

SIGNAL TO CONNECTOR	A1 8224	A2 8080	A3 8228	A4 8205	A5 8212	A6 8212	A7 1702	A8 1702	A9 8111	A10 8111	
RESET IN ×	1										TO 39K RESISTOR
READY IN ×	2	23									TO 10K AND 30 µf
READY ×	3	19									
	4										
	5										
	6										
TTL φ2 ×	7										
STATUS STROBE ×	8		1								
GROUND ×		2	14, 22	8	12	12			8, 10	8, 10	30 µf, TRANSISTOR EMITTER, FILTER CAPS. PIN 7-7404
+12 VOLTS ×	9	28	28								
	10	15	6								CRYSTAL
	11	22	19								30 pf CAP
+5 VOLTS ×	16	20	21	16	24	24	12, 13, 23	15, 22	18	18	FILTER CAP, 10K RESIS. 2-7404-16
	14	1	8			7					
	15	3	10								
		5	12								
		6	17								
		7	15								
		8									
		9									
		10									
		11									
		12									
		13									
		14									
-5 VOLTS 4 ×					22						FILTER CAP 7404-2
RESET ×											
HOLD ×											
INT R ×											

Fig. 10-3. Wire list for CPU portion of the system (contined on next three pages).

SIGNAL TO CONNECTOR		A1 8224	A2 8080	A3 8228	A4 8205	A5 8212	A6 8212	A7 1702	A8 1702	A9 8111	A10 8111	
INT E	x	16	4									
		17	3									
WAIT	x	18	2									
		21										
		24										
			25									
			26		3	3						
			27		5	5						
			29		7	22						
			30		9	16						
			31		16	18						
			32		18	20						
			33		20	9						
			34		22							
			35									
			36									
			37									
			38									
			39									
			40									
DB 4	x			5			8	8	14	11		
DB 7	x			7			11	11	11	12		
DB 3	x			9			7	7		14		
DB 2	x			11			6	6		13		
DB 0	x			13			4	4				
DB 1	x			16			5	5				
DB 5	x			18			9	9	13			
DB 6	x			20			10	10	12			
INT A	x			23								

Fig. 10-3. (continued).

219

SIGNAL TO CONNECTOR	A1 8224	A2 8080	A3 8228	A4 8205	A5 8212	A6 8212	A7 1702	A8 1702	A9 8111	A10 8111	
MEM R	X			24							
I/O R	X			25			9		9		
MEM W	X			26							
I/O W	X			27			16		16		
A8	X				1	4					
A 9	X				2	6					
A 10	X				3	8					
E1	X				4						
E2	X				5						
07	X				7						
06	X				9						
05	X				10						
04	X				11						
03	X				12						
02	X				13						
01	X				14			14	14	15	15
00	X				15						
A0	X					4		3	3	4	4
A1	X					6		2	2	3	3
A2	X					8		1	1	2	2
A3	X					10		21	21	1	1
A5	X					15		20	20	17	17
A6	X					17		19	19	5	5
A7	X					19		18	18	6	6
A8	X					21		17	17	7	7
A9	X						4				
A10	X						6				
A11	X						8				
A11	X						10				

Fig. 10-3. (continued).

220

SIGNAL TO CONNECTOR	A1 8224	A2 8080	A3 8228	A4 8205	A5 8212	A6 8212	A7 1702	A8 1702	A9 8111	A10 8111
A12	X									
A13	X					15				
A14	X					17				
A15	X					19				
-9 VOLTS	X					21	16, 24	16, 24		

TRANSISTOR COLLECTOR TO 10K AND 7404 PIN 1

NOTE: IF CRYSTAL FREQUENCY GREATER THAN 7 MHz, CONNECT A2 PINS 23 AND 24 TOGETHER EITHER ON THE BOARD OR AT THE CONNECTOR, TO ALLOW USING THE SLOWER EPROM MEMORIES SUCH AS THE 1702A.

Fig. 10-3. (continued).

221

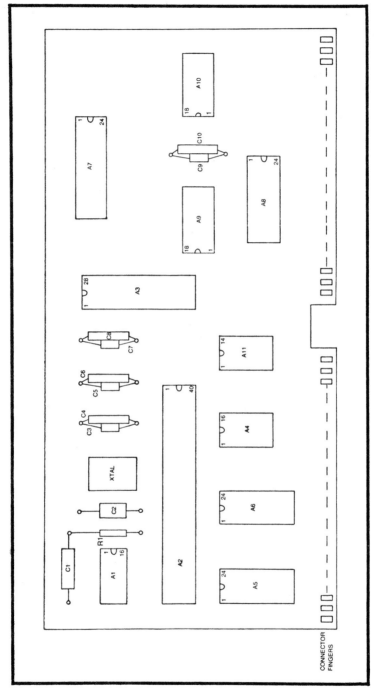

Fig. 10-4. CPU parts layout.

222

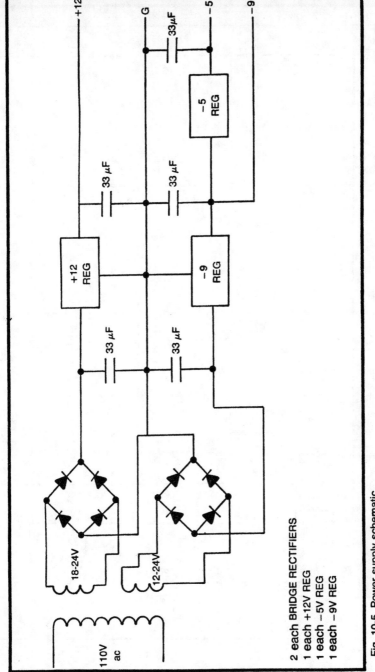

Fig. 10-5. Power supply schematic.

223

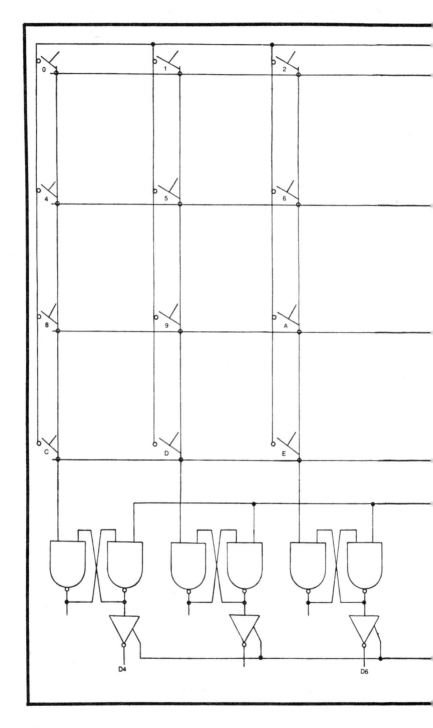

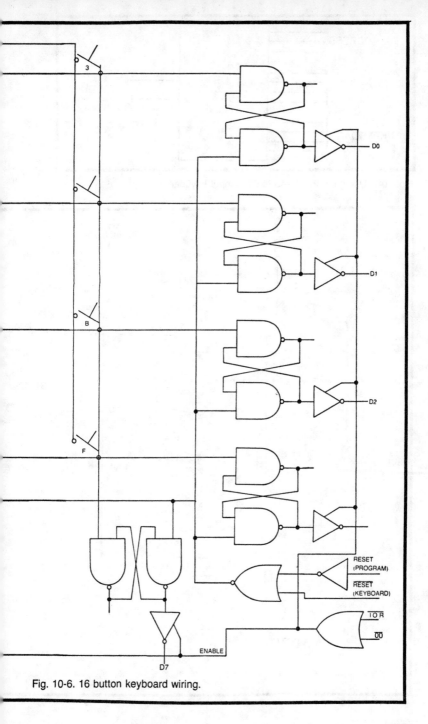

Fig. 10-6. 16 button keyboard wiring.

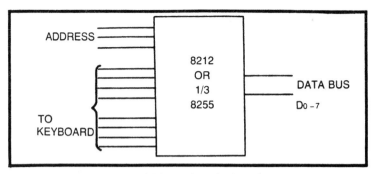

Fig. 10-7. Using the 8212 and 8255 to input keyboard.

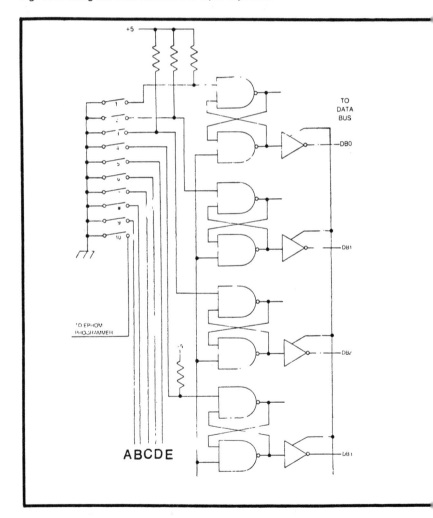

latches. The system reset provides the reset signal to the micro-processor, and sets the program counter to 00.

This keyboard is of the individual switch type, with each key an individual switch making contact with ground when the key is depressed. The eight data switches set the data latches in a similar fashion to the other keyboard. The enable pulse for the tri-state inverters is address $\overline{0}$ᵢ and $\overline{I/O}$ read.

Figure 10-9 shows the connections for using an 8255 or an 8212 chip in place of the latches and inverters. These chips are enabled by the same address (01) and the I/O read control signal.

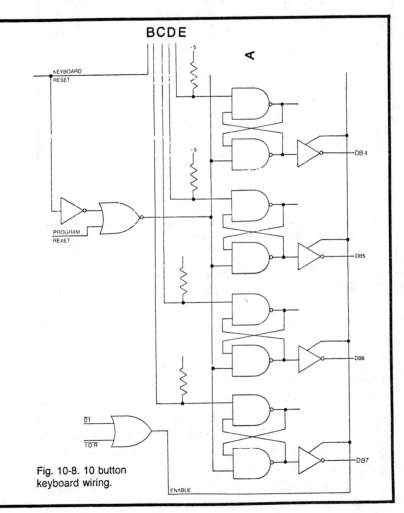

Fig. 10-8. 10 button keyboard wiring.

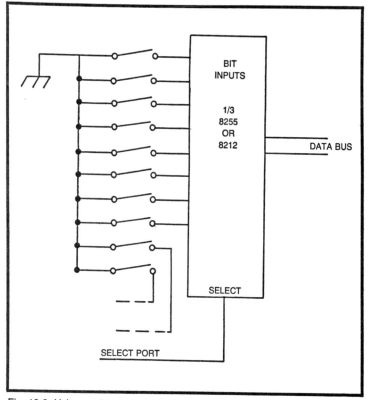

Fig. 10-9. Using an 8255 and an 8212 with the 10 button keyboard.

If the sixteen button keyboard is not of the type described, the standard switch closure type can be used. The connections to the port will be similar to the connections shown in Fig. 10-8, except that two ports are required. These should be assigned ports 0 and 1, with the ten button keyboard assigned as port 2. This will simplify the program slightly, but will make the hardware more complex.

A twenty button keyboard can be used, with four of the switches designated as momentary hardware switches. If the keyboard is constructed as a 4 by 5 matrix, the fifth row (or column) can be the special switches, with the 4 by 4 matrix as the sixteen data inputs. As shown in Fig. 10-10, the individual switches are sampled with OR gates to determine when they are depressed. If the keyboard is an individual switch type, connect it like the one shown in Fig. 10-8, leaving the four switches as special function switches.

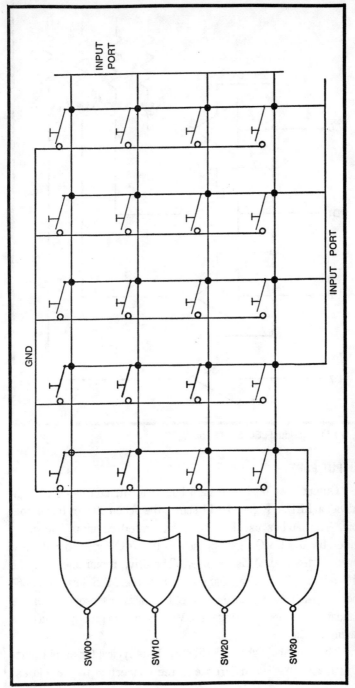

Fig. 10-10. 20 button keyboard connected as a 4 by 4 matrix.

229

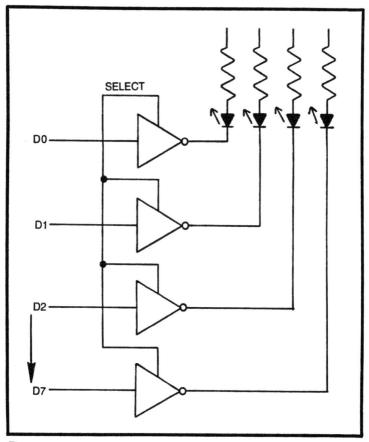

Fig. 10-11. Individual LED output port.

OUTPUT PORT

Output port 00 is the data bus readout, consisting of eight individual LEDs. Figure 10-11 shows the schematic for this output port. The latches use low drive integrated circuits. These are preferably the CMOS gates, such as the 74C series, but the low power series (74LS) can be used. The drive requirement for the 74C series is 5 to 10 microamps, and for the 74LS series it is 360 microamps. This compares to the 1.6 milliamps required for the standard 74 series. So using the CMOS chips can greatly reduce the loading on the buses.

The schematic shown in Fig. 10-11 is typical for output ports 00, 01, and 02. The difference is the connection to the address decoder, O_0, O_1, and O_2, respectively. The switch controls the function of the output port. If the switch is in the position shown, the circuits are connected to the buses and constantly display the data. This is used in manual loading and reading of the buses, and in single step. When the switch is in the other position, the ports are addressable output ports, displaying information only on command.

Figure 10-12 shows the connections for using the 8212 or the 8255 chips in the output ports. This takes three of the 8212 chips or one of the 8255 chips to service all three of the output ports.

Output port 03 has six individual LEDs, and two control bits. Bit 7 is for the programmed keyboard reset. Bit 6 is a commanded output for use by the user. Figure 10-13 shows the schematic for this port, which is under program control, and has no function switch.

Figure 10-14 shows the functional diagram for the input/output portion of the system. The address decoder for the I/O section is connected to the low order five address lines, and can address up to eight input and/or output ports. The EPROM programmer is both an

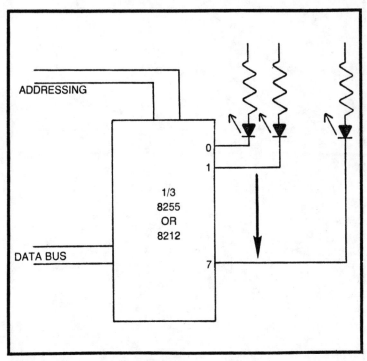

Fig. 10-12. Using the 8255 and 8212 for the output ports.

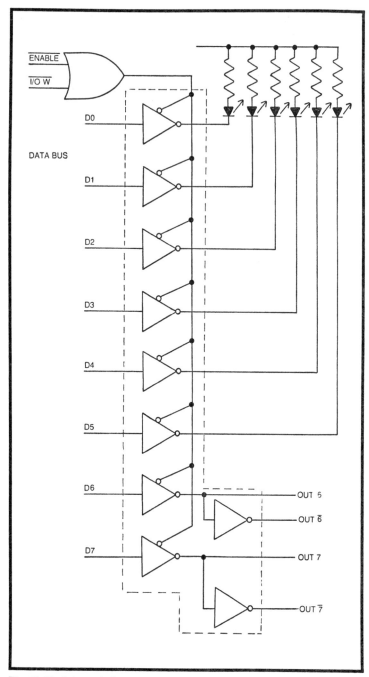

Fig. 10-13. Schematic for output port 3.

input and an output port because data is sent to it to load the EPROM, and read from it to verify the EPROM.

SYSTEM CONTROL

The hardware functions for the control of the system are:

- Reset
- Single step
- Memory read
- RAM load

These control functions assist in the using of the system, and are operator controlled.

The reset is a switch which grounds the reset input to the clock generator. This shorts out the capacitor, resetting the system. The capacitor eliminates the effects of switch bounce, and adds a time constant for the Schmitt trigger input circuit in the clock generator.

Single-step is a convenient aid for hardware troubleshooting and program development. To single-step the circuit requires controlling the ready input. When the ready input is low, the processor is in the wait state. To step the program one instruction requires pulsing the ready line. This pulse must be long enough to allow the processor to recognize the pulse, but short enough that the program does not address memory twice. A 1.0 microsecond pulse should fill the need for a machine operating at 0.5 microseconds. Figure 10-15 shows the schematic for this. The toggle switch selects the normal mode, or single step. The pushbutton switch triggers the dual one-shot. This provides a 1.0 microsecond pulse delayed 10 milliseconds from switch closure. This delay is to eliminate the effects of switch bounce.

To use the single-step, place the toggle switch in single-step. If it is desired to start from address 00, depress reset. Place the switches on output ports 00, 01, and 02 in the bus monitor mode. The address will be presented on ports 00 and 01. The data bus will be shown on port 02. To step the program, depress the single step switch once. This will step the processor to the next address read. This may be the instruction fetch at the start of an instruction cycle, or it may be the memory read or store, or it may be the I/O read or store. The processor stops on any addressing function. The address and the data are on the buses at that time.

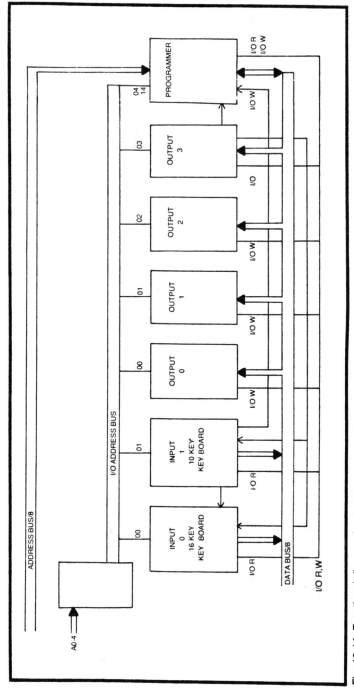

Fig. 10-14. Functional diagram for the I/O portion of the system.

234

The memory read function gives the capability of reading any memory location, and Fig. 10-16 shows the schematic for one method of accomplishing this. The switch disables the address bus drivers and places the processor in the hold state. Toggle switches select the addresses, and the pushbutton switch issues the memory read pulse.

The RAM load function is an extension of the memory read. Figure 10-17 shows the schematic for this function. A toggle switch selects read or write, disables the bus drivers, and places the processor in the hold state. Toggle switches select the addresses and set up the data. The pushbutton switch issues the memory read or memory write pulse.

If the switches on output ports 00, 01, and 02 are in the bus monitor position, the information being transferred, and the address

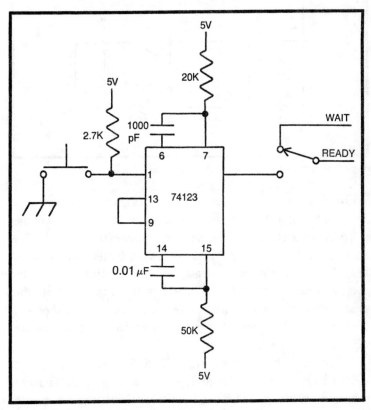

Fig. 10-15. Schematic for single step.

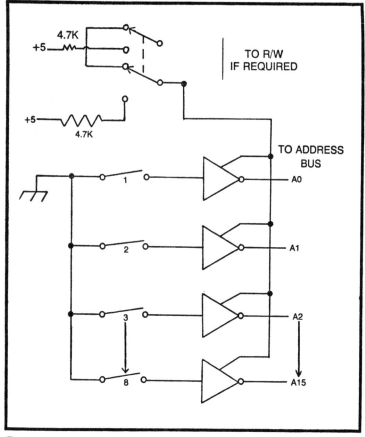

Fig. 10-16. Hardware memory read schematic.

will be displayed, in hexadecimal format. It takes twenty-four toggle switches to enter the address and data. If the keyboards are of the individual switch type, they can be used in place of the switches. The sixteen switches used for the address bus require the buffers shown in Fig. 10-17, connected in parallel with the existing buffers. The control circuitry shown in Fig. 10-17 is required to control the processor, and to provide the enable signals, with an added pole of the toggle switch connected to ground the enable line to the tri-state buffers shown in Fig. 10-8.

The type of keyboard shown in Fig. 10-6 requires considerable added circuitry to be useful as the input for this application. It is more convenient to use the added toggle switches than it is to incorporate

236

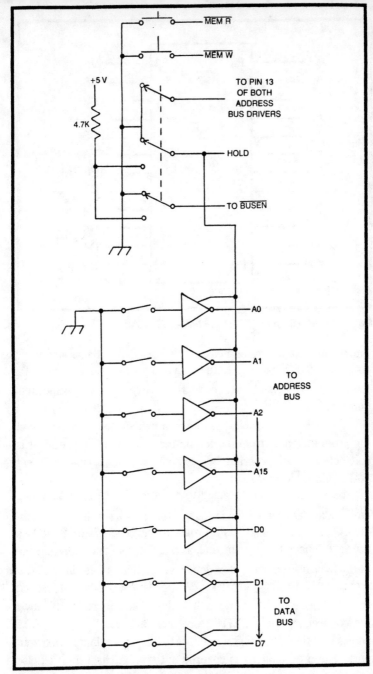

Fig. 10-17. Hardware memory load schematic.

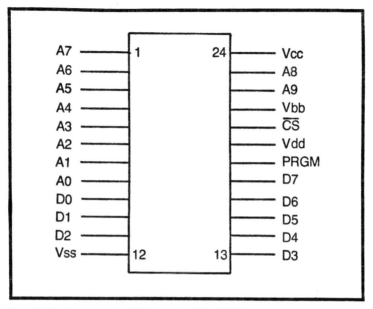

Fig. 10-18. Replacing the 1702As with 2708 EPROMs.

the required registers and circuitry to make the matrix keyboard output the individual lines to the data and address buses. Normally the program is used to decode the matrix into a hexadecimal number.

The self test capability is a program input, assigned as one of the program inputs from the ten button keyboard. The self test is conducted by the program, and exercises the input ports, output ports, and RAM memory.

Facilities must be obtained to program the EPROMs. Either have a knowledgeable friend program them, or have them programmed by someone who has a programmer. The 1702A EPROMs used are difficult to program, and, as a last restor, a programmer can be built using the guidelines given here. If there is no available programmer to program the 1702As, it is advisable to use an easier-to-program EPROM, such as the 2708. Figure 10-18 shows the connections for the 2708 to replace the 1702A. Figure 10-19 shows how the 2708 programmer fits to the system bus as an output port. The programming is covered in the next chapter. If all else fails, a programmer for 1702A can be built. The requirements for programming a 1702A are as follows:

1. Data to be programmed into the EPROM is placed on the input lines in complement form.
2. The address to be programmed is placed on the address bus in complement form.
3. When the programming cycle begins, the following changes in the static conditions occur:
   a. V_{cc} switches from 5 to 47 volts
   b. V_{bb} switches from 5 to 59 volts
   c. V_{gg} switches from -9 to 12 volts.
   d. V_{dd} switches from -9 to 0.6 volts.
   e. PRGM (the program signal) goes from 0 to 47 volts.
   f. Address data changed from 0 to 5 volts to 0 to 47 volts.

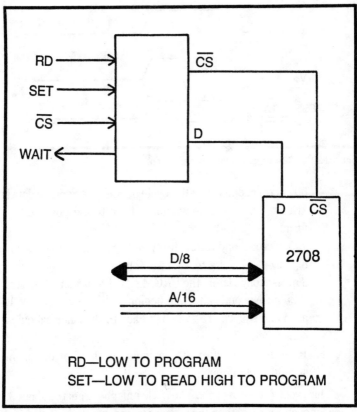

Fig. 10-19. The 2708 programmer connected to an output.

239

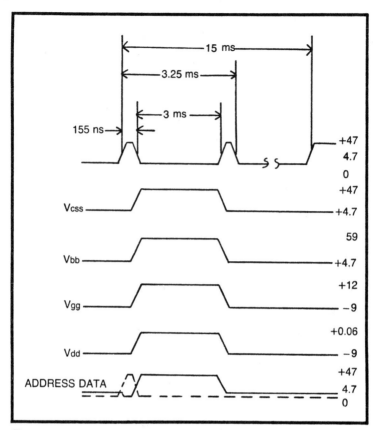

Fig. 10-20. 1702A programming waveshapes.

4. 60 microseconds after the cycle begins, the address data is switched from the complement form to the positive true form.

5. 155 microseconds after the cycle begins, the PRGM signal dips from 47 volts to about 9 volts.

6. 3 milliseconds later, the PRGM signal returns to 47 volts.

7. 3.25 milliseconds after the beginning of the cycle, all voltages and signals are switched back to their normal quiescent levels.

8. 15 milliseconds after the beginning of the first cycle, the second cycle begins.

This is one program cycle. The cycle must be repeated about 35 times for each address, then the address is incremented and the next address is programmed. Figure 10-20 shows the waveshapes associated with the programming requirements. The duty cycle is established by the 11 millisecond time between steps 7 and 8 above. If the duty cycle is too long, damage may result.

The details of a programmer for 1702 EPROMs are beyond the scope of this book. Some of the details have been presented, and some ideas about how to accomplish the desired end results will be given. From this, a working system can be developed. All the voltages are required to switch from the normal level to the programming level, at the start of the programming cycle. The timing required is given by the waveshapes of Fig. 10-20. The following timing signals are required; 60 microseconds, 155 microseconds, 3.15 milliseconds, 3.25 milliseconds, and 15 milliseconds. These are all initiated by the start of the program cycle. To switch V_{ccs} between the 47 volts and the 4.7 volts level, the regulator shown in Fig. 10-21 can be used. A similar circuit can switch V_{bb} from 59 to 4.7 volts. From the V_{ccs} voltage, the V_{gg} and V_{dd} voltages can be obtained with the circuit shown in Fig. 10-22. The input control pulse is connected to the emitter of the left hand transistor. This pulse must be low for the duration of the programming voltages, 3.25 milliseconds.

When this pulse is high, the left transistor is turned on, turning on the second transistor (the NPN). So the voltage at V_{dd} is 10 volts minus the V_{ce} drop across the transistor. When the pulse is low, the

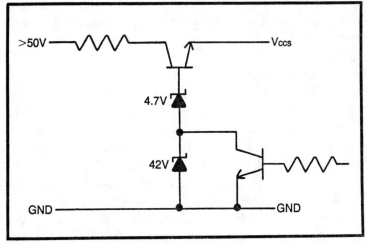

Fig. 10-21. Programmer regulator.

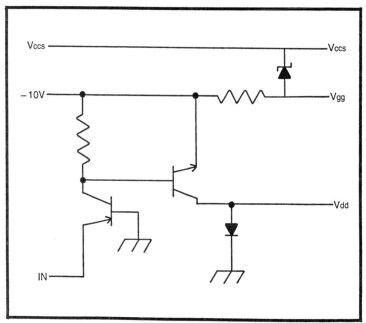

Fig. 10-22. Programmer circuits.

transistors are both off, so V_{dd} is clamped to ground through the diode. When V_{ccs} is above 36 volts, V_{gg} is equal to V_{ccs} minus the zener diode voltage drop (36 volts). When V_{ccs} is below 36 volts, V_{gg} is equal to 10 volts minus the voltage across the resistor.

The transistor in Fig. 10-21 is to short out the 42 volt zener diode after the programming sequence is over. This must be capable of carrying the sustained current for the long periods of time required.

To invert the signals to the data inputs and the address inputs, an exclusive OR gate can be used as shown in Fig. 10-23. The control signal is a low for non-inversion and a high for inversion. If the input is a low, then the output will be low when the control signal is low, and a high when the control signal is high. If the data input is a high, the output will be a high when the control signal is low, and a low when the control signal is high. This is because the output is low if both inputs to an exclusive OR gate are high.

Facilities should be provided at the end of the programming each word to check the data loaded against the data to be loaded. This can be done by treating the programmer as an input port, and

242

reading the port and address. If the data does not compare with the data loaded, then the program should stop, and the address and data of the error indicated. This checks the EPROM and the load to make sure the correct data is in the desired memory location.

A single toggle switch should apply programming power to the chip to be programmed. This chip should be plugged into a socket on the programmer, and not into a socket which is a part of the system. If it is desired to allow the program to read the EPROM plugged into the programmer, the voltages required for reading the chip must be applied when the program switch is off. This prevents accidental writing into the EPROM when it is being read.

The key, designated 'to programmer' on the keyboard, is wired into the power supplies. This loads the main power supply of the programmer, and indicates, via a LED, that the voltage is good. This gives a power supply check before programming.

INSTALLING THE CHIPS

After the system is wired and assembled, do not be too hasty about installing the chips. This can cost you chips that are burned out because of misapplication of voltages. First connect the power supplies and turn on the power. Measure the voltages at the power

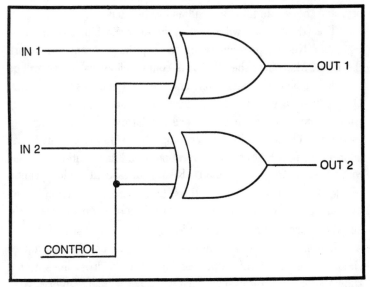

Fig. 10-23. Programmer circuits.

supplies, looking for high or low voltages. Next measure the voltages at the chips, using the ground on the chips as references. Look for low voltages and their cause, and for voltages at pins not connected to power. Also look for grounds using a ohmmeter.

When the power has been checked out, turn the power off and install the crystal and the clock generator. Place a scope on the $\phi2$ TTL lead from the clock generator. Then turn the power on, and look for $\phi2$ timing signal on the scope. This is a square wave, with a repetition rate of 1/9 of the crystal frequency, and a duty cycle of 5/9. This indicates that the clock is running, and that the clock signals are being generated. Touch the chip to make sure it is not overheating. This chip will run warm, but not hot.

Next turn the system off and install the 8080 chip and the 8228 chip, which are the system controller and the microprocessor. Turn the system back on, and check again for overheating of the chips. The 8080 will run warm, and the 8228 will not feel as warm. Turn the system off and install the memory chips. These must be connected up as addresses; but the EPROMs must be all zeros. Turn the system back on and depress reset. The reset signal should go high, then low at the microprocessor. The data bus should be all zeros until the addressing reaches the RAM memory, then it is hard to tell what will happen; the RAM will come up with random bits in memory, and these bits may be read as instructions.

The address bus will count up in binary fashion, for the first eight bits. Keep depressing reset, to keep the program cycling thru the EPROMs. Since the EPROMs contain all zeros, these will be decoded as NO OP instructions and the next address will be read. Once you are assured that the address and data bus are responding with the correct information, place the hardware load switch on. Insert the chips required to accomplish the hardware load, and address the first RAM memory location. Read this location, and load with all zeros. Do this for several RAM addresses, then load a jump to address 00 (C3-00-00) as a three byte instruction. Then let the system run. Occasionally, some bits will appear on the data bus, and the address bus will show cycling of the addresses.

If at any time the response is not as expected, the differences should be resolved before proceeding. If the address lines do not show the binary progression, (that is, A_0 has a change every cycle,

244

A_1 every other cycle, and A_2 every 4th cycle, etc.) then there is something wrong on the address bus. Using the scope, look at the signals at their source, and at the destination. The two should compare. Also look for signals that are not up to the voltage level of other similar signals. A low signal level can indicate a short on the line, or a gate that is in the tri-state.

LOADING RAM

Up to now, the only control signal used has been the memory read signal. This is working if the program jumps back to 00 and keeps cycling. The next step is to load the RAM with data by the program, and then read the data using the data read hardware function. A short data load program is to load the H and L registers with the starting address of the memory block to be checked, and the B register with the number of locations to be loaded. Then do an MVI M FF to load the locations with all ones. Check for B register zero, and see if it is halt. If it is not zero, decrement B and increment H and L. Then jump back to the MVI instruction. This loads the memory locations with all ones. Using the reset switch, kick the program off and let it run. It will reach the halt instruction almost immediately. The halt is indicated by all highs on the address bus.

Using the hardware read capability, read the memory locations loaded by the program. If the information is not as loaded, check the memory write control signal, and the addressing. Also check the program to make sure it was loaded correctly. When the data is correct, repeat using 55 in place of FF for the MVI instruction. This loads every other bit of RAM with a one. The alternate bits are loaded with zeros.

TROUBLESHOOTING

While doing the checkout, measure the power supply voltages occasionally. Also touch the chips to check for overheating. If any of the chips are painfully hot to the touch, immediately turn off the system. Some chips, such as the 8080, the 8224, and the EPROMs operate warm to the touch, but not hot.

Overheated chips can mean the wrong voltages, the voltages are too low at the chip, that something is loading the chip, or that a voltage is being fed into the wrong pins. Also if two or more signals are trying to drive the same pin, overheating may result. Carefully check the circuit and find the cause of the overheating before proceeding.

If the reset signal is not functioning correctly, strange things can happen, such as the program not starting at address 00. This can be checked by depressing and holding the reset switch. Then ground the reset input to the 8080, release the reset switch and remove the ground. This insures that a good solid reset is given to the microprocessor. If this clears up the problem, the reset circuitry is at fault, and must be corrected.

Electrical noise can cause the system to reset at the wrong time, and cause the wrong address or information to be on the buses. To correct noise problems, filter all power supplies with a large capacitor in parallel with a small one, typically, 33 microfarads in parallel with 0.001 microfarads. Larger capacitors may be required, depending on the interference frequency and amplitude, and small capacitors may be required at some of the chips, between the voltage pin and ground.

Ground loops may also cause noise problems. A ground loop is where the ground patch makes a loop, so that it is not one single continuous run. The ground path may branch out so that parallel branches exist, but these paths must have only one path to the ground at the power supply.

Sometimes it is required that the AC power for the system be isolated from other devices which produce noise. When motors are turned on, or fluorescent lights are turned on, large voltage transients may result. These transients may be induced into the system through the power lines, and filtering may not eliminate them.

Some EPROMs are sensitive to light. These may give the wrong information when read, but the contents of the location will not change. The simple method of correcting this is to place a strip of black tape over the window of the EPROM. This tape must be removed if the EPROMs are to be erased.

Whatever the problem, it is solvable. It takes patience, logical troubleshooting, and a thorough understanding of how the system works to solve some of the problems. Do not think that there will be no problems, especially on the first system, because there will

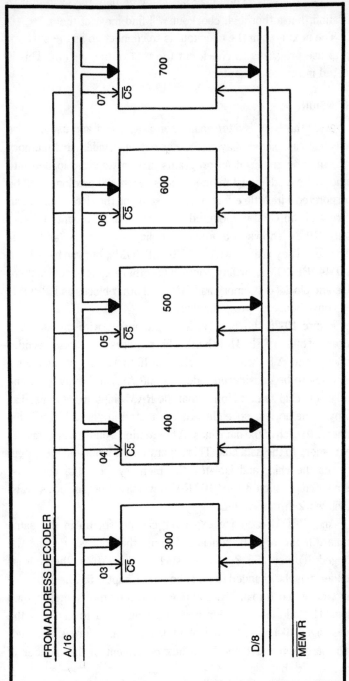

Fig. 10-24. Adding five additional 1720As.

always be problems. They may not show up until the system is in operation, but a thorough checkout will find most of them.

The next step in the checkout is to connect up all the system, and to use programs to check out the rest of the system. This is covered in the next chapter.

EXPANSION

After the basic system has been assembled and used, more needs and capabilities may arise. For example, additional memory space may be required as programs are written and loaded into memory. Five additional memory chips, each 100 hex long, can be incorporated with little effort. If room exists on the circuit board that the rest of the CPU is mounted on, these can be mounted there. Figure 10-24 shows the functional diagram for the additional memories. They are shown as 1702A EPROMs, but can be RAMs, PROMs, EPROMs, or any combination thereof. It is advisable to add some blocks of memory as RAM, and other blocks as EPROMs as a convenience to programming.

Figure 10-25 shows a 1K RAM expander, with the assigned address of 800 to FFF (1K in hex). This requires an address decoder connected to A_{10} thru A_{14} as shown. If there are no additional memories to be considered, address line A_{10} can be inverted and used as the chip select. Notice that the RAM chips are organized as 1K by 1 memories, so eight are connected in parallel. One chip connects to each of the data lines. A bidirectional bus driver connects the memory to the data bus. This separates the input and the output data for the chip, and isolates the memory from the data bus. Memory chips, such as the 2102 RAM, which are organized as 1K by 1, will work in this circuit.

An EPROM memory expander can be set up in the same manner. If the organization is different, the addressing must be changed. To use 256 × 8 chips, such as the 1702A, the address decoder must be changed to that shown in Chapter 5. The expander may contain more than 1K, and may be made up of some 1K by 8 chips. The address decoder must be connected to give, as the lowest signal (0_0), the hex equivalent of the lowest address assigned. Each increment must equal the hex equivalent of the number of addresses in the chip.

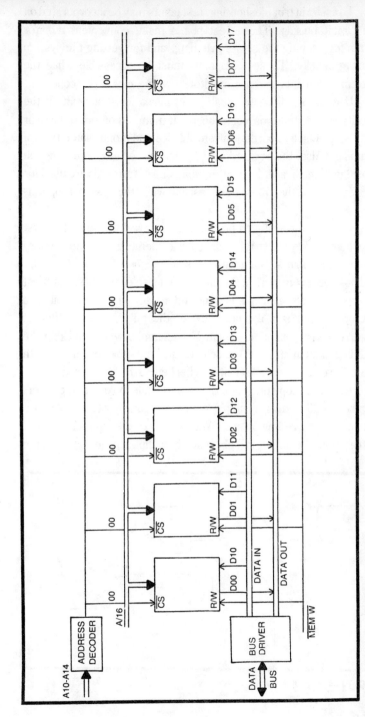

Fig. 10-25. A 1K RAM expander.

To assist in troubleshooting, test points may be incorporated on the circuit boards. These test points make convenient monitor points for keeping the system running, and for getting the system running initially. These test points must be accessible while the system is running, and are monitored with a meter or scope.

Use the small vector push-in terminals for test points if the circuits are mounted on vectorboard. If mounted on printed circuit boards or on solid boards, drill small holes and mount some type of terminals. Also, the small edge test points can be mounted along the top edge of the board. No matter what kind of terminals are used for the test points, they must be accessible while the system is operating.

Connect the voltages on each circuit board to the test points. Also connect key control signals, such as memory read and memory write to test points, along with the select signals for the I/O ports, and possibly even some of the memory chip select signals. For most of these signals a scope is required to see the pulse. Since a microprocessor is a dynamic device, the pulse, and the time of occurrence is usually important. For example, when checking the enabling of an input port, the select signal must be concurrent with the I/O read pulse. This can be checked with a triggered scope, triggering the scope on one of the signals while looking at the other. Figure 10-26 shows a simple concurrent pulse catcher for two concurrent active low pulses. When either of the inputs to the OR gate is high, the output is high. When both inputs go low at the same

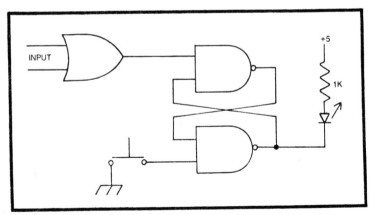

Fig. 10-26. A simple pulse catcher.

time, the output of the OR gate goes low, setting the latch and turning on the LED indicator. The pushbutton switch resets the latch. To use this unit, connect the inputs to the points being monitored, and watch the LED. It will turn on when both pulses occur concurrently.

If one of the signals is active high, feed that signal through an inverter to the OR gate. If both signals are active high, replace the OR gate with a NAND gate. To check addressing, or some function requiring concurrence of more than two signals, replace the OR gate with an 8 input NAND gate. This can check eight active high signals. To check an address, add inverters to the low address lines.

Chapter 11
Programming the System

◆◆

When the system is assembled and the static tests have been done, the system is ready for programming and checkout under program control. But first, all the checks detailed in the last part of the last chapter must be done to be assured that the hardware seems to be working.

CONTROL PROGRAMS

During the initial checkout, leave all the EPROM memory location at zero, so that the program can be written into RAM memory using the hardware RAM loading capability. The first step is to construct a chart showing the I/O port assignments and the memory map. This will aid in writing the programs for the checkout and use of the system. To this sheet add the capabilities of the system, and any special input or output assignments. This sheet will then become the guide for using the system, and should be taped to the wall above the system.

Output Ports

The first, and easiest thing to check out will be the LED output ports. This is done by sequencing a number through them, one at a time. This lights one LED of each of the displays at the same time, with a programmable delay built in the loop. This program loads a bit in bit position one, outputs this to the three 8-bit displays and the 6-bit display. The LED corresponding to bit position zero will light; then after a short delay it will go out and the next LED will light. This proceeds up to bit 7; then after a short delay it starts over again. The program listing is shown below. Notice that all the numbers in this listing are in hexadecimal, as will be the case for all the following listings. If there is confusion about the hex numbering system, consult the Appendix. If there is confusion or uncertainty about the program listing, consult the chapter on programming.

Mnemonic	Op Code	Address	Notes
MVI A	3E	200	
01	01	201	Initialize for bit 1
OUT	D3	202	
00	00	203	
OUT	D3	204	
01	01	205	
OUT	D3	206	
02	02	207	
OUT	D3	208	
03	03	209	
LXI B	01	20A	Set up delay time
3F	3F	20B	
FF	FF	20C	
DCR C	0D	20D	Delay loop
JNZ	C2	20E	
02	02	20F	
0D	0D	210	
DCR B	05	211	
JNZ	C2	212	
02	02	213	
0D	0D	214	
RAL	17	215	Move bit left one
JNC	D2	216	
02	02	217	
02	02	218	
JMP	C3	219	
02	02	21A	
00	00	21B	

This program is set up to start at address 200, since for the system specified in the last chapter, RAM starts at address 200. If this is not the first address of RAM memory, then change the addresses and the jump commands to the correct value.

Load the program using the manual RAM load capability. Place the switch in load, set up the address and data, and load using the load pushbutton. Then increment the address and repeat. This is the hard way to load a program; every time the power is turned off, the program must be reloaded. However, until the EPROMs are loaded, this is the way it must be done. When the program is loaded, read the locations using the memory read switch. When this is done, reset the system and let the program run.

If 7-segment displays are used in place of the eight individual displays for the first three output ports, the sequencing of the segments will be a, b, c, d, e, f, g. Reference is made to both the displays and the individual LEDs because either mode may be used for output ports 00, 01, and 02.

The 7-segment LEDs should all display the same segment and one of the individual LEDs should come on for each of the eight steps. Two of the steps, bit 7 and bit 8, will not light any individual LED, and the first bit will not light any segment on the displays. The time each step is held is determined by the constant in the delay loop. This is the data entered as bytes 2 and 3 of the LXI B instruction. If the timing is too short to make sure all the correct responses are obtained, increase the 3F entry in address 20B. If the time is too long, decrease this number.

If there are doubts about the program working correctly, single-step the program using the single-step capability. Place the system in single-step and do not depress reset. If reset is depressed the program will start at address 00, and you will have to single-step through the EPROM memory. When the program has stopped, the address that it stopped on and the data on the data bus will be displayed. The chances are good that this will happen in the delay loop, because most of the program time is spent in this loop. If this is a problem, set address 20B to 02 and address 20C to 02. This will shorten the delay loop to one loop so that the program will jump back through the loop once, checking out the JNZ instructions and their execution.

If the output seems to be working properly, this can indicate several things. If one of the displays is not correct check for the proper wiring, and check that the display is good. Use the single-step capability to verify that the program is being executed properly, and that the correct data appears at the output ports. Make sure that EPROM memory is all zeros, and that the program is not going astray there.

If EPROM is not all zeros, disable it by disconnecting the CS line from the address decoder from all the memory chips. Connect 0_0 from the address decoder to the RAM select line. This assigns RAM memory as addresses 00 thru FF. Then, when reset is depressed, the program will start with RAM memory. Do not forget to change all the jump addresses in the program to address block 00 instead of block 200.

Input Ports

When it is certain that the output ports are working correctly, it is time to start on the input ports. The logical starting point is with the sixteen button keyboard. The following program listing is for the matrix type keyboard with the automatic reset, manual reset, and program reset, and with the keyboard connected to input port 00. The program reset is connected to bit 7 of output port 03.

Mnemonic	Op Code	Address	Notes
MVI A	3E	200	
80	80	201	
OUT	D3	202	Reset high
03	03	203	
MVI A	3E	204	
00	00	205	
OUT	D3	206	Reset low
03	03	207	
IN	DB	208	Read keyboard
00	00	209	
OUT	D3	20A	Output on port 00
00	00	20B	
LXI B	01	20C	Set up delay loop
3F	3F	20D	

Mennonic	Op Code	Address	Notes
FF	FF	20E	
DCR C	0D	20F	
JNZ	C2	210	Delay loop
0F	0F	211	
02	02	212	
DCR B	05	213	
JNZ	C2	214	
0F	0F	215	
02	02	216	
JMP	C3	217	
08	08	218	
02	02	219	

This program will display the number of the key depressed as two bits on the individual LEDs or as two segments on the 7-segment displays. The zero bit will not be displayed if using the 7-segment displays, but can be displayed on port 03 by changing the 00 in address 20B to 03.

After the LEDs illuminate, they will stay on for a length of time determined by the delay loop. They will then turn off if no other keys have been depressed because of the automatic reset connected to the select line of the keyboard. To check the program reset, depress a key, then depress system reset before the number is displayed. This will initialize the program and reset the keyboard. So the display should be zero when the program executes address 20A. It will stay zero until a key is depressed and the program recognizes it.

To check out manual reset, depress a key, then depress the manual reset switch before the program recognizes the key. The program should display zero when address 20A is executed, and not the number of the key depressed before the reset.

To check that the proper LEDs are lit, consult the table in Fig. 11-1. This assumes that the keyboard is connected as shown in Fig. 10-6. This table shows the indications for both the individual LEDs and the 7-segment displays, along with the six LEDs of port 03. Check that the indications are as shown for the key depressed, and check all the keys.

KEY	INPUT BITS	SEGMENTS	PORT 03	LEDS
0	00010001	abcdef	0010001	00010001
1	00010010	bc	0010010	00010010
2	00010100	abdeg	0010100	00010100
3	00011000	abcdg	0011000	00011000
4	00100001	bcfg	0100001	00100001
5	00100010	acdfg	0100010	00100010
6	00100100	acdefg	0100100	00100100
7	00101000	abc	0101000	00101000
8	01000001	abcdefg	1000001	01000001
9	01000010	abcfg	1000010	01000010
A	01000100	abcefg	1000100	01000100
B	01001000	cdefg	1001000	01001000
C	10000001	adef	0000001	10000001
D	10000010	bcdef	0000010	10000010
E	10000100	adefg	0000100	10000100
F	10001000	aefg	0001000	10001000

Fig. 11-1. Input bits and LEDs illuminated for the 16 button keyboard inputs.

If the delay is short and the LEDs do not stay on long enough to check the displays, increase the constant in address 20D. Again, if it is desired to use the single-step capability to troubleshoot the system, set the delay constants to 02. Do not reset the system after entering single step, or all of the EPROM must be single-stepped through before encountering the program. Changing the memory addressing as described previously will eliminate this.

When the sixteen button keyboard is working, check out the ten button keyboard in the same manner. Change the IN 00 instruction to IN 01 by changing address 209 from 00 to 01. This enables input port 01, which is the ten button keyboard.

If this keyboard is the matrix type, two segments will be turned on for every key depressed, similar to the above example. If this is the individual switch type of keyboard, each key will turn on only one segment, because each key controls one bit of the output word. Bit 0 is controlled by the 0 key, 1 by the 1 key, etc. Here again, output port 03 will have to be used to check bit 0 for either type keyboard.

Remember the control signals required to route data from the keyboard into the system. These are the address and I/O read, and if either is absent the port will not be enabled. But these are pulses,

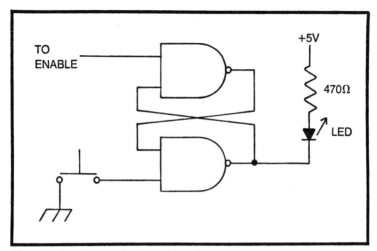

Fig. 11-2. Circuit to catch the enable pulse.

and must be observed with a scope. If there is doubt about their working, look for positive going pulses on the enable line going to the gated buffers in the port circuit. If a good scope is not available, the circuit shown in Fig. 11-2 will catch the enable pulse. Build it up on a breadboard, and connect the enable signal to the inverter input. The pushbutton switch is to reset the latch, and can be replaced by a wire, which is touched to ground to reset the circuit. This will catch any positive going pulse. To catch negative going pulses, such as the reset to the keyboard latches, eliminate the input inverter and connect the input signal directly to the latch. In either case, the LED will turn on when a pulse is received, and it will stay on until the latch is reset.

If the keyboard seems to be working, but it is doubtful if the correct information is getting into the system, single-step the program and look at the data on the data bus when the input port is read by the program. Also look at the data going to the output port when the output port is addressed. One common problem is that the address or data lines get crossed during assembly. This can be checked using this program.

When these interfaces are working, it is time to program the system with usable programs. These programs are usually developed using the RAM memory, then transferred to EPROM when the programs are completely developed. The programs given here will consist of subroutines to make up a monitor program. Parts can be chosen for incorporation as desired, and some of the subroutines can be eliminated if desired. An executor type program ties all the subroutines together, and a series of program pointers will call the various subroutines for the different commands. An easy way to call the pointers and the commands is to use the sixteen button keyboard, and assign commands 2-digit hex numbers which are larger that 64. This is larger than the higher order addresses, so the command will not be confused as the first two digits of the address.

One of the basic programs is to convert the keyboard reading into a hex number. The sixteen keyboard inputs four bits of an 8-bit word, so to compile a 2-digit (8-bit) data word requires two entries with the keyboard. The program shown in Fig. 11-3 reads the keyboard and converts it to four bits appearing in the low order four bits of the E register. The D register is used for temporary storage within the subroutine. Notice that at first glance that this program appears simpler than the one given in Chapter 8, but this only reads the keyboard. It does nothing about compiling the results into a data word. This is done by the subroutine which calls this subroutine. The information can mean anything at this point.

Twenty-four (hex) locations are required for this program. The addressing shown assigns the last of EPROM memory to this use. It is advisable to check the program out in RAM by changing the addresses and the jump commands to reflect RAM addresses, but some method is needed to check out the program to make sure the correct information is arrived at. One method of doing this is to write a small executor program to read the keyboard, store the information in temporary memory, then halt the program. When the program stops, read the memory address using the hardware memory read facilities to make sure the correct data is being inputted into the system.

Another method of checking the keyboard and input data is to read the data into the system, then to output it on one of the output ports. The program shown in Fig. 11-4 uses the program shown in Fig. 11-3 as the input subroutine, then outputs this on output port 00. Figure 11-5 shows the method of outputting to 7-segment displays for the same input. This program uses a table look-up, shown at address 1A0, to arrive at the correct segments for the

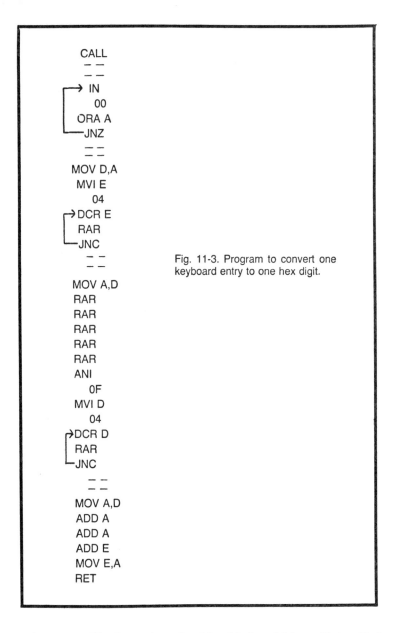

```
        CALL
         − −
         − −
  ┌──→   IN
  │       00
  │     ORA A
  └─────JNZ
         − −
         − −
        MOV D,A
        MVI E
         04
  ┌→ DCR E
  │   RAR
  └──JNC
         − −
         − −
        MOV A,D
        RAR
        RAR
        RAR
        RAR
        RAR
        ANI
         0F
        MVI D
         04
  ┌→ DCR D
  │   RAR
  └──JNC
         − −
         − −
        MOV A,D
        ADD A
        ADD A
        ADD E
        MOV E,A
        RET
```

Fig. 11-3. Program to convert one keyboard entry to one hex digit.

characters. The first pointer for this table is at 1A0, so this is added to the hex number to be displayed. The LDAX B instruction loads the accumulator with the contents of the location whose address is in the B C register pair. This is computed by the program. Then the

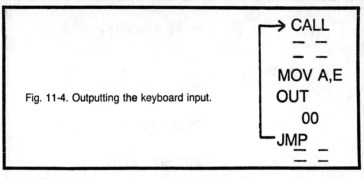

Fig. 11-4. Outputting the keyboard input.

accumulator is outputted to port 00 as a bit pattern representing the segments required for the character to be displayed.

The call reset keyboard is a subroutine which resets the keyboard by setting the proper bit of output port 03 high, then low.

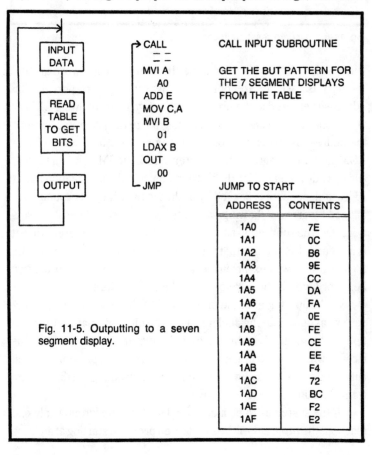

CALL — INPUT SUBROUTINE

GET THE BUT PATTERN FOR THE 7 SEGMENT DISPLAYS FROM THE TABLE

JUMP TO START

ADDRESS	CONTENTS
1A0	7E
1A1	0C
1A2	B6
1A3	9E
1A4	CC
1A5	DA
1A6	FA
1A7	0E
1A8	FE
1A9	CE
1AA	EE
1AB	F4
1AC	72
1AD	BC
1AE	F2
1AF	E2

Fig. 11-5. Outputting to a seven segment display.

```
LXI H                PORT 3 WORD ADDRESS:
 — —
 — —
MOV A,M
ORI                  SET BIT 7 HIGH
  80
OUT                  RESET HIGH
  03
ANI                  SET BIT 7 LOW
  F7
OUT                  RESET LOW
  03
RET
```

Fig. 11-6. Keyboard reset subroutine.

Figure 11-6 shows this subroutine. It assumes that a word in RAM memory is assigned to contain the bits outputted to port 3. This address is entered in the program in the two lines following LXI H.

Notice that no addresses are assigned to the programs because the address is dependent on the memory size, addresses of EP-ROM, and the programs to be entered in EPROM. The mnemonic and op code are given for the instructions, and the information that is address-dependent is flagged by dashes in the listing. The jumps are flagged by arrows showing where the jump is to. The call instructions give the subroutine name so the address can be entered when it is assigned. Remember that the address information is entered with the low order two hex bits in the first address, and the high order two hex bits (even if they are zero) in the next address.

Make up a folder of the programs as written, even if no addresses are assigned. In this folder include the memory map and instruction of how to use the subroutines and programs. These instructions include where the data is that is passing from the programs to the subroutines and back. For the program shown in Fig. 11-3, the data from the subroutine is in the E register.

If the system is to be a dedicated system, performing only one function, the program will be a dedicated program starting at address

0000. If it is to be a general purpose system capable of doing many things, a control or executor program is entered at location 0000. (This may just be a jump to a program if the interrupts are used.)

The executor program runs one of the various programs depending upon commands given by the operator. So it contains a keyboard read program, a command decode program, and an execute.

The keyboard read program reads two digits from the keyboard and compiles them into one 2-digit hex number. This program is shown in Fig. 11-7, and requires the input subroutine of Fig. 11-3

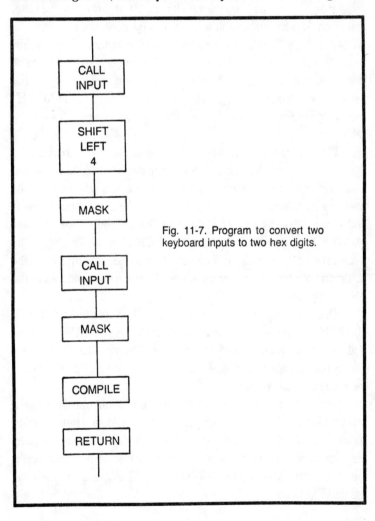

Fig. 11-7. Program to convert two keyboard inputs to two hex digits.

and the keyboard reset subroutine of Fig. 11-6. The data inputted is displayed on output port 00 by the executor program shown in Fig. 11-8. This uses the 0 key on the second keyboard as the execute, so the command can be changed by a system reset, and entering new data. If the second keyboard is not of the matrix type, where the input for key 0 results in an 11 into the accumulator, change the CPI constant to the correct value.

This program sets up the addresses of the starting points for the different commands as 2-byte pointers, with the low order two digits in the first byte of the pointer, and the high order address digits in the second byte. As written, the pointer table is set up to start at an address where the low order digits are 00. If this is not the case, insert an ADI instruction and the required constant between the ADD A and the MOV L,A instructions. This constant will be the low order bits of the address, and should be low enough so that the table does not spill over into the next higher hundreds (hex) or the program will require change. The constant entered in the MVI H* instruction defines the high order bits of the starting address of the table.

This program assumes that the commands are all greater than 70, and that the address pointer for command 70 is stored in the first two locations in the pointer table, for 71 in the second two, etc. The pointers are moved to the D and E registers, and moved on to the H and L registers (by the XCHG instruction). From there they are placed in the program counter by the PCHL instruction. Since the microprocessor gets the next instruction to be executed from the program counter, the program is transferred to the address in the pointer locations.

The stack pointer is initialized in Fig. 11-8 as the first step. It should be initialized to somewhere near the top of RAM memory, and the temporary storage locations should be placed at the bottom. Enter the address, if different than shown (02FF), in the proper locations in the program.

This executor does not allow the use of interrupts because it starts at location 0000. If interrupts are to be used, or if the capability to incorporate them at some later date is desired, place a jump instruction at the first three addresses, then start the executor at location 0040. At location 0040 place an EI instruction, then the executor.

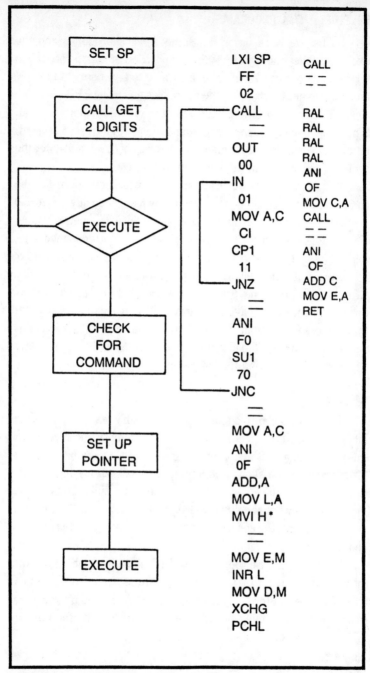

Fig. 11-8. Program to decode a 2 digit keyboard input as a command.

DEVELOPMENTAL PROGRAMS

So far we have discussed some small subroutines and the executor. These should be written and tried at this point. When trying out programs initially it is advisable to try them out in RAM memory, either by changing the addresses and using EPROMs with all zeros, or by changing the address of the RAM memory to 0000. When they have been checked out and memory addresses asigned, enter them on the memory map to keep track of them, and enter the program description in the program folder.

What follows are several programs which can be called by commands from the keyboard. When they have been developed and proven, they can be used in the development of additional programs. These programs can be compressed, changed, omitted, or added to, depending on the memory space available and the requirements of the user. But when enough programs are completed to fill one EPROM, program the first EPROM so that the programs are permanent and do not have to be hand loaded every time. Also enter the pointers in the pointer table, leaving the remaining pointers all zeros. Doing this will allow the pointers to be programmed later without reprogramming the total chip.

RAM Test

Figure 11-9 shows a simple RAM memory test program. One bit is sequenced compeltely through RAM memory and checked. If the bit affects any other bit in the same word, or if a bit does not program, it will be shown. The program stops, displaying the low order address of the error, what should be there, and the difference. Port 0 shows what should be there, port 1 shows the differences, and port 2 shows the address. If port 1 is all zeros, then the location and bit did not program.

This program can be useful if there is some doubt about the integrity of the RAM memory. Some systems use a RAM memory check in the executor to ensure frequent checking. To assign this as command 70, simply place the starting address in the pointer table.

Output Test

Figure 11-10 shows a simple output test program. This program turns on all the output bits for a short duration of time, one at a

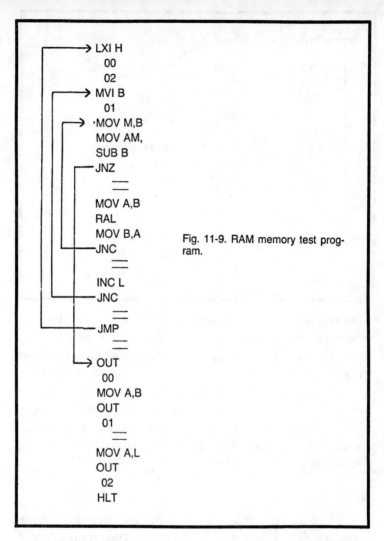

```
      LXI H
      00
      02
      MVI B
      01
      ·MOV M,B
      MOV AM,
      SUB B
     JNZ
      ──
      ──
      MOV A,B
      RAL
      MOV B,A
     JNC
      ──
      ──
      INC L
     JNC
      ──
      ──
     JMP
      ──
      ──
      OUT
      00
      MOV A,B
      OUT
      01
      ──
      ──
      MOV A,L
      OUT
      02
      HLT
```

Fig. 11-9. RAM memory test program.

time, by rotating a bit through the accumulator and outputting it. The length of time each individual light is on is determined by the length of the delay loop, as shown in Fig. 11-11. This provides a fixed delay determined by the constant loaded in with the LXI instruction. The length of time is determined by the cycle time used, which is determined by the crystal frequency used with the clock generator.

To make this a variable delay subroutine, preload the H and L register with the desired delay and CALL to the address assigned to Delay V, or to the DCR L instruction. In this manner a delay up to

```
┌── MVI A
│   01
│   OUT
│   00
│   OUT
│   01
│   OUT
│   02           Fig. 11-10. Output test program.
│   OUT
│   03
│   CALL
│     DELAY
│     ROUTINE
│   RAL
└── JMP
    ═══
```

about two seconds can be achieved. When incorporating this delay subroutine, program in some variables and measure the delay using the program in Fig. 11-10. Make a simple chart showing the delays and incorporate this with the program instructions in the folder.

The delay subroutine, if used, will not be a command accessed by the command switches. Instead, it will be a subroutine accessed from other programs by a call instruction. The test programs are commanded programs, accessed by a command and addresses in the pointer table.

GO TO

A very useful program, especially when developing other programs, is the GO TO program. This starts executing instrucitons at any desired address. This program is useful in developing programs because it allows the programs to be located anywhere in memory, and they can be accessed using this command and placing all four digits of the address in the keyboard. The program is shown in Fig. 11-12. The two high order digits are obtained from the keyboard and moved to the H register, then the two low order digits are obtained and moved to the L register. Then the PCHL instruction places this in the program counter. The execute block gives the operator a chance to check the digits and change them, by using the system reset and starting over again, before they are used by the program. This may save starting at the wrong point and destroying what is loaded into RAM. The output instructions display the digits before the execute is issued.

To use the program, enter the command on the keyboard, then enter the two high order digits in the address, starting with the highest order bit. If the displays show the correct numbers, depress execute and enter the two low order digits. If the display is correct, depress execute again, and the program will be entered.

The pointer for the program must be entered in the pointer table. To give this command 72, enter the starting address of the program in the fifth and sixth locations in the pointer table.

READ and LOAD

Another useful program is the program read and load. This allows the program to read any memory location, and to load any RAM location. This program uses the sixteen button keyboard to input the address and data. The address, as it is loaded, is displayed on output displays 0 and 1. When the location is read, the low order address bit is displayed on output display 2, while the data in memory is displayed on 0 and 1. The procedure is as follows:

1. Execute the proper command.
2. Enter high order two address bits.
3. Depress execute; the two bits are displayed on 0 and 1.
4. Enter low order address bits.

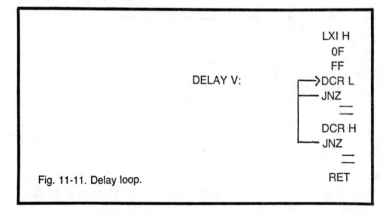

Fig. 11-11. Delay loop.

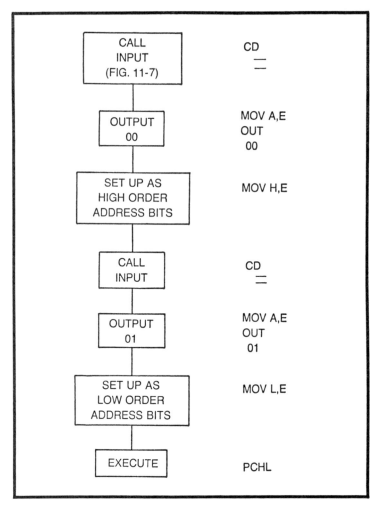

Fig. 11-12. Go To program.

5. Depress execute; the two bits are displayed on 0 and 1.
6. Depress read; the contents of the addressed location are displayed on 0 and 1, and the low order address digit is displayed on 2.
7. If data is to be entered, enter the data on the keyboard, and depress load.
8. The data is entered and read on displays 0 and 1.
9. Depressing the read increments and address and displays the contents.

So several consecutive memory locations can be read by simply depressing read. To load consecutive locations, enter and load data. Then depress r≈≈d to increment address. The data is displayed and the low order address digit is displayed. Figure 11-13 shows the program for this. To assign this as command 71, enter the first address in the proper command pointer locations.

This GO TO program gives the capability of loading development programs into RAM memory, and should be included if programs are to be written on the system. The programs can be accessed using the GO TO command.

Others

There are several other programs that may or may not be included, depending on the capability and requirements of the system. Some of these can be added at a later date as the system grows and the number of programs increases. One such program is a program to fill a number of consecutive memory locations with a constant. This program, called FILL, is often used to zero a block of memory locations in preparation to entering a program.

Figure 11-14 shows the flow chart for the FILL program. It is a matter of inputting the data and addresses with the keyboard. Then the data is entered when execute is received. The assigning of addresses and op codes is left to the user.

Another convenient program is one which moves a block of data from one series of addresses to another. Figure 11-15 shows the flow chart for this program. The starting and ending addresses of the data block are entered, and the starting address of the transfer to address is entered last. Then the first address is read and loaded into the new block. The addresses are incremented and checked for last address. The process is repeated until all locations have been transferred.

There are several more programs, such as a compare program, which are useful under some conditions. It is advisable to leave these programs until they are needed by system expansion. Then experience will be gained which is valuable in writing and developing programs.

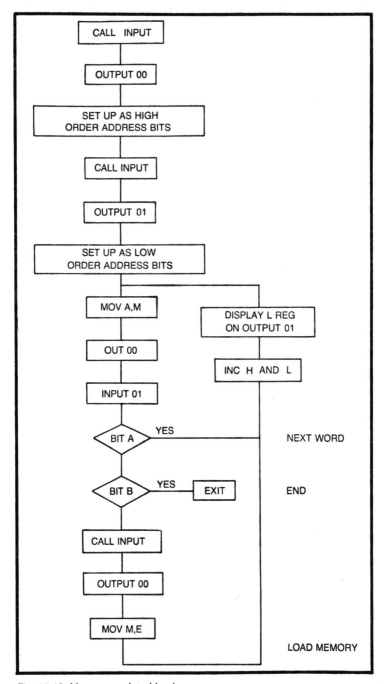

Fig. 11-13. Memory read and load program.

INTERRUPTS

To service interrupts, the registers and the PSW must be saved and restored at the end of the routine. This insures that the program status is the same as before the interrupt. The information can be stored temporarily in the stack using single-byte instructions, and restored using single-byte instruction. The following program gives the save/restore/enable/return portion of the routine. This is normally preceded by a jump instruction to the service routine.

PUSH PSW   Push program status word
PUSH B   Push B register

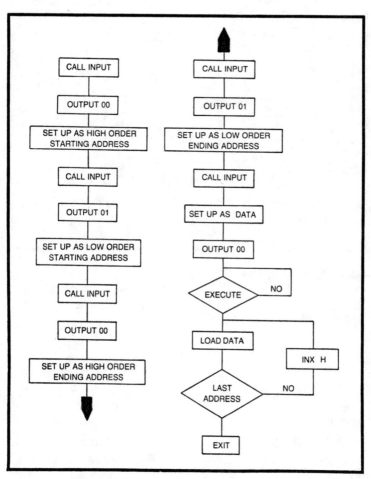

Fig. 11-14. Fill program.

273

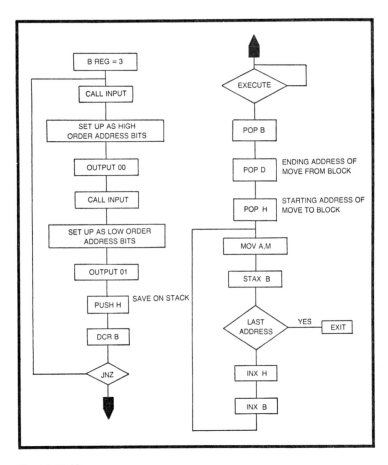

Fig. 11-15. Move program.

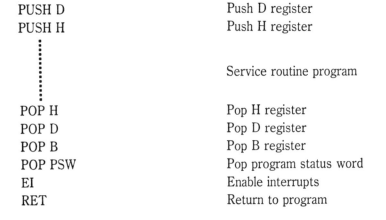

PUSH D	Push D register
PUSH H	Push H register
⋮	Service routine program
POP H	Pop H register
POP D	Pop D register
POP B	Pop B register
POP PSW	Pop program status word
EI	Enable interrupts
RET	Return to program

274

All PUSH and POP instructions place the referenced register pair contents either on the stack or from the stack to the register pair. These must be done because the only way to keep track of what is where on the stack is by the program instructions. If the last push instruction was a PUSH H and the first pop instruction is a POP B, the contents of the H and L register will end up in the B and C register.

Hardware is required to use interrupts. This hardware places the proper RST command on the data bus when the interrupt has been acknowledged by the processor. Interrupt zero cannot be used for anything except restart, unless special programming has been provided. This is because interrupt 0 takes the program to address 00, and this is the starting place for reset.

Chapter 12
Applications

++

Now that the microcomputer is assembled and checked out, what can it be used for? Just leaving it in a corner to collect dust is no fitting fate for a system built and checked out after long nights of frustration and hard work. It should be put to work doing something for the enjoyment of the builder.

This chapter is to give you some ideas on using your computers. Only generalized programs are presented, because it is up to you as to whether the programs are to be retained and where in memory they should go. If the programs are not to be permanent, they can be assigned RAM memory addresses and be accessed by the GO TO command. If they are written into EPROM, a command must be assigned so that they can be accessed by the command code; however, they must be placed in RAM for initial use and checkout.

GAMES

Simple games are the easiest applications. The computer can assist the operator in playing the game, or the operator can actually play against the computer.

ESP

In this game, the operator guesses 1 or 2, then the computer displays either a 1 or 2. The number of tries and the number of correct guesses are determined. The program can be restarted for another attempt, or the game can be resumed after reading the results.

Figure 12-1 shows the flow chart and program for the ESP game. To determine the number (1 or 2) for the computer, the B register is incremented each pass through the program. If bit 0 of the B register is set, the number is a 1; if the bit is low, the number is 2. This number is compared to the input from the keyboard. If they match, both the number of correct guesses (D register) and the

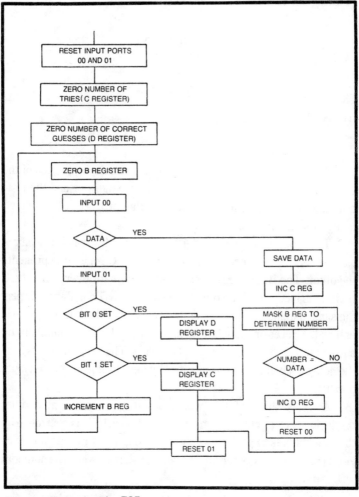

Fig. 12-1. Flow chart for ESP program.

number of tries (C register) are incremented. If the guess is wrong, then only the number of tries is incremented.

If key 0 on the second keyboard (port 01) is depressed, the number of correct guesses is displayed on output port 00. Key 1 displays the number of tries on output port 00.

As written here, the program does not use any subroutines. They can be used as long as register usage does not overlap. It may be necessary to store the number of tries and the number of correct guesses in RAM memory. If this is done, the increment instructions must include instructions for setting up the H and L register. The following list of instructions will accomplish this.

LXI H

(RAM memory)

(address)

INR M

The other places where the C and D registers are referenced must also be changed accordingly.

Rolling Dice

This is a simple program, not actually simulating the roll of the dice. That would require a random number generator and the programming that goes with it. However, this program comes close enough for most uses.

The program shown in Fig. 12-2 simulates the rolling of a pair of dice. B register represents one die, and the C register represents the other. The B register is incremented twice for every time the C register is incremented, so that the two dice will not always display the same number. The shake of the dice starts when the program is entered. Depressing any key on input 01 displays both numbers on output 00, representing the roll of the dice. The program holds until the next shake of the dice is initiated by depressing and key on input port 01.

A modification of this would be to roll one die at a time, displaying each as one digit on output 00. So each die is controlled by the time it takes to push a switch. If the length of time spent in each loop is made slightly different, the relationship between the numbers will be random.

278

CONTROL: MODEL RAILROAD

One large area in computer application is in the control field. Here, the control of model railroad trains will serve to demonstrate the use of the microprocessor in the control of devices. The basic

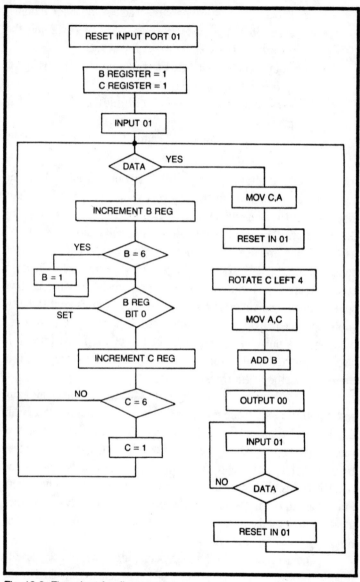

Fig. 12-2. Flow chart for dice program.

task of the control system is to keep the trains from colliding, to sequence the track controls for the proper train routing, and to control the speed of the individual trains.

The basic controls are:

- Insulators: isolate sections of the track from other sections.
- Reverse blocks: provide the capability of reversing the polarity of the voltage to each track.
- Turn out switch: switches the track so that the train will take one branch or the other.
- Markers: magnetic switches which indicate if a train has passed over.
- Speed controls: a means of controlling the train speed by changing the voltage applied to the track.

Figure 12-3 shows a simple track layout, complete with the standard representation of the controls. This consists of a double loop track and a reverse loop. The track is broken up into sections by the insulators, and each loop is fed by a speed control.

Switches are used to control the turn out blocks, the speed control, and the polarity of the voltage applied to the track. The track is broken up into blocks by the insulators. Each block has its own speed control and reversing switch, so each train is controlled by controlling the individual blocks of the track. Turnouts are switched by applying a pulse in one direction or the other. If the turnout is already switched to the direction desired, it does not switch. If it is in the other position, the track switches.

The basic loop consists of blocks 1, 3, and 4. A train in this loop, with the turnouts set and the speed controls set, will run forever in this loop. The siding, consisting of block 2, gives the capability of running two trains. Once train can take the siding while the other train runs the main loop. The turn around (block 5) gives the capability of turning around a train to run in the opposite direction. For a train to run in the opposite direction, the polarity of the track must be reversed. So each block must be reversed ahead of the train.

To control the track by microcomputer, it is necessary to replace the switches with electronic switches, each controlled by the computer. One method of doing this is to use an output circuit, such

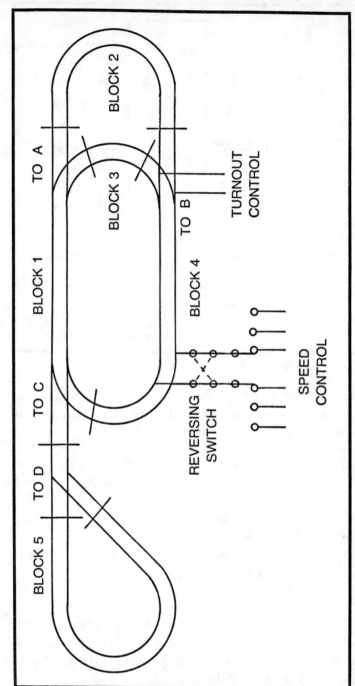

Fig. 12-3. Simple track layout.

281

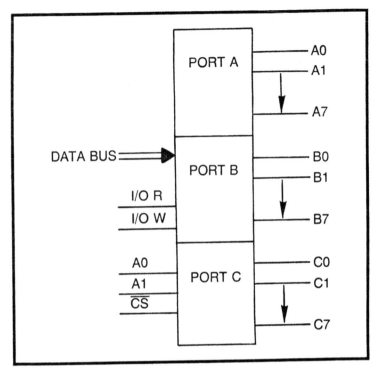

Fig. 12-4. Using an 8255 for control.

as an 8255, connected to the data bus, as shown in Fig. 12-4. The bits required to control the track, and their functions, are itemized in the table below:

Control	Number required	Bits per control	Total bits
Speed control	5 (one for each block)	3	15
Reversing switch	5 (one for each speed control)	2	10
Turnout	4	2	8

From this it can be seen that it will require 33 bits to control the track. This requires five computer output ports to control all the functions. Seven bits are left over which can be used for such things as signals, track lights and the like.

Typically, the switches are controlled by relays, each control-led by a bit of the computer output word. This is convenient if the controls are operated from low level AC signals. But if DC can control the turnout switch and the speed control, then solid state devices, such as transistors or SCRs, can be used. Figure 12-5 shows using relays to apply power to each of the controls. Figure 12-6 shows using transistors and SCRs, while Fig. 12-7 shows using opto-isolators to isolate the control and power circuits.

Markers are small magnetic reed switches taped to the track at various points. These switches are activated by a small magnet on the underside of the train, to give an indication of when a train passes over them. Figure 12-8 shows reed switch mounting and connection to computer. The switch is connected at one bit of an input port. This tells that a train has passed over, but does not identify *which* train has passed over.

Other, more complex markers can be built to identify which train has passed over. One method is to use photocells imbedded in the track and to use coded light sources mounted on the bottom of the trains. Another is to mount the switches on the sides of the

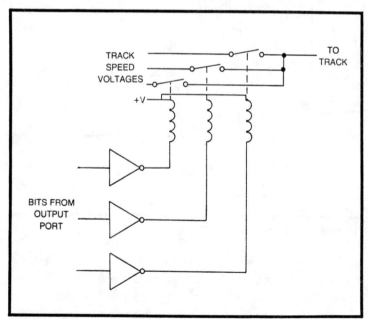

Fig. 12-5. Using relays for control.

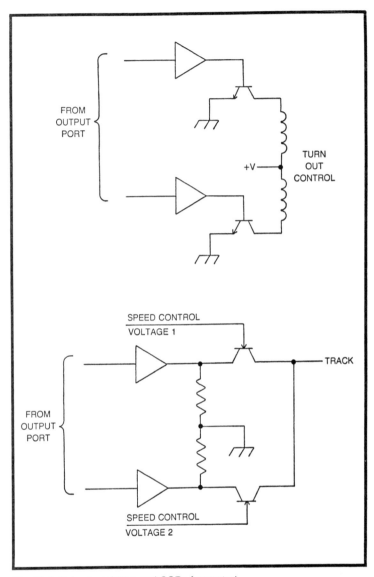

Fig. 12-6. Using transistors and SCRs for control.

track, and to mount the magnet on one side or the other of the train. This gives the capability of determining which one of two trains has passed over the marker if the direction of train is known.

The markers are set in the track to determine where each train is. Figure 12-9 shows one marker placement for the track layout of

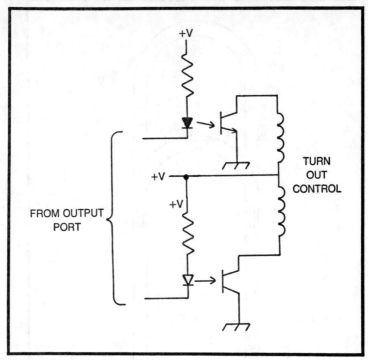

Fig. 12-7. Using opto-isolators for control.

Fig. 12-3. Only eight markers are used, and this makes one input word for the computer. For this simple track layout, five output ports and one input port are required. This can be achieved using two of the 8255 type output/input chips, as shown in Fig. 12-10.

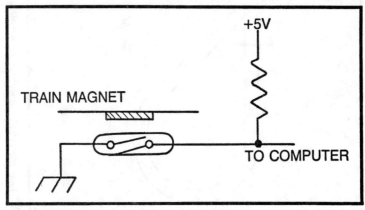

Fig. 12-8. Marker circuitry.

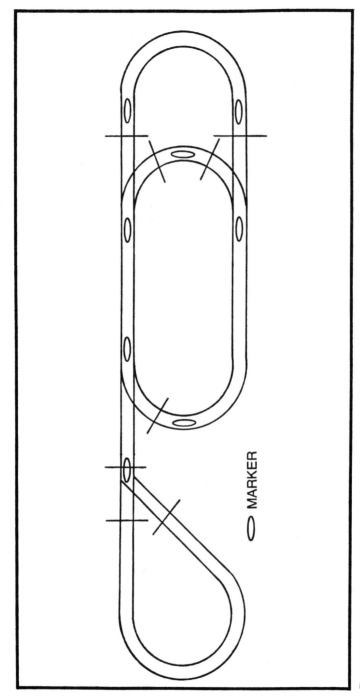

MARKER

Fig. 12-9. Marker placement for the simple track.

Address lines 3 and 4 are inverted and used as the chip select for the chips. Address lines 0 and 1 are connected as the address inputs. So the table below gives the addresses and port numbers:

Address	Port number	Chip	section
08	08	1	A
09	09	1	B
0A	0A (10)	1	C
0B	Control	1	
10	10 (16)	2	A
11	11 (17)	2	B
12	12 (18)	2	C
13	Control	2	

Port C of chip 2 is the input port, so the control word is 89 for that chip. The control word for chip 1 is 80. So the following sequence of instructions must appear in the program before the chips are used:

```
MVI A
  80
OUT
  0B
MVI A
  89
OUT
  13
```

This writes the control words into the 8255 chips. They must be initialized only once during the program, so these instructions should be at the start of the program.

Typically, this type of control program maintains status quo until a command is given to change the operation. The keyboard (or switches) connected to input port 01 can be used to issue these commands. These commands can be simple, such as "move one train to the siding." Or they can be complex, such as "turn both trains around without collison." This depends on the programming.

The control program is to maintain status quo; that is, the markers are read to make sure that the trains do not run into each other, and the track is set for one run. The commands may change the status quo of the track, so that a new set of conditions exists.

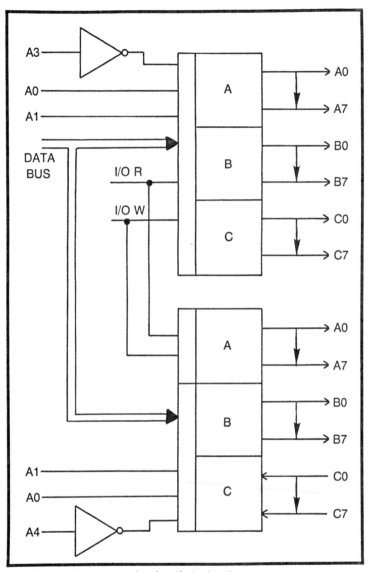

Fig. 12-10. 8255s connected as input/output ports.

Typically, all the output ports have an output word stored in RAM memory.

OTHER APPLICATIONS

Most computer applications are presently in the industrial and commercial fields because the development time and money are available there. These application range from the simple microwave oven controller to the sophisticated test sets, and more applications are announced daily.

One of the major applications of microcomputers is in the data handling field. This requires the use of a terminal of some type, such as a keyboard and display. One such application is an editing program, where letters, reports, recipes, or anything composed of text, can be stored on a cassette tape unit, and searched under program control. With the proper programs, the text can then be corrected, edited, and typed, or the results can be displayed on a video terminal for use, as with recipes.

For the home experimenter and hobbyist, the applications are a result of the ingenuity of the user. The most intriguing applications require additional input and output devices such as the video monitor, cassette tape, and printer output. These devices, and the programs required to interface and operate them, are as complex as the microprocessor itself. They are beyond the scope of this volume and will be covered in a later book.

Appendices

Appendices

◆◆◆

Just as the decimal, or base 10, system uses ten numbers (0,1,2,3,4,5,6,7,8,9), the *binary*, or base 2, system uses two numbers (0,1). Base 10 is undoubtedly the most convenient for 10-fingered human beings, but base 2 is more efficient for a digital computer. The 0 and 1 equate to off and on, low and high, false and true, and to the two state digital circuit.

A number is defined as each digit times the base of the number to the power of the place. For example, the number 53926 in the decimal system is:

$$53926 = (5 \times 10^4) + (3 \times 10^3) + (9 \times 10^2)$$
$$+ (2 \times 10^1) + (6 \times 10^0)$$
$$= 50000 + 3000 + 900 + 20 + 6$$
$$= 53926$$

Remember that any number to the first power is that number, and any number to the zero power is one. For example $10^1 = 10$ and $10^0 = 1$.

THE BINARY SYSTEM

This same procedure works for numbers to other bases. If you will refer to Table A-1, you will find that 110111 binary is defined as:

$$110111 = (1 \times 2^5) + (1 \times 2^4) + (0 \times 2^3) + (1 \times 2^2)$$
$$+ (1 \times 2^1) + (1 \times 2^0)$$
$$= (1 \times 32) + (1 \times 16) + (0 \times 8) + (1 \times 4)$$
$$+ (1 \times 2) + (1 \times 1)$$
$$= 32 + 16 + 0 + 4 + 2 + 1$$
$$= 55 \text{ (decimal)}$$

Table A-1. The Binary System.

Binary	Place Value	Decimal Equivalent	Bit Position
1	2^0	1	0
10	2^1	2	1
100	2^2	4	2
1000	2^3	8	3
10000	2^4	16	4
100000	2^5	32	5
1000000	2^6	64	6
10000000	2^7	128	7

Addition and subtraction in binary is simple and it is used quite a bit for checking microprocessor operation and troubleshooting systems.

Binary Addition

To add two binary numbers, add the individual bits one digit at a time starting at the far right with the least significant bit. Incorporate any carry in the next high order bits. The rules for binary addition are as follows:

1: $0 + 0 = 0$ carry 0
2: $1 + 0 = 1$ carry 0
3: $0 + 1 = 1$ carry 0
4: $1 + 1 = 0$ carry 1
5: $0 + 0 +$ carry $1 = 1$ carry 0
6: $1 + 0 +$ carry $1 = 0$ carry 1
7: $0 + 1 +$ carry $1 = 0$ carry 1
8: $1 + 1 +$ carry $1 = 1$ carry 1

Two examples of binary addition are:

$$
\begin{array}{r}
110010111 \\
+ \ 11110010 \\
\hline
1010001001
\end{array}
\qquad
\begin{array}{r}
100100100 \\
+ \ 111000110 \\
\hline
1011101010
\end{array}
$$

Binary Subtraction

To subtract two binary numbers, subtract the bits, one digit at a time starting at the far right with the least significant bit. Use the rules given below, and always carry forward the borrow to the next higher order digit.

1: $0 - 0 = 0$ borrow 0
2: $1 - 0 = 1$ borrow 0
3: $0 - 1 = 1$ borrow 1
4: $1 - 1 = 0$ borrow 0
5: $0 - 0 - 0$ borrow $1 = 1$ borrow 1
6: $1 - 0 -$ borrow $1 = 0$ borrow 0
7: $0 - 1 -$ borrow $1 = 0$ borrow 1
8: $1 - 1 -$ borrow $1 = 1$ borrow 1

Two examples of binary subtraction are:

$$
\begin{array}{r}
110011101 \\
-\ 11100100 \\
\hline
010111001
\end{array}
\qquad
\begin{array}{r}
100100100 \\
-\ 100011111 \\
\hline
000000101
\end{array}
$$

The answer can be checked by adding the lower two binary numbers.

THE HEXADECIMAL SYSTEM

Binary numbers can grow quite unwieldy; for example, 6 digits are required to represent 32 decimal. Most computers and microprocessors use bits in multiples of 8. Although handled easily by computer, these long binary numbers are difficult to manipulate with pencil and paper. The hexadecimal system is therefore used as a shorthand method for such documentation as program listings and data compilations.

The *hexadecimal*, or base 16, system includes 16 numbers: 0 through 9, and A through F. Since 16 is 2^4, 4 binary bits can be represented by a single hexadecimal digit, as illustrated in Tables A-2 and A3.

To convert a binary number to a hexadecimal, separate the binary number into groups of four digits, beginning at the far right with the lowest order bit. Then convert each group of four to its single hexadecimal equivalent, using Table A-3.

Any binary number can be easily converted to decimal by first converting it to a hex number. For example, to convert the binary

Table A-2. The Hexadecimal System.

Hexadecimal	Place Value	Binary Equivalent					Decimal Equivalent
1	16^0					0001	1
10	16^1				0001	0000	16
100	16^2			0001	0000	0000	256
1000	16^3		0001	0000	0000	0000	4096
10000	16^4	0001	0000	0000	0000	0000	65536

number 10110001001111 to hex, first divide it into groups of 4 bits: 10-1100-0100-1111. Then look up the hex equivalent for each group of binary numbers in Table A-3: 2-C-4-F or 2C4F. To convert this number to decimal, look up the decimal equivalent for each hex digit in Table A-4. Then add these numbers together. For this example, 2C4F (hex) = 8192 + 3072 + 64 + 15 = 11343 (decimal).

To convert a decimal to a hex number, use Table A-4, and successively subtract the largest decimal number. The hex equivalents form the hex digits. For example, to convert 3862 from decimal into hex:

Decimal numbers	Hex equivalent
3862	
− 3840	F00
22	
− 16	10
6	
− 6	+ 6
0	F16

Table A-3. Decimal and Hexadecimal Equivalent of Some Binary Digits.

Decimal	Binary		Hexadecimal	Decimal	Binary		Hexadecimal
0	0000	0000	0	17	0001	0001	11
1	0000	0001	1	18	0001	0010	12
2	0000	0010	2	19	0001	0011	13
3	0000	0011	3	20	0001	0100	14
4	0000	0100	4	21	0001	0101	15
5	0000	0101	5	22	0001	0100	16
6	0000	0110	6	23	0001	0111	17
7	0000	0111	7	24	0001	1000	18
8	0000	1000	8	25	0001	1001	19
9	0000	1001	9	26	0001	1010	1A
10	0000	1010	A	27	0001	1011	1B
11	0000	1011	B	28	0001	1100	1C
12	0000	1100	C	29	0001	1101	1D
13	0000	1101	D	30	0001	1110	1E
14	0000	1110	E	31	0001	1111	1F
15	0000	1111	F	32	0010	0000	20
16	0001	0000	10				

The main difficulty with hex addition is to remember to carry 1 for each multiple of 16, not for each multiple of 10. For example:

$$
\begin{array}{r}
\text{F9216} \\
+ \; \text{2163F} \\
\hline
\text{11A855}
\end{array}
\qquad
\begin{array}{r}
\text{FBDE} \\
+ \; 1942 \\
\hline
11520
\end{array}
$$

You can convert a decimal to a hex number by using hex addition and Table A-5, which gives the hex equivalents for decimal numbers, digit by digit. For example, to convert 3862 to hex, look up the hex equivalents of the decimal digits, then add these hex numbers. In this example: 3862 (decimal) = BB8 + 320 +

Table A-4. Decimal Equivalents of Some Hex Digits up to 10000 Hex.

Hex	Decimal	Hex	Decimal
1	1	100	256
2	2	200	512
3	3	300	768
4	4	400	1024
5	5	500	1280
6	6	600	1536
7	7	700	1792
8	8	800	2048
9	9	900	2304
A	10	A00	2560
B	11	B00	2816
C	12	C00	3072
D	13	D00	3328
E	14	E00	3584
F	15	F00	3840
10	16	1000	4096
20	32	2000	8192
30	48	3000	12288
40	64	4000	16384
50	80	5000	20480
60	96	6000	24576
70	112	7000	28672
80	128	8000	32768
90	144	9000	36864
A0	160	A000	40960
B0	176	B000	45056
C0	192	C000	49152
D0	208	D000	53248
E0	224	E000	57344
F0	240	F000	61440
		10000	65536

Table A-5. Hex Equivalents of Some Decimal Digits.

Decimal	Hex	Decimal	Hex
10	A	400	190
20	14	500	1F4
30	1E	600	258
40	28	700	2BC
50	32	800	320
60	3C	900	384
70	46	1000	3E8
80	50	2000	7D0
90	5A	3000	BB8
100	64	4000	FA0
200	C8	5000	1388
300	12C	6000	1880

3C + 2 = F16 (hex). To check the answer, use the procedure for converting hex to decimal. For example: F16 (hex) = 3840 + 16 + 6 = 3862 (decimal).

Index